THE MARY FLEXNER LECTURES

Established in 1928 at Bryn Mawr College to
promote distinguished work in the humanities

T0335215

A FEMINIST THEORY OF REFUSAL

BONNIE HONIG

HARVARD UNIVERSITY PRESS

Cambridge, Massachusetts | London, England   2021

First printing

Library of Congress Cataloging-in-Publication Data

Names: Honig, Bonnie, author.
Title: A feminist theory of refusal / Bonnie Honig.
Description: Cambridge, Massachusetts : Harvard University Press,
    2021. | Includes index.
Identifiers: LCCN 2020043824 | ISBN 9780674248496 (cloth)
Subjects: LCSH: Feminist theory. | Autonomy. | Justice, Administration
    of—Political aspects. | Political participation.
Classification: LCC HQ1190 .H667 2021 | DDC 305.42—dc23
LC record available at https://lccn.loc.gov/2020043824

THE MARY FLEXNER LECTURESHIP was established at Bryn Mawr College on February 12, 1928, by Bernard Flexner, in honor of his sister, Mary Flexner, a graduate of the College. The income from the endowment is to be used annually or at longer intervals, at the discretion of the Directors of the College, as an honorarium for a distinguished American or foreign scholar in the field of the humanities. The object of the Lectureship is to bring to the College scholars of distinction who will be a stimulus to the faculty and students and who will help to maintain the highest ideals and standards of learning.

For Judith Butler, Adriana Cavarero, Jill Frank,
Miriam Leonard, Lori Marso, and James Martel,
whose work I read and in whose company I wrote this book

I want to give
Everything away. To wander forever.
Here is a pot of tea. Let's share it
Slowly, like sisters.

—Tracy K. Smith, "Interrogative"

Contents

Preface

Bartleby and Antigone, the great canonical refusers with their "I prefer not to" and "Enough! Give me glory," are unblinking in their refusal to yield to injustice even in the face of force. But their capacity to inspire a politics seems limited or problematic. Both have long been seen as solitary actors rather than as contributors to larger movements. I have argued elsewhere for a more expansive reading of Antigone as a political actor *in concert*, and I will argue here that Bartleby, too, can be read more expansively, as representing a postwork ethic that exceeds his solitary (un)doings.[1] That said, in this book I take a different tack than earlier with Antigone and now with Bartleby. Beyond reading these two great refusers against the grain of convention, I propose we theorize feminist refusal in connection with a new figure: Euripides's Agave.

In Euripides's play the *Bacchae*, Agave and her sisters lead three tribes of women, bacchants (sometimes called maenads), out of the city of Thebes to Cithaeron, where they dance beyond the reach of King Pentheus (Agave's son) before joining together to kill him. Agave then returns to the city, demanding glory for herself and all the women involved, only to be expelled from Thebes, her native city, and sent off to wander waywardly into the unknown with her sisters, perhaps holding hands.

Agave and the bacchants provide a vital contrast to Bartleby's and Antigone's mortal examples. The bacchants feast and rejoice in plenty on Cithaeron while Bartleby and Antigone both refuse food provided them in captivity. Antigone, with her suicide, ignores the several days' ration provided to sustain life in her burial cave. And Bartleby hungers in prison, ignoring the food his former employer has arranged for him. When Bartleby hungers, that is the last iteration of his iconic "I prefer not," though this one is unspoken. For most readers, Bartleby's final silence completes his evacuation of language, which empties the world as he repeats rotely "I prefer not to."

Notably, when Bartleby refuses to explain his refusal, he is told he speaks too little, while Antigone, who gives herself a dirge that runs through the reasons for her refusal, is told she speaks too much. By contrast, the bacchants' work refusal is tied neither to a nearly silent refusal nor to a wordy explanation, but to a sung chant that calls others to "gather round!" and provides a thrum for the women's dance: *"Eta Bakkae, Eta Bakkae."* Yopie Prins calls the chant "one of the most mobile passages in the *Bacchae*," and indeed it intensifies the women's collectivity and lures them from Thebes to a heterotopia, Cithaeron, where they are free to worship Dionysus away from the gaze and interference of men.[2] The bacchants eat and drink to their hearts' content, unleash desire, generate collective power, and host new practices of mutuality that express care but also unleash violence.[3]

Because the women follow Dionysus, explore his mysteries, turn to violence, and are punished at the end of the *Bacchae*, and because they are often, if not always, described in the play as mad, they have not been taken seriously by political theorists as political actors. The women are commonly dismissed as misguided, manipulated, or insane. But when refusal, especially women's refusal, is pathologized, that calls for counter-reading and scrutiny. Do the women of the *Bacchae* refuse work because they are under the influence of Dionysus? Or do they choose to follow Dionysus because they want to refuse work? Worshipping Dionysus can be seen as a precommitment of sorts, the women's version of Homer's Ulysses arranging to be bound to the mast.

I propose we take seriously the bacchants' refusal as a refusal. A refusal reading of the *Bacchae* notes the significance of the fact that what happens on Cithaeron does not stay on Cithaeron: it is one stop on a larger arc of refusal that includes the bacchants' work stoppage, escape from the city, fugitive experience on Cithaeron, violence against the king who first sought to tame them in the city and then to watch them in the wild, and finally, their return to the city to claim it. The city is unready or unwilling to receive the women, however. First its old king, Cadmus, tries to recuperate them back into their traditional roles; then Dionysus intervenes and sends Agave and her sisters into exile.

Its exemplary arc of refusal is why I turn to the *Bacchae*. But although I work with the play, this is not a book about the *Bacchae*.[4] *A Feminist Theory of Refusal* is a book about three refusal concepts in the contemporary refusal literature: inoperativity, inclination, and fabulation. I assess the strengths and limitations of these refusal concepts in connection with the *Bacchae* and in connection with other texts I think of as "Bacchaes." In the book's three main chapters, I enlist a refusal concept to highlight some unappreciated dimensions of the play which I read as a drama of refusal. Each chapter then turns to two "*Bacchae* readings" of the refusal concept in question, which put pressure on the concept from the vantage point of feminist theory. In conclusion, I argue that the three recovered concepts can themselves be seen as moments on an arc of refusal in which each depends on or postulates the others.

In Chapter 1, I recover inoperativity, Giorgio Agamben's refusal concept. In place of his emphasis on suspending use, I see inoperativity as an agonistic feminist practice of intensification that subverts and recovers use.

In Chapter 2, I recover inclination, arguing that it is Adriana Cavarero's refusal concept. But in place of the pacifist maternalism offered by Cavarero, I suggest we do better to treat inclination as an agonistic sororal practice of peaceful and violent mutuality.

In Chapter 3, I recover fabulation, Saidiya Hartman's "method of refusal," as a meaning-making practice that postulates the return to the city that Hartman does not embrace but Euripides's bacchants are willing to risk.

Why these three?

Inoperativity is important to a feminist theory of refusal for its critique of use, since use is a particular mode of subjection for women and other minoritized peoples both historically and in contemporary liberal democracies.

But inoperativity as we find it generates no assembly and seems to abjure power. Our second refusal concept, inclination, better provides for the mutuality and care on which any feminist theory of refusal depends. We end with fabulation because without it, women who rise in rebellion against a king will be remembered as merely drunk and mad, their example lost along with the work of inoperativity and inclination. It is important to note that in the *Bacchae*, fabulation coincides with the women's return to the city, which means fabulation's refusal is not a new beginning or a fugitive practice. It is an entry into a contest over meaning, a bid for the posterity that might make a past episode into the start of a feminist future.

Introduction

The *Bacchae*'s Arc of Refusal
and the Tragedy of the City

ALL OUR SOURCES ARE MALE

—HELENE FOLEY, "THE POSITION AND CONCEPTION OF WOMEN
IN CLASSICAL ATHENS"

THE FEMINIST CRITIC MUST DO ALL SHE CAN TO RESCUE THE
EMANCIPATORY POTENTIAL OF THE TEXTS SHE READS.

—PATRICIA YAEGER, *HONEY-MAD WOMEN*

Refusal in Euripides's fifth-century tragedy, the *Bacchae*, occurs when the women (1) refuse work in the city, then (2) move outside the city where they live otherwise, then (3) return to the city with a set of demands. The first two actions violate King Pentheus's orders. By the time of the third, Pentheus is dead and Cadmus, his grandfather, has stepped into his place. As I read the play, the three refusals are connected stops on a single arc of refusal. Indeed, the work-refusal and heterotopian escape set up the return to the city that follows. In this book, I make the case for reading the *Bacchae* this way. I also argue that depicting refusal as an arc conveys a normative, civic, and feminist obligation to risk the impurities of politics on behalf of transformation. The effort may fail, but the return to the city, I claim, is fundamental to a feminist theory of refusal that aims to transform the city, not abandon it. The city, in this book, is a figure for political community. It may be an actual city, but it may also be a state, a town, a village, or a neighborhood.

Not all admirable refusals follow this arc. Indigenous theorists of refusal, for example, have argued in favor of developing or recommitting to their own sovereignties rather than working to ameliorate or infiltrate those of settler societies. In some areas of Black studies, the city is seen as so unsalvageable that fugitivity is embraced as the only way for Black life to flourish. The arc of refusal that I trace here may not serve the needs of such theorists and practitioners of refusal.[1] Even so, my hope is that some may find something useful in the agonism of Euripides' bacchants and the audacity of their refusal.

It was Euripides's play that first led me to think about refusal as having an arc and of the city as its destination. In the *Bacchae*, the arc belongs to the women, the bacchants, but their refusal has not received any serious attention as such, because (1) the women are assumed to be mad, in thrall to Dionysus, and unaware of what they are doing when they defy and kill the king, (2) the tragic ending means most readers see not an arc but a restoration or reprimand, and (3) although the play is named for the bacchants, most readers take the focus to be the play's remarkable agon between Thebes's male rivals: Pentheus, the king, and Dionysus, a foreign god who is (unbeknownst to Pentheus) the king's cousin. For these reasons, most readings of the *Bacchae* prioritize its lessons about religion, kinship, recognition, or hubris but not refusal. But what happens when we switch the focus from the male rivals' quest for power to the women's collaborative experiments? From male hubris to women's agency? From heterotopia as fugitivity to a space / time of rehearsal? From women's singular madness to refusal's arc?[2]

Reopening the *Bacchae* as a drama of refusal requires first and foremost that we depathologize the conventional picture of the women as mad or deluded. Once we do that, all the other objections lose their grip. When it is said that the women do not know what they are doing, we may recall Hannah Arendt's insistence that in acting politically in concert with others, we are self-forgetting. Caught up in action, we are not in charge of it; we may be its initiators, but we are not its authors. Indeed, we may well be surprised later to realize what we have done. This is why action, on Arendt's account, postulates forgiveness. The example of Agave, Pentheus's mother, reminds us it may also postulate mourning.

The *Bacchae* dramatizes the difficulty that Arendt recounts. That the bacchants know not what they do is not reason enough to dismiss their political agency; it is also a reason to consider it seriously. Once we do so, the bacchants' return to the city stands out more starkly as a political action. They could have stayed away. They lack for nothing outside the city. But they return. Why? Perhaps to claim equality, perhaps to demand their story be told, perhaps to alter the city. Approached this way, the bacchants seem to be more worldly than worldless. Indeed, as I read it, the *Bacchae* teaches how even when refusal *seems* to reject the world, it betrays a deep attachment to it, if not to the world as it is, then surely to a more just world that is not yet.

From the perspective of an arc of refusal, the bacchants' time outside the city appears not as ventilation but as preparation: a re-formation of the body and steeling of the mind to one day alter the everyday, not just rejoin it. When the women leave Thebes and repair to Cithaeron, I argue, their purpose is to prepare a storm of transformation and not just gather a breeze of fond memories that will occasionally stir the windless "safety" of home.[3] The latter reading is recuperative. The former is transformative. The transformative intent is clear, as we shall see, in Agave's address to the city when she returns to Thebes.

Although I follow the lead of Agave and the bacchants, and trace the arc of their refusal, I want to make clear that the subjects of a feminist theory of refusal need not be women as such, but those shaped by feminist theory and practice. In the *Bacchae*, as we shall see, even the bacchants, who are women in the city, are not always women outside of it. Their experiments in living on Cithaeron traverse conventional categories of sex/gender and human/animal. We may see promise in their gender and species crossing while still seeing their dissidence as a feminist refusal. The term *feminist* here refers to the project of enacting sex-gender equality, which includes pluralizing sex-gender practices and identities, in the face of governing powers that insist on gender binarism, heteronormative sphere separatism, patriarchal kinship, and the instrumentalities and inequalities they secure. In some sense, I will argue, feminist refusal is, as such, a regicidal project because it seeks to put an end to the old order. In the *Bacchae*, when the bacchants kill the king, it seems they do so unknowingly. But I am not so sure.

In the chapters that follow, I connect the three moments in the bacchants' arc of refusal—(1) refusing work, (2) leaving the city (Cithaeron) and (3) returning to the city—with three refusal concepts, respectively: (1) Giorgio Agamben's inoperativity (which suspends use and offers up new (post) uses of the body), (2) Adriana Cavarero's inclination (which represents a new moral geometry of relationality and care "completely apart" from the autonomous verticalism of the city), and (3) Saidiya Hartman's fabulation (her "method of refusal," which can also be the basis for the story told of an action that becomes part of a web of meaning). In each of the three numbered chapters, the selected refusal concept— inoperativity, inclination, or fabulation—presses us to a new reading of some aspect of the *Bacchae*, and then the *Bacchae*, along with other contemporary "Bacchaes," in turn force a critical rethinking of the concept. To the latter end, Agamben on inoperativity is here joined with Judith Butler (*Notes toward a Performative Theory of Assembly*, on assembly), Cavarero on inclination with Sara Ahmed (*Queer Phenomenology*, on dis/orientation), and Hartman on fabulation with Hannah Arendt (*On Revolution* and *The Human Condition* on the city that fabulation postulates and fabulates).[4] The idea is to explore the three refusal concepts' promise and limitations in order to recover them for current use and illumination.

One particular focus throughout is on how refusal is remembered or erased. It will come as no surprise that the *Bacchae*, which tells the story of Dionysus, the god of forgetting, can be read through the lens of memory and forgetting. But in Chapter 3, on fabulation, we will see that memory is not enough: the story's emplotment matters, too. This comes out in my reading there of the seldom-noted agon in the *Bacchae* between Agave and her father, Cadmus. The agon is seldom noted because the consensus is that "the principal axis of the play is the protracted contest between the two young cousins, Pentheus and Dionysus." It is a good scene; Robin Robertson is right about that.⁵ But the later agon between Agave and Cadmus is worthy of attention, too, precisely because it *shifts* the play's principal axis and focuses attention on the politics of storytelling.

The contest between father and daughter is over how to tell the story of the women's action. A feminist theory of refusal notes the practices by which memory and forgetting are shaped and enjoined because these affect not only the past but also the future. In the *Bacchae*, as we shall see, the techniques by which the story is shaped include the pathologization of the women (by Pentheus), their maternalization (by Cadmus, Agave's father, and by Pentheus, her son), and, ultimately, their exile (by Dionysus). The *Bacchae* documents a "splendid failure" (to borrow W. E. B. Du Bois's term) in which a possibility first nurtured outside the city is extinguished, but memory of it remains. A women's refusal is rendered unimaginable but it nonetheless haunts the very present that denies its possibility. It may even seed a future.⁶

But the *Bacchae* is less well known than other dramas of refusal such as "Bartleby" or *Antigone*. I turn now to summarize the play before taking up in detail this book's work of counternarration, conceptual critique, and recovery.

IN THE *Bacchae*, a festival of Dionysus goes terribly wrong, or possibly terribly right, depending on how we interpret the play. The play begins with the arrival in Thebes of Dionysus, a foreign god followed by bacchants from Asia who travel with him spreading his mysteries. Dionysus is the god not only of theater, music, and poetry but also of wine and forgetting. Tiresias, the blind seer, explains early on, "the goddess Demeter—she is the earth, but call her whatever name you wish; she nourishes mortals with dry food; but he who came afterwards, [Dionysus] the offspring of Semele, discovered a match to it, the liquid drink of the grape, and introduced it to mortals. It releases wretched mortals from grief, whenever they are filled with the stream of the vine, and gives them sleep, a means of forgetting their daily troubles, nor is there another cure for hardships."[7] The chorus echoes Tiresias's appreciation of the gift: "To the blessed and to the less fortunate, he gives an equal pleasure from wine that banishes grief."[8]

Dionysus is not really a foreign god, however. The drama turns on his native city's failure to recognize him as one of its own. In fact, he is, as Tiresias says, the son of Semele, one of four daughters of Cadmus, Thebes's founder and grandfather of the current king, Pentheus. Years earlier, as Dionysus explains, Semele had been "visited" by Zeus and became pregnant with Dionysus. She told her story, claiming Zeus was the father of the child, and was challenged by her three sisters, Agave, Ino, and Autonoe, to prove it. The sisters dared Semele to call Zeus to come to her, surely knowing the danger, since calling on Zeus is a perilous act. And sure enough, when the god did come, proving the truth of her claim, Semele died in the encounter. Was this an act of sororicide? Did the sisters instrumentalize Zeus to their purpose?

There is a shrine of sorts in Thebes for Semele, with a flame that is tended, so we may infer she is not forgotten. Yet no one seems to have inquired into the wrong committed against her nor into what might have become of the baby she was carrying when she died. After Semele's death, Zeus took the fetus into a womb of his own and birthed the baby (or something like that; in the play, Tiresias notes that story has been garbled over the years, suggesting the plurality of myth and the unreliability of reports).[9] The child grew up to be the wine god, Dionysus, who now returns to Thebes seeking recognition and vengeance. Cadmus, king at the time of Semele's death, never addressed his daughters' violence, which was left open: unadjudicated, unresolved, poised to return. Thus, we know that the women who join up with Dionysus in the *Bacchae* already know how to act in concert with murderous intent.

The lack of an inquiry and the denial of his cult by Thebes, first under the leadership of his own grandfather, Cadmus, and now under Cadmus's heir and Dionysus's cousin, Pentheus, outrages Dionysus, who returns in disguise to seek the recognition due to him both as a god and as a Theban, son of Semele. It is perhaps ironic that he represents forgetting when forgetting is precisely what he seeks to correct. For Dionysus, Pentheus's rejection of the Bacchic rites reiterates that earlier offense committed against Dionysus's mother, Semele, by her sisters, Agave, Ino, and Autonoe, Pentheus's mother and his and Dionysus's aunts.[10]

The Dionysian rituals attract the three remaining sisters, Agave, Ino, and Autonoe, who, along with the rest of Thebes's women, abandon their work, violating Pentheus's order to return to their looms. Pentheus has some of the women imprisoned, trying to contain them and preserve order, but they all escape to Cithaeron where they party like it's 405 B.C. Says the servant to Pentheus, "And the bacchae whom you shut up, whom you carried off and bound in the chains of the public prison, are set loose and gone, and are gamboling in the meadows, invoking Bromius [aka Dionysus] as their god. Of their own accord, the chains were loosed from their feet and keys opened the doors without human hand."[11] Or in a different translation: "The chains fell from their feet and the bars of their cells were withdrawn as if by magic."[12] It seems Dionysus is also the god of prison abolition. The women's escape is a gift of the god, Dionysus, the play suggests. That may be. But Dionysus is also a gift the women give to themselves: he is summoned by their desire.

I will detail further in Chapter 1 what happens on Cithaeron, the inoperative space / time outside the city to which the women repair, while tracking the power of Euripides's play to press on us a critique and recovery of inoperativity, Giorgio Agamben's refusal concept. For Agamben, inoperativity means the suspension of the ordinary (the "no" of Melville's Bartleby, with his formal formula: "I prefer not") and its replacement by a kind of "new use" that is useless or post-use. In the *Bacchae*, however, the inoperativity that the women enjoy involves not just the *suspension* of use but also a kind of *intensification* of use. Away from patriarchy's sex-gender enclosures, the women experience leisure and pleasure in new, intensified ways that alter their experience of space and time. Their power is suggested by the messenger's report to Pentheus that when the women chased away the herdsmen spying on them, the women ran, and "the world ran with them."[13] He is clearly stunned by the swerve he has witnessed. The bacchants exert a gravitational pull on the world from which others think they only flee.

They also learn to police their own boundaries, outside the city, away from the boundaries of public and private that once confined their movements and spaces. When they are spied on by those herdsmen "camouflaged with leaves," whose "good idea" it was to "lay in ambush" hoping to "hunt down Agave, Pentheus's mother, and drag her from the dance," the women attack. The herdsmen's foiled plan prefigures what will later happen when the women encounter Pentheus, also up to no good, also spying on what he should not see. In the earlier scene, the men, once discovered, flee in fright ("they would have torn us to pieces"), and the women attack the men's cattle in a horrifying way, dismembering rather than slaughtering them. "A single woman pulled a mewling calf in two, while others clawed apart a full-grown heifer. . . . Then they rose like birds," flew to towns in the foothills, and "snatched children from their homes and pillaged houses."[14] The men fought back with spears but drew no blood, while the women's "flung wands" in turn "ripped open flesh, and the men turned and ran. Women routing men! Some god was there with them," says the messenger.[15]

Duly warned and frightened, the men who witnessed the horrors retreat and then report to Pentheus on the wildness of the women. This episode of violence against the animals is like a blooding of the hounds, a rehearsal for the more profound violence to come, when the bacchants will kill Pentheus. Indeed, arguably everything on Cithaeron is a rehearsal, perhaps even also for the return to the city that will follow. Having erected a para-polis outside the city, the women will soon risk their hard-earned inoperativity in order to preserve and practice it *in* the city. They won't succeed fully. It is a tragedy after all! But whose tragedy is it? We have long assumed it is Pentheus's, since he overreaches and pays with his life; or that of the women, who also overreach, and will be exiled, and Agave's, in particular, since she will lose her son, Pentheus, the king. Pentheus withheld the recognition due a god, and the women dabbled in mysteries that were beyond them. But neither the women's violence nor their "splendid failure" means the women were wrong to leave the city and then return to it. It could simply mean the city was not ready for them, in which case, the *Bacchae* is not the women's tragedy at all, nor Pentheus's, but the city's.[16]

Pentheus at first wants to battle the bacchants directly, but his desire to *see* and maybe even *be* one of them is stoked by Dionysus, who lures the king, his cousin, into a trap. Thinking he is talking to a stranger who follows Dionysus and not to the god himself, Pentheus listens to the stranger's advice and agrees to dress as a woman so as to be able to observe the women on Cithaeron surreptitiously without offense. Dionysus in disguise says, "I'll dress you up as a woman, and then you can go see what they are up to." Pentheus seems drawn to the stranger whom he admires as womanish ("such long hair . . . Not a wrestler, then, I take it? . . . Such pale skin," says Pentheus when they first meet).[17] And then Pentheus clearly enjoys the cross-dressing he initially resisted as unbefitting a king. He moves and adjusts his costume under Dionysus's direction, practicing his gestures. "So how do I look? A little like Aunt Ino, or a bit more like my mother?"[18] Still under the direction of the god, but unknowingly also under his divine influence (but then, according to Tiresias, all the god does is to uninhibit our own secret desire), Pentheus follows Dionysus's instruction and hides in the top of a tree (it might even be a phallus tree[19]) on Cithaeron so as to get a good view. Dionysus calls to the women, notifying them that a "creature" is watching them, and the women attack the creature, at first singly and without success, then together. "Once they saw [Pentheus] . . . they started pelting him with stones, throwing fir branches over like javelins." Notably, the bacchants begin singly, pell-mell, each one throwing branches and rocks at the figure high above. But "all fell short." So they try another tactic: "they sheared the limbs off an oak and tried to lever the fir [tree] up by its roots. But that failed, too." So Agave calls on the women to join together. "'Come, my maenads, *gather round this tree and all take hold. . . .*' And with that, *countless hands* pulled and pushed." Only by acting in concert do the women succeed in bringing down the tree and Pentheus from its top: "and from his high roost Pentheus fell."[20] They then kill Pentheus, whom they seem not to recognize. They certainly do not respond to his cries. When the sisters kill Pentheus, they reperform their terrible violence against Semele, but this time they do it—as they did with the cattle—with their own bare hands, and this time the victim is Agave's own son. Thus, loss is repaid with loss.

The earlier murder of Semele and the exile of Dionysus that ensued are repaid now with the murder of Pentheus and the ensuing exile of the remaining royal family. Cadmus and his wife, Harmonia, are fated, Dionysus pronounces in the aftermath, to become wandering, conquering snakes. Their daughters, Agave, Ino, and Autonoe, are exiled out of the city. The sisters leave Thebes together, perhaps holding hands.[21] Their performance of sorority will be important to our recovery of inclination, in Chapter 2, where I argue that the refusal concept should figure not just maternal pacifism, as in Cavarero, but also the agonistic sororal ties that enable intimate dance and worship as well as violence and murder. These three sisters are on intimate terms with mutuality in all its violent ambiguities. Why doubt their taste for violence?

The play's most famous scene offers instruction here: when Dionysus seduces Pentheus into dressing as a woman, we see the king enjoys it as an expression of his own secret desire. Might the same be true later, when the women direct their violence against him? Tiresias claims early on that this god permits what his followers secretly want: "she who is modest will not be corrupted in Bacchic revelry. Do you see?"[22] Is the bacchants' refusal, which includes their violent murder of the king, an expression of *their* own secret desire? To borrow Tiresias's formulation, she who is pacifist cannot be corrupted to violence via revelry.

Judith Butler differs: the violence is regretted, she says in her reading of the play, rightly noting that what follows for Agave "is an infinite sorrow and remorse."[23] But what do the sorrow and remorse mean? And are they the only feelings that count? When Agave mourns her son, it may mean she regrets murdering the king. But she could also be seen as mourning her situation in which she cannot kill the king without sacrificing her son. Regicide and filicide are inextricably intertwined. This is Sara Ahmed's "double bind," described strikingly by Maurice Merleau-Ponty, whom Ahmed cites, as "the vital experience of giddiness and nausea, which is the awareness of our contingency and the horror with which it fills us."[24] The giddiness and nausea that are experienced simultaneously in Merleau-Ponty are pried apart in the *Bacchae* and sequenced in time. The women are giddy at the murder of Pentheus, and only later are they nauseated by what they have done. Such sequencing invites a moralized reading in which the later nausea is regret for the prior giddy act. But the simultaneity that Merleau-Ponty and Ahmed assume invites us to delve more deeply into giddiness and nausea as a "vital" response to the double bind of women acting free in patriarchy.

Alternatively, we may reconsider Butler's reading of Agave in loose connection with Bernard Williams's "tragic situation," which forces a choice between two oughts, and there is no single right thing to do because whatever we do will be attended by moral regret.[25] In the case of Agave, she committed regicide and killed her son. Although this is not what Williams had in mind when he explored the tragic clash of oughts, his approach may be helpful here. Since Agave's son is the king, regicide and filicide are one and the same act: she could not do the former without also doing the latter, and so she has reason for regret. But, arguably, as in a tragic situation, had she chosen the alternative course, she would have regretted that, too. Not taking down the tyrannical king would also be cause for regret, since ending his tyranny is also a normatively compelling act.

On this reading, the women who oppose the king but love Pentheus both desire the regicide they commit (un)knowingly *and* mourn the consequences. Their tragic predicament is clarified when we note that the bacchants commit regicide long before they kill the king and only commit murderous violence against him when he forces their hand.[26] It is regicide when the women refuse the king's orders to work (inoperativity) and when they set up a para-polis outside the city in which they rehearse new comportments and inaugurate new temporalities (inclination).

These more or less nonviolent acts are regicidal in that they deny recognition to the king and refuse his authority. The later violence just literalizes, in a way, what has already occurred.

When they kill and dismember Pentheus, the bacchants advance an arc of refusal that began when they, together, broke out of prison and left Thebes en masse. Actually, it began when they first defied Pentheus to worship Dionysus. Pentheus has lost his monarchy, though he doesn't know it, well before he dares to disguise himself as a woman to spy on the bacchants only to be murdered by them in the most horrifying way. In Thebes, his orders are not followed and his words are impotent. Dionysus, the bull/[wo]man/god Pentheus aims to net with his mortal power, will tie him up in a trap like a spare piece of string. Pentheus' rule is in pieces.

In the moment of his murder, Pentheus calls out, "Mother, Mother, look, it's me, your son, Pentheus!" and Agave wrenches his arm from its socket. Agave's nonrecognition of Pentheus suggests there is a problem with kinship or maternity (Butler) or with Agave (most readings). But what if we switch Agave's identity from mother, which is the interpellation that fails, to subject, an interpellation that seems to succeed? What if Agave *did* recognize Pentheus and still, *or therefore*, went on to dismember him? Then the seeming nonrecognition would be a recognition—not between mother and son but between subject and king.

I return to the scene several times in the following chapters, from the distinct vantage points provided by inoperativity, inclination, and fabulation, to consider what it would mean to see the women's violence as, in some way, deliberate and free: a refusal. This means approaching Euripides's play as an imaginative exploration of what is needed to render patriarchy inoperative, to engage it agonistically with inclination, and to demand or propose the fabulations that record it and support the effort to move past it.[27] Let us start, though, by acknowledging that the murder of Pentheus is nauseatingly horrifying. Its horror, which is surely the point, leads most readers or viewers to condemn the women who committed the violence and to see them as mad. But is it right to be shocked by the women's violence, and not by the king's?

If we hold off on the urge to moralize about the play (is it really necessary to *say* that murder is wrong?), then we create space to see that the *Bacchae* illustrates, metaphorically speaking, the breadth and depth of patriarchy's grasp, its imbrication in everything we love as well as in the structures and powers we resist. The play's horror is its powerful lesson: breaking with patriarchy means breaking (with) the fathers, sons, brothers, neighbors we love. It is difficult and awful, nauseating. The women's horrific killing of Pentheus allegorizes the double bind that goes beyond the tragic situation theorized by Williams, and it shows how the breaks necessitated by equality tear us apart, rip apart loved ones, and destroy the conjugal and communal bonds we value even though they make us unequal.[28] This is not a conflict between two oughts so much as it is a depiction of a double bind. The scene of dismemberment vivifies the fears that stop us, the reluctance to lose loved ones that renders us complicit with oppressive structures, and the anxieties that can keep us compliant with our own and others' subjugation. I suggest, in any case, that the overt violence on which so many focus when they encounter the *Bacchae* is less radical than the relaxation and rehearsal on Cithaeron that precede the regicide and the claim to the city that comes after it. When the women return to the city to demand to be feasted and have their story told not as one of madness but of sex equality or even of women's superiority to men, they are, in a way, killing Pentheus again. This, too, is part of the bacchants' *arc of refusal*.

1 Inoperativity and the Power of Assembly
Agamben with Butler

ONE VENTURES FROM HOME ON THE THREAD OF A TUNE.
—DELEUZE AND GUATTARI, *A THOUSAND PLATEAUS*

WE CAN SHARE A REFUSAL.
—SARA AHMED, *LIVING A FEMINIST LIFE*

WE WANT TO CHANGE EVERYTHING.
—NON UNA DI MENO

Refusal is one of the virtues necessary to democracy, and to feminist theory in particular, but it takes many forms: Agamben's "inoperativity" is the first of three refusal concepts to be critically examined and recovered for a feminist theory of refusal.[1]

Why start with Agamben? Because his work has inspired what I think of as the Bartleby Left, for whom refusal is something of an end in itself, and Melville's Bartleby is a hero. Bartleby's "I prefer not to," a celebrated example of inoperativity, responds to the concern that giving reasons and making demands just enters would-be dissidents into the tradeoffs of their opponents and compromises projects of radical transformation. Inoperativity is a key concept of refusal in Giorgio Agamben's work because he advocates a politics or ethics of pure means, rejecting instrumental and teleological approaches to ethics or politics.

To render something inoperative, Agamben says, is to suspend its old use, and ideally, repurpose it to a new use that is post-use, not a means to any end. What would that look like? Often, on Agamben's account, to render something inoperative means removing it from use by exhibiting it or reiterating it in festive form where it cannot be a means to anything.[2] This means Agamben's refusal concept is vulnerable to charges of aestheticism, purism, or passivity.[3] In a world of use that demands hyper-doing, refusal may well find expression in aestheticism, purism, or passivity; but the risk is that embracing these *as* refusal ends up dismissing as merely instrumental or teleological all actual, active efforts to refuse. With the help of the *Bacchae*, I make the case here for a feminist inoperativity willing to risk implication in means and ends on behalf of equality, power, and transformation. An inoperativity that abandons the city, or suspends the everyday, is a move in the feminist arc of refusal, not its destination.

Recall the refusal of the Occupy Wall Street movement in 2011 to make specific demands in return for which they would leave New York's Zucotti Park and the festival-like protest that started there. Revisiting the movement four years later, Michael Levitin argues that "Occupy was, at its core, a movement constrained by its own contradictions: filled with leaders who declared themselves leaderless, governed by a consensus-based structure that failed to reach consensus, and seeking to transform politics while refusing to become political." In 2011, the mainstream media mocked its Bartleby posture, faulting it "for its failure to produce concrete results." But in the years that followed, several focused means-end movements grew out of Occupy, including those advocating for student debt forgiveness and the movement to raise the federal minimum wage. Occupy is the Cithaeron that rejects means-ends; but the Debt Collective, Rolling Jubilee, and the Fight for Fifteen represent the movement's return to the city. Have they sold out? Or do they bring Cithaeron home by way of a transformative politics of equality named by the call "we are the 99 percent"? If the latter, their political vision of a more equal society is not reducible to their demands. The demands are steps in a larger politics of transformation.[4]

The purism of Agamben's version of inoperativity is evident when he locates all his examples of inoperativity in exceptional, liminal times and spaces: outside the city or in the time or space of festival or resurrection, on the verge, threshold, or precipice of (in)action. Festival, exception, precipice, and exhibition are central to his effort to refuse means-ends politics and modernity's conversion of everything into use, accelerated under contemporary neoliberal capitalism. To feminists, however, it matters that the problematic paradigm of use is specifically gendered and raced (the historic leashing of women and people of color to reproduction and production) and that it predates the modern era by centuries. Feminists' different diagnosis of the problem of use—as part of raced and gendered patriarchal histories and ongoing practices—leads us to prioritize action on behalf of equality over what Agamben favors: the suspension of use, as such. Or better, we insist the suspension of use is part of a larger arc of refusal.

I will argue here for a feminist take on inoperativity that takes its bearings not from Agamben's examples—Melville's Bartleby and the Christian glorious body are the two examined here—but from the *Bacchae*. The play is well-served by an inoperativity reading, since the women's Dionysian festivities inspire them to refuse work (unproductive) and to abandon conventional norms of sex-gender (unreproductive). But in this Greek tragedy inoperativity is not just the suspension of use; it involves also and more significantly the intensification of use. As we shall see, Agamben's turn to exhibition and spectacle to suspend use is countered by the bacchants, who have their own critique of exhibition and have reason to suspect that spectacle is invariably a carrier for the male gaze. The bacchants find their way to a different inoperativity.

After offering an inoperativity reading of the *Bacchae*, I turn to two *Bacchae* readings of inoperativity. First, I examine, through the lens of the bacchants' version of inoperativity, Agamben's account of the "glorious body," noting the contrast between the post-mortem perfection he marvels at and the bacchants' more vital version of festive embodiment. I then turn to *The Fits*, a 2015 film by Anna Rose Holmer. *The Fits* is a modern *Bacchae* which imagines what it might look like to be released from the daily demands of use without falling back on exhibition or festival as the antidote. Instead, *The Fits* trains our attention on the motions and gestures of refusal, relying on the camera's gaze and also intensifying or troubling it so that the young women at the film's center are not simply used or watched.

Some of the film techniques used in *The Fits* recall and may even cite those used by nineteenth-century sciences of motion, which Agamben comments on in his early "Notes on Gesture."[5] Agamben says these new studies of motion robbed the bourgeoisie of their gestures. I read *The Fits* as closely in conversation with Agamben's essay and with this history, and I show how the film can be seen as a reclamation of those gestures, a taking back. Thus, *The Fits* offers a way out of Agamben's impasses that he does not. A close reading of Agamben's essay and the film together highlights the gendered history of the study of gesture, and helps to finalize Chapter 1's recovery of inoperativity for a feminist theory of refusal.

The turn to motion studies sets up the two chapters that follow, focused, respectively, on gesture (inclination) and gait (fabulation's wayward wanderers). But I begin with Melville's Bartleby to detail the difference between a Bartleby politics of inoperativity and the bacchants' arc of refusal.[6]

Queer Escapes: Bartleby or the *Bacchae*?

> "Are you going to do something?"
> —LAWYER TO BARTLEBY

Agamben's most well-known example of inoperativity is Herman Melville's Bartleby who "prefers not to." Melville's story tells what happens after a Wall Street lawyer advertises for a clerk and Bartleby answers the ad. Bartleby starts out as a furious copyist who works ceaselessly. He ends as a destituent subject whose seeming self-evacuation, ultimately suicidal, discomfits and disorients those around him. This may be part of the attraction for Agamben, that destituency—a kind of inoperativity—has consequences. But Melville's Bartleby has more to offer inoperativity than Agamben realizes: fossilized in that short story is a more agonistic sort of inoperativity than the one Agamben excavates.

For Agamben, inoperativity is "the hardest thing to consider. For if potentiality were always only the potential to do or to be something, we would never experience it as such; it would exist only in the actuality in which it is realized."[7] And that would betray it so, Agamben explains, inoperativity must be poised on the verge, in a kind of suspended animation. Hence Agamben's attraction to Bartleby who famously prefers not to but never actually says no.[8]

Bartleby can also be read, however, not as a figure of suspension but of intensification. His refusal to comply with his employer's demands and requests, while also refusing to *not* comply with them, intensifies a situation already ongoing in an office that is "postwork" well before Bartleby's arrival.[9] Other employees have outmaneuvered their boss to negotiate a limited freedom, never saying an outright yes or no either. Ginger, Nippers, and Turkey, especially the latter two, work the least amount possible while keeping their jobs. They hoard time to waste, seemingly enjoying their theft, if not their freedom, as would-be wastrels. Thus, Bartleby's arrival does not introduce refusal to the office; it magnetizes and intensifies a refusal that is already in play.

The lawyer hopes his new industrious hire will be an example to the others, that Bartleby will accomplish by example what he, the boss, cannot accomplish by power or authority. And Bartleby *will* be an example to the others, just not in that hoped-for way. When the lawyer asks Bartleby to do more than copy, Bartleby refuses. Responding virtually identically to kindness ("Are your eyes recovered?") and to threats ("Will you, or will you not, quit me?"), Bartleby refuses to give reasons for his noncompliance; he is silent or only repeats his *formula*, as Deleuze calls the famous "I prefer not to."[10] Soon, everyone in the law office is using that "queer" word: *prefer*. Eventually, the law office is relocated in response to Bartleby's *occupation* of the workplace, and Bartleby is finally evicted and arrested. This is the arc of refusal in Bartleby: first, specific work refusal (he will copy, but he will not join with others to check the copies), then no work and no justification (he will not even copy and he will not say why), then occupation (he will not work at all, but neither will he leave the office). The final move in the arc is his hungering to death in prison after the lawyer has visited him there and made provisions to be certain that Bartleby receives food.

For Agamben, as for Deleuze before him, the radicality of Bartleby's refusal is precisely in its pure roteness, which empties language of meaning, rendering it inoperative.[11] What begins seemingly as a refusal in language becomes, or turns out to be, a refusal *of* language. When Bartleby repeats virtually the same words, "I prefer not to" or "I would prefer not to," without explanation or e*labor*ation (which would involve *labor*), he switches language from communication to catechism (though it is always both: what are J. L. Austin's performative utterances if not magic-making repetitions of language?).[12]

Consider by comparison the bacchants' repeated chant, "*Eta Bakkae.*" Like Bartleby's formula, the women's chant becomes hypnotic thrum, but the bacchants' chant also performatively collects the women together.[13] Where Bartleby's phrase seeks freedom, first, in the solitary control over the terms of work existence and then in their evacuation, the women worshippers of Dionysus seek freedom in work refusal, then in abandon as assembly, and then in defense of their new form of life against sovereign intrusion.

In her *Notes toward a Performative Theory of Assembly*, Judith Butler notes the power of such collective chants. They gather people in assembly and focus their energies, she says. For her, what is important about the chant is its power to keep the assembled crowd nonviolent when events might otherwise take them over. The chant helps those gathered to "resist the mimetic pull of military aggression . . . by keeping in mind the larger goal: radical democratic change." The chant is a source of power and discipline for actors in concert. "To be swept into a violent exchange of the moment was to lose the patience needed to realize the revolution."[14] The chant binds people together and collectivizes their resolve.

When Butler says that what interests her about the chant is how "language worked not to incite an action, but to restrain one," to contain what might otherwise explode, she in effect splits the difference between

Bartleby and the bacchants.[15] Bartleby's singular phrase restrains, but it gathers no one together, and the bacchants' *Eta Bakkae* does gather people together, but we cannot say it restrains them. It incites them, surely, and they do commit violence. Butler wants to affiliate the chant with pacifism, but the bacchants show the chant is undecidable. It restrains those it gathers *and* it can urge them to violence. Like all performatives, the chant is part of a larger action and context. In this sense, we may say that we need not only what Butler offers here—"a performative theory of assembly"—but also an "assembly theory of the performative" (surely what she offered in *Gender Trouble*). The latter emphasizes what J. L. Austin notes in his work on speech acts: the dependence of performatives on an audience, listeners, interlocutors, contexts, moods, sensibilities, larger arcs, rites, rituals, worldly (in)capacities for responsiveness, contingency, and more. *Eta Bakkae*, which gathers the bacchants to common purpose, is neither essentially pacifist nor violent. There is restraint in the habitus of Cithaeron and propulsion in defending it from intrusion. In Austin's terms, we may say the bacchants are performatively gathered by the chant whose perlocutionary force (its uptake by others) is not secured by the chant. When the chant is let loose in the world, anything, or many things, may happen.

In the end, both Bartleby and the bacchants fail Butler's assembly test of restraint. Bartleby intensifies the lawyer's violence and turns it inward on himself. The bacchants violently attack the sovereign when he comes to spy on them. Although neither ends happily, exactly, there are nonetheless reasons to prefer the bacchants to Bartleby. Freedom from work, the enjoyment of dance, worship, and new ways of being, a return to the city, and then exile from it (the fate of the bacchants, whose exile tells us the world is not yet ready for them) surely offer a better arc to a feminist theory of refusal than isolation, self-fortressing and death (the fate of Bartleby, whose fate tells us there is no place for him in this world).[16]

The lawyer's sentimental elegy, "Ah Bartleby, Ah Humanity!" (humanism's own catechism), disavows his implication in the violence, but Bartleby intensifies it with his hungering death so that it cannot quite be covered up. Pentheus tries to do something similar once he is top-pled. Switching from violent, entitled, illicit observer hiding in a treetop to loved and loving son, Pentheus's "Mother, Mother," occludes his im-plication in the violence he himself launched and now ruefully suffers. But it is too late. Not because the women are too wild, as so many say, but rather, I would venture, because they are not wild enough! Their "queer escape" succumbs to cyclical endless vengeance and routine vio-lence.[17] It would be wilder still, in the sense of not so predictable, were the bacchants not to react violently to the king who spies on them. But that is not to be. Instead, they will try to break the cycle of violence only later, when they return to the city, but Cadmus will keep them in it. He is a cannier foe than his too-young grandson, as we shall see. But we need not give such prominence to the bacchants' direct, murderous encounter with Pentheus. Indeed, doing so occludes the affirmative dimensions of their refusal, which are broad and deep, and neglects the regicidal nature of their refusal's long arc. This is made clear by the in-operativity reading of the *Bacchae* to which I now turn.

The Slow Time of Slow Food: An Inoperativity Reading of the *Bacchae*

> In our society where leisure is the rule, idleness is a sort of deviation.
> —MICHEL FOUCAULT, "OF OTHER SPACES"

> In consuming honey so avidly, the honey-mad woman . . . consum[es] a substance like herself [and] usurps her society's right to consume her.
> —PATRICIA YAEGER, "HONEY-MAD WOMEN"

The comparison of Bartleby and the bacchants shows how, Agamben's embrace of Bartleby notwithstanding, Melville's character is removed from key components of inoperativity as theorized by Agamben himself. Agamben says inoperativity involves not only the suspension of use (evac-uating signifying systems, or undoing the law) but also the generation of "new use" (new nonutilitarian ways of doing something *like* what was once done); specifically, Agamben says in *Nudities*, inoperativity is "new use in common."[18] Bartleby's formulaic language may seem to pass this test since, as the lawyer says, it is a "queer" phrase, and perhaps it becomes common—and not just contagious—when it is taken up by his office mates. But there is no concertedness here. Bartleby also lacks the enjoyment that Agamben associates with new use, as for example when Agamben approvingly affiliates inoperativity with the messianic vision of one day playing with the law.[19] For that, I suggest, and for the "turn" or "swerve" that Butler elsewhere calls "queer," we do better to turn to the bacchants.[20]

The *Bacchae* offers a gendered example of inoperativity. In Euripides's tragedy, the women of Thebes escape the bonds of household reproduction, defying King Pentheus's orders to stay home, work at their looms, and care for their children.[21] So far, their refusal suspends use. But what the women enjoy at Cithaeron, relaxing outside the city apart from its structures and strictures, illustrates the "new use in common" that is supposed to be a feature of Agamben's inoperativity. How the women enjoy themselves, however, presses further, beyond inoperativity's two-step suspension of old use and inauguration of new (post-)use, and toward the *intensification* of use.

The women's work refusal in Thebes, which includes their escape from imprisonment and their flight from the city, is part of that first suspensive step of "no use." Fearlessly, they defy orders and abandon the instruments of work, the loom and shuttle. Locked up, they break out and flee imprisonment to escape the city. Once outside it, on Cithaeron, the women move to inoperativity's second step: "new use." They establish a heterotopia where they can practice another way of living. Organized into three women-led bands rather than male-headed households, the bacchants together transgress all the norms by which they were governed in Thebes and they ground new normativities.[22] The women flee the city that maternalizes them, but rather than refuse to nurture, which would be a "no use" refusal of maternalism, they breastfeed animals out in the wild. Their nursing refuses the maternalism of heteronormative reproduction but not the intimacy of care. They throw out the baby, we might say, but keep the bathwater. Repurposing the breast out in the wild, they violate the practices of enclosure that prohibit women being out of doors and they ironize familiar patriarchal practices that force women into domesticity.

The women also act wild. Pentheus imagines them wild with sex, but the wildness of the women is that they nurse in the required way but with the "wrong" object. This does not simply broaden the circle of who counts (animals, too!); it goes further to disorient the human as such. Recall Agamben's position that sovereign power, as Guillermina Seri puts it, "reproduces itself by distinguishing between human and inhuman, and makes clear that there is no humanity outside this decision." The bacchants who nurse wild animals rework the "anthropological machine" to contest sovereignty.[23] On such a reading, their regicide is a slow regicide. It occurs long before they attack Pentheus, and it is the express aim of the women's actions, not an unfortunate error into which they inadvertently stumble when they are spied on by Pentheus.

Victoria Wohl highlights the importance of wildness in the *Bacchae*, seeing in the play evidence of an unnoted "anti-Oedipal strain in Greek thought" and a rejection of the structuralist binaries in terms of which Charles Segal interprets the play.[24] Wohl juxtaposes two approaches to the play, one oedipal and the other anti-oedipal. The former puts the play in the company of many other classical tragedies, which explore tensions between fathers and sons. The latter singles out what is unique about the *Bacchae*, specifically its wild de-oedipalization of desire. Says Wohl, "the bacchants' pleasure lies not in sexual objects [i.e., it is not oriented by the phallus of oedipal desire], but in movement or intensities: in rushing, whirling, yelling, hunting." That is to say, its logic is not "the either-or logic of sexual difference, but the logic that for Deleuze and Guattari characterizes desiring-production: 'and . . . and . . . and.'"[25]

For Wohl, the many "bizarre gender permutations in the play" and the often "terrifying mutations" generate "exhilarating new sensations" and promote a new view of sexual difference as "no longer a mysterious union of [binary] opposites" but rather "as a series of transformations."[26]

Deleuze and Guattari call such beings *bodies without organs* or BwO.[27] The BwO rejects the normative organ/ization of the body according to oedipal desires and opens the body to new pains, pleasures, and worlds beyond the binary of sexual difference and beyond structuralist categories of kinship. The best example of this, Wohl says, is Pentheus's dismembered body, which becomes "a smooth surface that registers no social status or gender but pure and fleeting energies."[28] (In Chapter 2 I will offer a different reading of the corpse as a queer registry of multiple statuses and genders.)

Where Charles Segal sees sexual difference as tested but restored in the play (in the "deliberate destructuring of the familiar patterns of order," he claims, the binary of sexual difference survives),[29] Wohl sees such structuralist readings as "complicit with the social and psychological normativity of Oedipality" and asks: what normative restoration can be said to occur when Cadmus and his wife end up in exile as snakes?[30]

The oedipal and anti-oedipal approaches are not the only choices, however. The *Bacchae* also offers a third option, a post-oedipal reading focused on the gynocentric nature of the gathering on Cithaeron, the particulars of the women's suspension of use and their experience of intensification, not the mad whirling that Wohl singles out but specifically: their honey-mad chants, the slow time of their leisure, and the generative powers of their assembly.[31]

Before the quick violence and mad gender dispersions, or alongside them, come the women's relaxation and its slow temporality, to which Wohl does not attend. Here is the herdsman's account of what he saw before he and his mates were discovered and fled. He saw three bands of women, each one led by Agave, Pentheus's mother, and her two sisters, Ino and Autonoe. "They [the women] lay exhausted, some resting on fir branches, others sleeping among oak leaves. They were modest and composed, not drunk with wine as you [Pentheus] say, not dancing wildly to pipe music, or chasing Aphrodite in some ecstasy."[32] No wild dancing, no ecstatic chasing? Not busy with worship? Not mad with activity? What were they *doing*? In her *Notes toward a Performative Theory of Assembly,*

Butler notes the power of "the simple act of sleeping there" as part of the assembly's prefigurative institution of new "horizontal relations."[33] On Cithaeron we see it: the simple act of sleeping there, and the enjoyment of relaxation, are radical. Might they prefigure a new horizontality?

When Agave is awakened from her daytime rest, perhaps by the noise of the spying herdsmen's cows, she lets out a cry that stirs the rest of the women from their sleep. Agave is startled and quick, "springing to her feet [she] let out a cry," but the women's awakening is languorous.[34] Awake but unaware of the men nearby, the women make move to worship, bringing forth water, milk, and honey from the ground with their thyrses, and then "waving their wands for the start of the ritual."[35] Their *slow* awakening and languorous movements are worth recounting:

> One by one they woke, rubbing their eyes like children, and rose— tall and straight. What a sight it was: old and young, some still unmarried. What a sight. First they stretched back to loosen their hair and let it fall over their shoulders, and those whose fawn-skin straps had slipped in sleep, secured them again with snakes that licked at their cheeks. New mothers who had left their babies behind at home, drew gazelles and wolf cubs to their swollen breasts and let them feed.[36]

Wohl rightly highlights the species dispersion reported here, distinct from the gender dispersion represented by Pentheus's later cross-dressing. The women use snakes to belt their dresses and offer their breasts to young gazelles and cubs. But also striking is the doldrum-like temporality of the women's sleep and awakening. In this scene, everything happens in slow motion.[37]

The slow time of Cithaeron is also subtly suggested by the food there, where "the plain flows with milk, with wine it flows, flows too with bees' nectar."[38] This list—milk, wine, and honey—calls to mind Lévi-Strauss's *The Raw and the Cooked* and its companion volume, *From Honey to Ashes*, the latter a source for Patricia Yaeger in her work on honey-mad women.[39] The connection between honey and inoperativity is noted by Norman Bryson, too, in connection with another work of art: "What have in common," Bryson asks, "the wine and the honey, the cheese and the milk, if not that they are all *culinary invocations of a world without work?*"[40] So, too, in the *Bacchae,* on which Bryson comments as well: when the women leave the city, he says, "all toil is forgotten: scratch the soil with bare fingers and milk comes welling up, strike a thyrsus in the earth and a spring of wine springs forth, pure honey sprouts from the wands. The honey and the milk are raw and their richness testifies to the dispensability of culture. The wine and the cheese require, by contrast, elaborate preparation, but they are foods produced by fermentation, a process which leaves the work of transformation to nature."[41]

The bacchants' later return from Cithaeron to Thebes is a transition from the raw to the city's cooked. It will begin, notably, with the women's murderous encounter with the raw flesh of the king's body, and it will end when Agave returns to Thebes and calls, first of all, for a feast. This is more than a call for celebration. Calling first for a feast, Agave shows she knows the price of reentry to the city involves trading the raw for the cooked, which means, very roughly, nature for culture and all that is implied. But for whom does such a call have implications?

An answer is suggested by Véronica Gago's account of the recent experience of Argentine feminists planning for a general strike on behalf of Not One (Woman) Less. A group of women wanted to join the women's strike but were committed to cook for a soup kitchen. How could they participate in the strike and not leave others hungry? Gago says, what "at first seems contradictory—'We want to strike but we cannot strike'—broadens the strike, [and] an idea emerges. . . . Why don't we just distribute raw food? We will leave the food at the soup kitchen door, but raw. Taking away all the labor of cooking, serving, washing . . . unblocks the situation and adds another level to the practice of the strike. The idea becomes a graffiti throughout the neighborhood. 'March 8, today, we distribute raw food. Ni una Menos.'" In sum, Gago says, "the assembly thus becomes a way of evaluating the logic of the sensible qualities of things—the raw and the cooked—from the point of view of women's labor."[42]

Here, we see it is women's *labor*, and not just fire, and not just culture, that distinguishes the raw from the cooked. In Thebes, among the family of Cadmus, it is surely the labor of slaves. But on Cithaeron, there is no labor in food preparation at all. Food is readied to be eaten neither by the fast heat of fire nor by the labor-intensive preparations that go with it in the city but by the slow heat of fermentation, which is a kind of intensification. Fermentation chemically breaks down substances. Its agents include bacteria and yeast, microorganisms that are effervescent or heat producing.[43] Since Agave will later be said to foam at the mouth as she dismembers Pentheus, it may matter that foam is fermentation's by-product; and it is fitting, surely, that fermentation's archaic meanings are "agitation" or "excitement." Fermentation's microorganisms excite a reaction, offering chemical parallel to what happens when dissenters assemble: nutrients enrich life and cause breakdowns.[44]

It is not clear whether a community that lives on slow time chooses slow food or whether the community's dependence on slow food, as it were, slows time.[45] The latter is in keeping with Bryson's great phrase, "culinary invocation," which suggests the food calls for a different time and opens the way to a new world: without work, we are off the clock. Regardless, intensification here offers a new take on inoperativity—not on the verge, like Agamben's inoperativity, but rather in the dirt of experience, where what is can be broken down and what is not yet may be invoked.[46]

Without endorsing structuralist binaries like the raw and the cooked, we can with the help of Bryson's idea of a "culinary invocation" see through their lens that Cithaeron is characterized not just by the miracle of plenitude (Wohl's "miraculous flows"), nor just by the festive suspension of work characteristic of Agamben's inoperativity, but also by the distinctive plenty of slow food and slow time.[47] Pentheus claims that the women on Cithaeron are in a perpetual frenzy of activity and transgression, but they are mostly not. And this is their third radicality: beyond or apart from the dispersal of gender and/or the mutation of the human to human/animal, to which Wohl calls attention, and beyond the suspensive inoperativity of work refusal, lie the women's relaxation and its intense, slowed time. In her *Notes toward a Performative Theory of Assembly*, Butler notes the power and desire of assembly "to produce a new form of sociality on the spot."[48] On Cithaeron the new sociality is a slow sociality.[49] The women of the *Bacchae*, figures of a feminist, agonistic inoperativity of intensification, are closer to Butler's assembly, which has its own inoperativities, than to Agamben's inoperativity, which lacks its own "assembly."

Glorious Bodies, I: A *Bacchae* Reading of Inoperativity

> Are we human? Or are we dancer?
> —THE KILLERS, "HUMAN"

I turn now from my inoperativity reading of the *Bacchae* to two *Bacchae* readings of inoperativity. The first I develop with the *Bacchae*; the second will draw on a contemporary *Bacchae: The Fits*. Both help us see how Agamben's effort to neutralize use by way of a new use that is more spectacle than experience actually allows use to slip back in. It is against such slippage that the *Bacchae* ironizes spectatorship, by using metatheatrical references to highlight spectacle's artifice and by underlining the bacchants' outrage at being watched. For its part, *The Fits* furthers that outrage by ironizing and problematizing the gaze of the camera so that it both shows and does not show the mystical Dionysian experience of its protagonist, a member of a local dance troupe.

Agamben does not discuss *The Fits*, a film about a young African American dance troupe in Ohio. But he does discuss dance, which is one of his examples of inoperativity. He notes how dance choreographs the body into a new use out of which it is impossible to discern the pedestrian body that precedes it.[50] However, Agamben focuses not on the experience of dance and how it transports the dancer (that would be an intensification reading) but rather on the experience of the spectator watching the dancer, being transported by it to apprehend a kind of embodiment that is new use (a suspension of use reading). In place of dance as a religious or political *experience*, Agamben offers dance as an aesthetic object or *spectacle*. This switches the focus from experience to gaze, participation to contemplation. In keeping with Agamben's approach to inoperativity (and his broader commitment to an ethics and politics of pure means), dance is suspended, poised on the cusp of action, but not thrust into activity: "What is essential here is a dimension of *praxis* in which simple human activities are neither negated nor abolished but suspended and rendered inoperative in order to be exhibited, as such, in a festive manner." Exhibition *suspends* use.[51]

This is evident also in another of Agamben's key examples of inoperativity, the glorious body, which is the Christian theological term for the body of Christ after Resurrection. Rehearsing early church debates about why the body of the risen Christ has its organs if they are no longer needed postmortem, Agamben sides with Aquinas who says the organs are there not to be used but to be seen.[52] Precisely in its uselessness, the glorious body exhibits the perfection of God's creation. "The glorious body is an ostensive body whose functions are not executed but displayed," exhibited, not used, Agamben says.[53] Because it is a body without (working) organs, the Christian glorious body makes it "possible for the first time to conceive of the separation of an organ from its physiological function," Agamben says.[54] It is as if the liver could say "I prefer not to."[55]

With its post-use organs, the glorious body may be *inoperative* in Agamben's sense of suspended use, but it remains normatively *organized*, with everything in its proper place, its enjoyments suspended (a priesthood of the postmortem) but still harnessed to useful reproduction. This body is an aesthetic object for exhibition. For contrast, we may think of Deleuze and Guattari's body without organs, the BwO, which is an intensified, erotic, and dis-*organ*-ized object for enjoyment, not contemplation.

Similarly, the bacchants in Euripides's play render the quotidian inoperative, not suspensively but intensively. Rejecting spectacle and doubling down on experience, they re-organ-ize their bodies for new pleasures, fast and slow, on Cithaeron.

Consider another example alongside these. La Furiosa, an Argentine feminist effort to render inoperative the country's nationalist, patriarchal dance. One of the movement's members recalls how in her childhood, when Argentina was governed by a junta and her father was one of its generals, he made sure that the tango, televised every Sunday night, was required family viewing. The traditional dance is still part of Argentina's imagined national community, but a new tango feminist movement is seeking "to make tango halls less dogmatic about traditional gender roles and more assertive about rooting out sexual harassment and assault." The movement seeks not to suspend the tango but to recover it. In July 2019, one member of the collective, Ms. Furió, "started renting venues for [an] event earlier this year, calling it La Furiosa—or the livid woman."[56] The new venues assemble women for a tango in which new modes of comportment swerve off the strictly guarded path of Argentina's heteronormative nationalism. Rather than just abandon the old tango, where it could go on constituting the mainstream meaning of nation and circumscribing the terms of membership in it, and rather than suspending it, the movement agonistically offers up not only a new use of the body, the experience of dance, but also more than dance. This is La Furiosa's version of returning to the city, as the bacchants will do in the end as well. The feminist reoccupation of the tango is a *queer escape* and a grounded normativity.

La Furiosa and the *Bacchae*, together, call attention to the *politics* of ostention or spectatorship as such. In the *Bacchae*, father figures tell the women where they may be and what they may see: this is the work of both Cadmus and Pentheus, his grandson (in patriarchy, even the son can be the father—that is to say, head of household). The bacchants respond by opposing display and spectatorship in favor of the transformative *experience* of their own dance. Similarly, in Argentina, Ms. Furió moves from watching television under the watchful eye of a Penthean father who chooses what the family will watch to herself setting the scene for a feminist, agonistic tango that aims to decenter the patriarch.[57]

In the *Bacchae*, when the herdsman tells of the bacchants' secret rites, he reports the bacchants' outrage at being made a spectacle for men in hiding. The play's references to secret *watching* render transgressive the audience's own illicit observation of the play's daring spectacle.[58] At that very moment, after all, other men are also watching, as spectators of this theatrical performance. There are many references in the play to its own artifice as spectacle. One oft-noted example is Dionysus taking on the role of director when he instructs Pentheus in how to play his role as a woman ("*Dionysus:* Let me be your hairdresser. Hold still. . . . *Pentheus:* You arrange everything. I'm in your hands").[59] This, in a play in which all the women's roles are played by men who have, presumably, been similarly instructed backstage and in rehearsal. Thus, we may see in the play a metatheatrical rumination on the politics of spectacle and a warning about the just deserts of illicit onlooking.

Or we may see in its looped interrogation of these matters a rather different lesson about the unavoidable, problematic ethics and politics of spectacle. Privileging the exhibitive over the experiential, Agamben positions us with Pentheus on his treetop: watching. But the women of the *Bacchae*, who do not want to be watched by seeing eyes (they *will* later want their story told to listening ears), conjure a different inoperativity.[60] When Euripides's wine-god women refuse work and gather together to worship Dionysus on Cithaeron, they use their bodies in new ways, unleashed from normative use: sleeping in the daytime, moving languorously not efficiently, nursing wild animals not babies, and using snakes to clothe themselves with those creatures' live bodies and not just their dead skins. None of this is exhibitive or ostensive. That Pentheus wants to watch is one of his many errors, a sign of how deep is his misunderstanding, how out of his element he is. We might say that Pentheus wanting to watch is a sign that he mistakes the bacchic women for Agambenian glorious bodies, as if they were to be exhibited in a post-use context and *seen*, when they are more like Butler's assemblies, intent on *enjoying* themselves in proximity to each other in ever new, queer, nonreproductive ways that are irreducible to use and hopefully prefigurative.[61]

The problem for Agamben's affiliation of inoperativity with exhibition is that although exhibition is opposed to use, it restores use and traffics in it.[62] In the *Bacchae*, observation is a problem because it returns us to a world where women exist to be watched and are designated for men's use and oedipal pleasure.[63] This is what the women leave behind when they flee to Cithaeron. As bacchants, the women are animal mothers and lovers, providers of interspecies care, celebrators of regeneration, and capable of great destruction; their bodies are natal, vital, and mortal. If their retreat on Cithaeron is short lived, at least we may say it is short *lived*. When they are watched, however, their actions are measured not by a standard of vitality but by one of patriarchal normativity. The power of Euripides's play, as I read it, is its indication that what begins as work refusal in the context of patriarchal normativity may go further to change the standards by which it is judged and issue in a generative, amorous, and transformational experiment in living, perhaps even a rehearsal for something more.

Or not: When a few years after his essay on Bartleby, Agamben turns to write on nymphs, what he finds there is tellingly more Bartleby than bacchant, quite different from the overflowing vitality of the women seeking to idle outside the city (Mount Cithaeron is said to be the location of the "groves of the nymphs").[64] Opening his essay on nymphs with a quotation from Giovanni Boccaccio, Agamben writes, "It is quite true," says Boccaccio, "that they [nymphs] are all female but they don't piss."[65] Possessed of bladders, but for no purpose, these nymphs are little more than a female iteration of the Christian glorious body. Is there no way out of inoperativity's maze or gaze?[66]

Glorious Bodies, II: *The Fits* as a *Bacchae* Reading of Inoperativity

Whereby the muscles seem to dance (*chorea*) quite independently of any motor purpose.

—AGAMBEN ABOUT TOURETTE SYNDROME, "NOTES ON GESTURE"

Must we choose to be slaves to gravity?

—*AURORA*, SUNG BY KIAH VICTORIA IN *THE FITS*

To produce a new form of sociality on the spot.

—JUDITH BUTLER, *PERFORMATIVE THEORY OF ASSEMBLY*

The Fits finds a way out. The film explores the cultural politics of Black girlhood and queer life through the story of Toni, a young Black girl who is drawn both to boxing, with her older brother, and to dancing, with the local dance troupe called the Lionesses.[67] "At the threshold of adolescence, Toni is confronted with conflicting models of bodily expression and belonging. What matters is how she works it out," says Patricia White.[68]

When she boxes, Toni moves fluidly and easily memorizes combinations. When she dances, she moves awkwardly at first and is unable to integrate the steps. Belonging comfortably to neither group, Toni moves back and forth between them, between boxing and dancing, boys and girls, in the sex-segregated spaces of a local community center in Cincinnati. The film closes with Toni experiencing the fits, a kind of seizure that has been moving through the dance community and finally lands on her. The title of the film, however, refers not only to those seizures but also to the demand of mandatory heterosexuality that Toni pick a side and fit in. She tries to do so, observing and mimicking the behaviors and comportment of the older girls in the dance troupe (with their talk of boyfriends and bodily markings of nail polish and earrings), but she does not always do so successfully or wholeheartedly.[69] Thus, the title— *The Fits*—names that demand, the demand to fit in, the innervations that result for those like Toni who don't, and what can happen when the demand is met with a mystical, even Dionysian experience.

In addition to its Dionysian ex-centricities and fitful fluidities, *The Fits* strikes me as a *Bacchae* because it takes up the *Bacchae*'s critique of spectacle by way of an inoperativity that is intensive not suspensive. Even while the film tells its story visually, it rejects conventional cinematic and other demands for the exhibitive, complicating rather than rewarding or indulging spectatorial desire.[70] The film has a unique way of *showing* its protagonist, Toni (whose own gaze is an act of intensification), while *fending off conventional spectatorial looking* and the cinematic gaze. Thus, the film both depicts and performs inoperativity. As Rizvana Bradley notes:

> From the beginning, [Toni] unsettles habitual dynamics of looking and being looked at, of seeing and being seen. The viewer is absorbed and troubled by Toni's defiant outward gaze. *As the concentration of her look gradually intensifies,* Toni's relentless gaze induces a palpable sense of unease. The power of Toni's look redoubles the effects of the cinematic close-up. [This is her deployment of intensification.] The opening shot collapses and dissolves perspectival time and space, as the slow zoom brings us into visceral contact with the timing and consistency of Toni's breathing and counting [as she does sit-ups], measuring her unremitting physical approach, which feels like an affront to the viewer's gaze in the way that *it challenges the film's voyeuristic separation between the audience and what is seen onscreen.*[71]

Contesting the voyeurism that another film might merely exploit, *The Fits* notably does not show most of Toni's body when she finally experiences "the fits." For a significant amount of time, we see only Toni's feet, in close-up, walking down a community center hallway and in slow motion.[72] The long slow hallway walk, the beginning of Toni's experience of "the fits," recalls Agamben's discussion in his "Notes on Gesture" of

Gilles de la Tourette's 1886 study of the human gait, which Agamben points out, is the second of two studies for which Tourette is known. The first is his study of the collection of tics, involuntary bodily shaking, and spasms—the fits—that would come to bear his name: Tourette syndrome.[73] Tourette described the syndrome in detail, providing, Agamben says, "a staggering proliferation of tics, involuntary spasms and mannerisms that can be defined only as a generalized catastrophe of the gestural sphere."[74]

Both of Tourette's studies are relevant to *The Fits* obviously, but it is Tourette's use of the "footprint method" in his second study of walking that is called to mind when Toni walks the community center's long hallway. Tourette used "a roll of white wallpaper, around seven or eight meters long and fifty centimeters wide . . . nailed to the floor and split in half lengthwise with a penciled line" to record the footprints of his subjects, whose feet he "sprinkled with powdered iron sesquioxide." The footprints could then "be measured with perfect precision according to different parameters," Agamben says.[75] In *The Fits*, it is not paper and powder but the slow-motion camera that records Toni's steps as it follows her down the hall. In that final sequence, Toni's steps leave no footprints, and behind her slow-motion feet, in soft focus, we see not Tourette's pristine white-papered walkway but bits of trash scattered on the floor of a well-used community center.[76]

Although Tourette did not use a camera for his studies, Agamben says, "the gaze at work is already prophetic of the cinema."[77] Pasi Väliaho explains what he means, mapping out the work of Vincenzo Neri who, in the early twentieth century, "following Gilles de la Tourette's footsteps," as it were, not only used footprint tracings, too, but also film and photographs to study the contorting bodies of his neurologically challenged patients. "It was precisely these kind of curiously arrhythmic motions that cinema was able to capture into the realm of knowledge and visibility; and here, one could say, we can see the cinema's capacity to take hold of the instantaneous, the accidental, the involuntary, and the irrational employed in its full power."[78]

For Agamben, who invokes not only Tourette but also Muybridge, Charcot, Marey, and others, these neurological studies of human movement are responsible for Western bourgeoisie's irretrievable loss of its gestures in the nineteenth century.[79] The cinematic gaze, discernible avant la lettre in Tourette's studies, is the problem, but Agamben looks nonetheless to cinema to record and repair the loss it has caused: "In the cinema, a society that has lost its gestures seeks to reappropriate what it has lost while simultaneously recording that loss," he says.[80] *The Fits* rejects such (anti-)cinematic nostalgia and invites us to see the attenuation of gesture, contra Agamben, not only in connection with mechanizations or biopoliticizations of the nineteenth century's new motion studies but also in connection with then-current and ongoing histories of race and gender injustice.[81] The film reclaims what has been stolen from its subjects, a community of Black adolescents in Cincinnati, by borrowing from the vocabulary of ordinary gesture for dance and cinema. As Patricia White notes, "The incorporation of everyday gestures—brushing one's hair or throwing a punch (Toni's best move)—into the choreography of stand battles is mirrored in reverse by the film's incorporation of dance into ordinary actions. The stylization of gesture, its communicability, comes to define the film's aesthetic as well as its themes."[82] *The Fits* takes back the gestures Agamben describes elegiacally as lost.

This is the film's response to the raced and gendered history that Agamben does not discuss while focusing with fascination on the particular history of Jean-Martin Charcot and others as dehumanizing. By contrast, let us consider the history of the neurological gaze recorded in André Brouillet's painting, A *Clinical Lesson at the Salpêtrière* (1887). The painting depicts a female hysteric, Blanche (Marie) Wittman, who has fainted. "Before her passing out there must have been some intense frantic gesturing," says Väliaho.[83] In the painting, we see Wittman, eyes closed, leaning back, fallen into the arms of one of Charcot's assistants. This is the "*arc en circle*, the hysteric's classic posture." A drawing of it hangs on the back wall in Brouillet's painting.[84] At the center of the painting, a light shines on Wittman's nearly bared breasts and opens her

André Brouillet, *A Clinical Lesson at the Salpêtrière* (1887). Paris Descartes University / Wikimedia

both to the clinical gaze and to the artist's and spectators' views. In *The Fits*, Toni is similarly positioned, leaning into a backward propulsion that mimics the *arc en circle*. Could *The Fits* be in dialogue with the famous depiction of one of Charcot's Tuesday lessons in which a woman's "fits" are subjected to the clinical "neurological gaze"? If so, *The Fits* rebukes Charcot and Brouillet. Toni is not similarly lit. Unlike Wittman, Toni moves at this moment from lit to silhouette. She is first shown (never exposed) and then obscured: the light that opens Wittman to view is so intense in *The Fits* that it blinds the viewer. Here, the film enacts its refusal of the exhibitive: by occluding the spectatorial gaze.[85]

But the film does not just refuse to intrude on its subject. Its refusal is not just suspensive. It employs the light to blind the viewer, but its camera does not stop. The camera is repurposed so that it is not only a device of clinical inspection or cinematic gazing but also a device of care. Significantly, no one catches Toni when she falls, and when she hits the

Stills from *The Fits,* directed by Anna Rose Holmer, Oscilloscope Laboratories, 2015

floor, the girls rush to her aid, moving from watching her to caring for her. This move from watching to caring is prefigured or modeled by the camera itself, which enlists ambiguous modes of display to counter the neurological and cinematic gaze of movement studies' cameras, lest their historic harms be repeated. Awakened by her fall, Toni's eyes open to look directly at us, unnervingly again (who is looking at whom, we wonder, not for the first time); her mouth's corners, almost out of the shot, twitch a bit into the beginning of a possible smile. Is it a twitch, perhaps a tic, or a smile? Who can say?

Thus, *The Fits* rewalks the endless hallways of the history of female hysteria, replacing the clinical gaze of Brouillet's painting (the men who grip Wittman with their eyes or arms) with the caress of the camera first and then with the assembly of girls who will gather Toni from the floor in a gesture for which we have no better word than sorority.

The camera caresses Toni throughout the film, but it is during her hallway walk that it asserts its new powers most forcefully. Toni begins moving from heel to toe, just as Tourette described, but soon strange things start to happen. Not tics, not yet, but what we might call an uprising.[86] Toni will hover for a while above the floor before succumbing to the spasmodic movements that are her version of the fits. It is important, as a matter of what Bradley calls the film's "cinematic knowledge" *and* as a critique of Agamben's inoperativity that Toni's suspension is achieved not by a camera that dissects or segments Toni's movements so that they can be *known* but by a camera that levitates, caresses, and obscures her: focusing on some of her parts, it makes her whole, precisely while shielding her from our view.[87]

With its caress, the camera refuses the neurological gaze of nineteenth-century movement studies and puts itself in that place.[88] The camera provides Toni with something like but not like the holding that Charcot's assistant provides Wittman in Brouillet's painting, that mise-en-scène of female hysteria, part of the history of female madness and contagion that runs, in all its variety, from the *Bacchae* to *The Fits*.[89]

Toni's fits partner with Black social dance, described by Bradley as "collectively enunciating the pain that marked the historical infliction of inhumane violence upon the body."[90] This second racial history, unmentioned by Agamben, is brought to mind when, during Toni's mystical hallway walk, her feet suddenly stop moving and she is suspended in midair, seemingly lifeless.[91] Patricia White calls this "the most spectacular fit yet witnessed" and notes that "Toni walks on air."[92] She does.[93] Toni's feet walk so high off the floor that they are almost out of reach of the camera. But then, as Toni turns a corner and the bodies of other girls assembled in the gym come into view, her feet stop moving.[94] They hang, just dangling. She is now not walking at all and suddenly, the film's mythic beauty is interrupted by the suggestion of the hard history that is one of the contexts that made Toni (im)possible.[95]

Has she become a glorious body in Agamben's sense? If Toni's "muscles seem [until now] to dance (*chorea*) quite independently of any *motor* purpose" (as Agamben says of Tourette syndrome),[96] they surely do not do so with no purpose. They cite a history of violence raced, sexed, and misogynistic, and depict the determination to triumph over it. Indeed, Toni's convulsions, which overtake her at the end of the hallway walk, and those of the other girls as well, call to mind Frantz Fanon's observation, in *Wretched of the Earth*, that the "muscles of the colonized are always tensed." For people who exist in a "constant muscular tonus," the "symbols of society" are not just "inhibitors but also stimulants."[97]

An Agamben style inoperativity reading of the sequence might privilege that moment of the cusp, between the hallway walk and the ultimate return to the gym. But the sequence as a whole suggests an encounter with the intensification, not suspension, of use. Toni drops back to earth. In the gym, she drops down, first moving in dancelike ways and then landing hard on the floor. The girls gasp, shocked by what they witness, perhaps in relief to realize she is still alive. Releasing Toni from its levitation of her body, the camera gives her up to gravity, and what might have been Agamben-style suspension gives way to Euripidean / Deleuzean vital intensification. This is cinema's bacchic refusal of

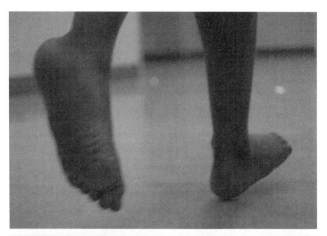

♪ Shouldn't we be treasure? ♪

♪ We were once the dream ♪

Stills from *The Fits,* directed by Anna Rose Holmer, Oscilloscope Laboratories, 2015

Tourette's and Charcot's and all the others' hallways of female hysteria and anti-Black violence. It is also arguably Toni's return to the city. The girls' gym in the community center is not her Cithaeron because it has offered not refuge but a series of tests that her adolescent queerness does not pass. To land there finally, loudly, is to make her claim.

Perhaps, like the bacchants who also float above others as they experience ecstasy and then return to the ground, ultimately even to claim the city, Toni, too, will exert a gravitational pull on the community assembled before her.[98] It is not clear. She has experimented with conventional femininity's nail polish and earrings, but the earrings infect her and the nail polish feels wrong. She scratches off the polish while she sits on the edge of the boxing ring. She may continue to tack between the community center's sex-segregated activities and communities. She may come out one day. She may fit in. She may be exiled. Who knows?[99]

What is clear is that Toni's experience of the fits is not like the others. But then, none of the others is like the others either. Even though the fits are contagious, each girl is individuated by their visitation. The fits belong to no one tempo; they do not obey Tourette's rules. For some of the girls, the fits quicken time; for others, they slow it down. The first to experience the fits looks like she is having an epileptic seizure on the gym's floor. Later, Toni's friend, Beezy, is also catapulted down to the floor, though her movements are less innervated than those of the first girl and jerkier. For Beezy, "it was crazy; it was like I was watching it from above, like I had two sets of eyes." For Maia, the third friend in Toni's little social circle, the experience "was, like, serene." Maia's eyes look up as she stands in a trance. An older girl describing her own experience says she woke up in the morning and her teddy bears were strewn all over her bedroom. Rather like Dionysus in the *Bacchae*, the fits may well permit what those visited by them secretly desire. For Maia, serenity. For Beezy, to be watched. For the older girl, to grow up. And for Toni, to struggle, to belong, and to be free.[100]

The Fits asks without elegy the question Butler poses in connection with assembly: what do bodies need to support themselves in this world?

Agamben's analysis of cinema suggests the answer is the restoration of the gestures upended by a technological capture.[101] Locating gestural dispossession in nineteenth-century studies of nerve diseases, Agamben preserves cinema as a kind of remediative apparatus, a *pharmakon* with the power to reconnect what it has segmented by providing an archive of lost gestures to be reanimated one day.[102] But *The Fits* contests such an approach when, entering into this cinematic archive of inoperativity, it illustrates the undecidability of suspension (when Toni is suspended, is she dead or living?) and enacts its own cinema of refusal. Taking back the camera, the film replaces cinema's originating neurological gaze with a technological caress.

Altering the lighting and the framing that conventionally govern viewing, using slow motion (like the doldrums of Cithaeron), soft focus, and blinding light, *The Fits* discredits old narratives and opens new possibilities.[103] It does so by enlisting techniques of refusal that might be said to be borrowed from the *Bacchae*: inoperativity, inclination, and fabulation. Moving inoperativity from suspension to intensification, shifting the powers and protocols of watching to something more like inclination's practices of care, and fabulating Toni's return, *The Fits* triumphs over the alienations Agamben mourns. It plays with conventional protocols of spectatorship on behalf of the *Bacchae*'s arc of refusal.[104] Where the bacchants chase off those who would watch, *The Fits* veils its protagonist in light. This is what we learn from rethinking inoperativity in connection with the *Bacchae*'s arc of refusal, an "arc" that might displace the *arc en circle* that has long hystericized women.

I have in this chapter offered an *inoperativity reading of the Bacchae* to show the power of inoperativity's lens to highlight previously underestimated agencies of the women in the play. One example of feminist inoperativity was the women of the *Bacchae* nursing not dependent infants, as would be normatively expected of them, but infant gazelles and wolf cubs. Another was the slowed time and slow motion of Cithaeron, the slowed tempos of transcendence that refuse, by intensifying, everyday normativity and make alternatives imaginable. These examples put pressure on inoperativity, moving it from an ethics or politics of pure means into a more worldly and impure agonistic and feminist politics of refusal.

I then made clear the limits of inoperativity as a refusal concept by developing two *Bacchae readings of inoperativity*, each one moving us further from suspension to intensification, from a faith in the neutralizing powers of exhibition to the agonistic empowerments of experience. I suggested that the *Bacchae* is actually a better fit even for Agamben's own idea than is Bartleby, though I showed we could develop a more intensive rather than merely suspensive reading of Melville's character, too.

I turn now to Chapter 2 and the next refusal concept, inclination, developed by Adriana Cavarero. I focus on one of her examples of inclination, Leonardo da Vinci's painting of the baby Jesus with Mary and Saint Anne (also known as his Madonna). Cavarero attends in particular to the inclination of mother to child in the painting as an image of care's gesture. In his "Notes on Gesture," Agamben turns to da Vinci, too, casting another of his paintings, the *Mona Lisa*, as an image of lost gesture: "Even the Mona Lisa," he says, "can be seen not as timeless static [form] but as fragments of a gesture or as frames of a lost film solely within which they regain their meaning."[105] By contrast with Agamben, what Cavarero finds in da Vinci is not the mother of a lost gesture but the gesture of a(n almost) lost mother: maternity, she says, finds expression in the inclination of da Vinci's Madonna. Rather than lament our condition of gestic alienation, Cavarero celebrates a broader gestic repertoire not cataloged by Agamben—the gestic repertoire of care.[106]

2   Inclination and the Work of Dis / orientation
Cavarero with Ahmed

ALL TRUE RADICALISM HAS TO BEGIN IN THE BODY.

—SAMUEL DELANY, INTERVIEW WITH JUNOT DÍAZ, *BOSTON REVIEW*

I'VE NEVER BEEN THIS HIGH BEFORE. I'M TALKING ABOUT THE ALTITUDE.
THERE IS A LESSON IN BRINGING PEOPLE TOGETHER WHERE THEY CANNOT
GET ENOUGH OXYGEN, THEN HAVING THEM TRY TO FIGURE OUT WHAT THEY
ARE GOING TO DO WHEN THEY CAN'T THINK PROPERLY.

—BERNICE JOHNSON REAGON, "COALITION POLITICS"

MOMENTS OF DISORIENTATION ARE VITAL.

—SARA AHMED, *QUEER PHENOMENOLOGY*

As we saw in Chapter 1, Agamben's inoperativity fell short of the needs of a feminist theory of refusal because his new use looked a lot like the old (nymphs), was solitary rather than common (Bartleby), and tended toward the suspensive / exhibitive (the glorious body) rather than intensive / experiential (the *Bacchae* and *The Fits*). We saw how, when the objects on display are female bodies, the suspensive / exhibitive easily gave way to an untransformed "use," as in the *Bacchae*, for example, when the bacchants are watched, illicitly, first by the herdsmen and then by Pentheus, the king. We concluded that a more agonistic and feminist understanding of inoperativity might do better, finding examples in the *Bacchae* and in the innovative camera work of *The Fits*. For a feminist theory of refusal, there is promise in the herdsman's frightened observation that "when the women ran, the world ran with them." The world ran not to see a spectacle but because it was drawn by refusal's propulsion. What so disoriented the herdsman was the idea that the bacchants' "fits" might be not a personal affliction but signs of a worldly transformation that could sweep everyone up.

Now, in Chapter 2, I canvas the powers and limitations of Cavarero's refusal concept, inclination. If I turn to inclination after inoperativity, it is because inclination does not reject use; it offers a way to rethink or recover use as care and mutuality. Inclination asks the other "how may I be of use?" (D. W. Winnicott would say to his patients "use me"). Juxtaposing Agamben on inoperativity and Cavarero on inclination, we see how their orientations to refusal differ. In *Inclinations: A Critique of Rectitude*, Cavarero's aim is to intensify the body, not suspend it. She seeks not to undo or suspend normativity but rather to reorient normativity toward care or altruism.[1] Inclination is a maternal gesture, for her, and the inclined body of the mother is not glorious or exhibitive; it is intimate. Its organs are not perfect and suspended; they are functional and nourishingly vital. It is in their use that they and others live. Cavarero's maternal or caring bodies are for the most part not positioned on the verge but in the dirt of experience.[2] Instead of Agamben's politics or ethics of pure means, Cavarero prioritizes love, not as a formal or abstract affect but as an embodied feeling for a child. She works in Hannah Arendt's tradition of world care, even if she argues in *Inclinations* for moving from Arendt's famous focus on *natality* to *maternity*.

I begin this chapter with an exploration of the promise and limits of Cavarero's refusal concept, inclination, which refuses the traditionally privileged upright posture and ethics of moral rectitude. I reread the myth of the Sphinx from the perspective of inclination, and argue for seeing it not as a tale of Oedipus' triumph (the conventional reading), but as the seed of his tragedy and the tragedy of uprightness, as such. I then turn to an inclination reading of the *Bacchae* and two *Bacchae* readings of inclination.[3] The inclination reading of the *Bacchae* highlights how Cithaeron is for the bacchants a refuge where they can enjoy the peace of inclination. But inclination is also the posture of the women's regicide and of Agave's burial of her son, the king. Maternalism encompasses all of these and presses Cavarero's inclination from its professed pacifism to something more agonistic. Moreover, the kinship most evident in Euripides' drama is not mother, but sister. What happens when we shift inclination from the maternal to the sororal plane? Crucially, as I show in the first *Bacchae* reading of inclination, Leonardo's *Madonna*, one of Cavarero's own examples in *Inclinations*, can itself be read sororally: as a *Bacchae* image of sororal agonism, not pacifist maternity. The second *Bacchae* reading of inclination draws on the myth of Procne, in which sisters Procne and Philomela are able to act in concert thanks to the festival of Dionysus. The festivities provide the cover of darkness and disguise needed to birth the sisters' regicidal conspiracy. As I read it, the myth serves as a prequel of sorts for Euripides' play. Together, the two *Bacchae* readings of inclination, along with Sara Ahmed's work on disorientation, help disorient inclination from a maternal gesture of pacifist care to a sororal, agonistic gesture of feminist refusal made up of love, care, and violence.

Disorienting inclination in this way confronts Cavarero's aspiration to a feminist ethics of non-violence with what I take to be the inescapable violence of politics and recovers inclination for a feminist theory of refusal.

Postures of Refusal

> We tend to slip out of togetherness the way we slip out of the womb, bloody and messy and surprised to be alone. And clever—able to [un]learn with our whole bodies the ways of this world.
>
> —ADRIENNE MAREE BROWN, *EMERGENT STRATEGY*

Inclination is Adriana Cavarero's refusal concept. It is the inclined posture of maternity which she contrasts to the erect or vertical posture that philosophy associates with autonomy. Each posture, she argues, represents a distinct normative ontology. In place of autonomy's rectitude, Cavarero favors maternity's gesture of care in which she sees the basis of a subversive ethics of altruism and pacifism. Cavarero's focus on a gesture, inclination, calls us to attend to refusal's corporeal choreographies, pos-

Leonardo da Vinci, *The Virgin and Child with Saint Anne.*
Louvre Museum / Wikimedia Commons

ture, and plane. From the perspective of inclination, then, texts we thought we knew are opened to new readings and subjected to productive dis/orientations.

Take, for example, Cavarero's reading of Leonardo's Madonna, focused on posture and plane.[4]

There, she says, "Right at the heart of the self-sacrificing stereotype [the patriarchal view of maternity], right there where patriarchalism seems once again to triumph," we find in the women's "enigmatic smiles," "the imaginary resources for pacifism," there, "in the face of the mother inclined over her child." The posture of inclination is mistakable for subservience, but it is not that. "To think the maternal merely as care . . . risks repeating the stereotype of the self-sacrificing woman." Recall Hegel's claim that the lamenting Antigone is the *eternal irony of the community*. Antigone seems only to lament, but she brings down a king. Similarly, for Cavarero, we might say Leonardo's Madonna is the *eternal irony of the community*: enigmatically caring but not subservient, and possibly possessed of some radical powers. Could she, too, bring down a king?

We can develop further the tension between rectitude and inclination with the help of Thoreau in whose work the two meet. In *Walking*, Thoreau describes how he and his walking companion wonder how other men can live so cooped up in their workplaces all day but then, even more, how women, whose confinements are even worse, can stand to be in the house all day long. "How womankind, who are confined to the house still more than men, stand it I do not know," says Thoreau. The answer, he jokes, is that "most of them do not *stand* it at all."[5] On the contrary, the women are lying down! The secret is disclosed to Thoreau by his walking companion: as the two men pass "those houses with purely Doric or Gothic fronts, which have such an air of repose about them, my companion whispers that probably about these times their occupants are all gone to bed." The joke erases the possibility that the women's daytime napping is itself a refusal, though napping does refuse the busy work and office confinement against which Thoreau himself rails.[6] We know daytime napping was part of the bacchants' arc of refusal, one of their many offenses against Pentheus on Cithaeron. And, Cavarero points out, inclination is actually etymologically connected to the Greek *klinē*, which means "bed" or "couch."[7]

Perhaps, however, Thoreau does discern the refusal his joke denies, since he responds to the image of women in bed, or in each other's beds, by reaching for rectitude. Contemplating the scene, he says he is grateful for architecture, "which itself never turns in, but forever stands out and *erect*, keeping watch over the slumberers."[8] This positions Thoreau, the civil disobedient, uncomfortably close to Pentheus, the law-and-order ruler in the *Bacchae* who is also uncomfortable with women's inclination and also reaches for (e)rectitude—a tall tree—to counter it.[9]

The tall tree is where Pentheus is positioned by Dionysus, who has promised the young king a great view of the bacchants below. Three of the women below Pentheus are sisters. He knows them. One, Agave, is his mother and two are Pentheus's aunts, Ino and Autonoe. When Dionysus lets the women know they are being watched, the women attack Pentheus, or maybe it is his verticalism they attack: "Once they saw [Pentheus] . . . they started pelting him with stones, throwing fir branches over like javelins. . . . But all fell short. Finally, they sheared the limbs off an oak and tried to lever the fir [tree] up by its roots. But that failed too." In order to bring down Pentheus, the women must incline to each other and act in concert together to force down the tree. Agave shouts, "'Come, my maenads, gather round this tree and *all take hold. . . .*' And with that, countless hands pulled and pushed . . . and from his high roost Pentheus fell."[10] Thus, the women dethrone Pentheus. They go on to dismember him, too, as he futilely pleads with them to let him live. "The air was full of yelps and cries and he heard what must have been his last scream, delivered to the world with his last breath."[11] It is quite a scene. It is as if the women Thoreau imagined napping at home at midday had suddenly exited their houses, gathered themselves together, reached for the symbols of erectitude, toppled them, and then found they had committed the regicide that Cavarero never *names* as the true outcome of inclination.[12]

Regicide is not Cavarero's aim. Her ethical orientation is pacifist, and she seeks, by way of inclination, not to extinguish alternatives but to seed new possibilities. But the *Bacchae* reminds us that verticalists will not tolerate such pluralization; it is an existential threat. Besides, verticalists think they have refusal covered. Isn't the vertical itself associated with refusal? Think of the raised revolutionary fist, for example, or Jean Cocteau's iconic rendering of Antigone and Creon, each rigid in the face of the other, or of Sara Ahmed's example: the Grimm brothers' story, "The Willful Girl."[13] In the Grimm brothers' horrible fable, a girl who has died from being beaten by her mother is buried, but the girl's arm refuses to go down into the grave. Her mother is brought to the graveyard with a rod to beat her defiant daughter, postmortem, until the girl's upraised arm is finally withdrawn, underground. Ahmed admires the girl's refusal; it *is* admirable, but the girl's stiffened arm *mirrors* the mother's weapon of the stiff rod. Stiff-armed refusal sometimes wins, sometimes loses, but always risks reproducing what it opposes.[14] How to break out of the cycle?[15]

Cavarero offers inclination as a way out of such mimetic violence. She situates inclination in a space apart. She identifies it with heterotopia. But this leaves inclination vulnerable to mocking dismissals like Thoreau's. Or to murderous triumphs like Oedipus's. It happens in the story of the Sphinx, the ancient myth that prefigures the clash between the vertical and the inclinational that will later be taken up by the Greek tragedians. Approached from the perspective of inclination's attention to posture, gesture, and ethos, the myth of the Sphinx opens in new ways that bridge to recent work in queer theory and disability studies.

The Sphinx, a monstrous, female (maternal? foreign?) creature, part woman/part (in the Greek context) vulture, has a riddle that only Oedipus proves able to solve. "What crawls on all fours in the morning, walks on two legs midday, and then in the evening on three?" asks the Sphinx (posing what Cavarero elsewhere calls the riddle of the legs).[16]

"Man," is Oedipus's correct reply.[17] If this was a test, he certainly passes it, and he is rewarded with the throne of Thebes and marriage to its widowed queen.

But there is more going on here than the usual mythic test of a hero's cleverness. The riddle has a teaching and its wisdom is needed for good governance. One element of the tragedy of Oedipus is that he is clever enough to solve the riddle but not wise enough to apprehend its lesson. What the Sphinx offers to Oedipus by way of the riddle is the wisdom of inclination. The key to solving the riddle, after all, is knowing that uprightness is only a *part* of a human life and not its essence or telos. To move on all fours while dependent on the mother, or on three legs while dependent on another, is not a failing or a weakness; it is part of human life, as much so as the two leggedness that, for most but not all people, comes between them. This means that infancy and old age, which are figures for human natality and mortality, are on a par with autonomy, not deviations from it.[18] Thus, the riddle teaches how temporary is the rectitude that humans (mis)take for our species essence when we call ourselves *Homo erectus* and moralize our stature.[19] The lesson of the riddle is the mutual dependence that rectitude disavows and pathologizes.

That the Sphinx is Egyptian and Oedipus the whitened primogenitor of Western philosophy's rapturous attachment to male autonomy makes all the more poignant the fact that although Oedipus triumphs over the Sphinx, he does not absorb her wisdom. Perhaps this is also because his knowledge is not experiential. Oedipus himself probably did not crawl on four legs as an infant. His father, Laius, frightened by a prophecy that his son would one day kill him, wanted the infant abandoned and had his infant son's ankles pierced and tied together, likely disabling Oedipus's infant crawl and leaving Oedipus with a lifelong wound and limp. In his old age, Oedipus, in exile, walks with the help and support of his two daughters, Ismene and Antigone, suggesting he walks on six legs in the evening of his life, and not just on three, like most old men, with a cane.[20] Oedipus's tragedy will turn not on the temporariness of his (limping) two-leggedness but on his mistaking it for his life's entirety or its essence, as all verticalists do. He underrates relationality, for which inclination is a figure, and puts his faith in his autonomy. He can stand on his own two legs, except he couldn't and soon enough he can't. His inflexibility is his undoing when he dismisses the counsel of Tiresias, who is blind and himself inclines.[21] Tiresias has come to deliver a prophecy that would prove instructive if Oedipus were to listen. But the prophet's real lesson, which Oedipus also misses, is the mutuality shown by Tiresias when he leans on another.

The Sphinx, on this reading, teaches the lesson of pluralization that Cavarero sets out to teach by way of inclination: that a human life is made up of a spectrum of postures, none of which is its essence. It is a lesson the tragedians may have understood, since they contrast corporeal inclination and verticality. It is this idea that today's verticalists oppose when they privilege mind over body and affiliate the intellect with the head not the gut. The point made by inclination, however, is not just about posture; it is about how the denial of mutuality is corporealized and how the verticalist understanding of moral maturation undoes mutuality's relations of care. I turn now to assess the impact of inclination's switch in perspective by way of an inclination reading of the *Bacchae*.

Pentheus's Queer Corpse: An Inclination Reading of the *Bacchae*

> [Canetti] can only see what his imaginary allows him to see: certain postures, but not others; certain warlike scenarios but not domestic or more reassuring ones; images of death and terror but not those involving the fragility of birth.
>
> —ADRIANA CAVARERO, *INCLINATIONS*

Inclination's postural perspective calls attention to the arrangement of bodies. Attention to choreography, corporeal arrangement, plane, and posture brings out the importance of one subtle detail in the agon between Agave and her father, Cadmus, that I discuss fully in Chapter 3. For now, let us note the detail: as the play moves toward its denouement and Cadmus confronts his daughters' violence, seeking to correct Agave's moral failings, he does so, first, by correcting her posture. Agave has proudly carried her son's "hopeless head" back to Thebes, crowing about how the women are great hunters, better than men, and deserving of glory. Cadmus, her father and founder of Thebes, seeks to make her understand that what has occurred is something to be mourned, not celebrated. He begins by saying, "First, turn your eye to this *upper* air" (emphasis added). Agave looks up and says, "Why did you suggest I look on this?" Good question. Is it to see the sun? Or is it that, in order to look up, Agave would have to, like Plato's first philosopher, stand up straight and exit the cave of inclination?[22] It is not clear, in fact, whether Agave's coming alteration of perspective is enabled by the luminosity of the sun—"It is brighter than before and more translucent," she remarks—or by the erect posture entailed by her having to look *up* to see the sun. When Cadmus asks, "Is this fluttering still with your psyche?" Agave says, "I don't understand what you say; but I am somehow coming to my senses, am altered from my previous mind." Standing up straight straightens her mind.[23]

The "previous mind" from which Agave is altered is inclinational in its orientation. Among the many moments in the drama that depict inclination in agonistic contexts of care, four stand out. In one, the women of Thebes ally with the bacchants from Asia, illustrating a kind of inclination in their willingness to join with the newly arrived in violation of the dividing lines of polis membership normally dictated by the sovereign. We may look at the Theban women's affiliation with these newly arrived foreigners as part of the women's refusal to be domesticated; it is surely a refusal of sovereign line-drawing. The bacchants would rather take the risk of foreignness than retreat to the domestic space (what Sara Ahmed dubs "habit spaces") of enclosure, which is scripted as safe but is not safe for them, not if safe means vital and free from coercion.[24]

The second moment is on Cithaeron when, as we saw in Chapter 1, the women join together in dance, worship, and sleep and in caring for the animals in whose midst the women find themselves.

The third and fourth moments, which I focus on here, are when Agave leans over Pentheus, first with others, to kill him, then alone to bury him.

In the former, she is assumed by most interpreters of the play to be mad, in the latter regretful. This is an example of what we saw earlier, in the Introduction, with Ahmed and Merleau-Ponty, as the sequencing of disorientation's ambivalence. But we see now that the sequencing of giddiness and nausea, madness and regret, not only avoids the unnerving disorientation that Merleau-Ponty discusses; it also elides the possibility that Agave actively desires Pentheus's destruction. This elision is what prepares us to see Agave's handling of the dead body of Pentheus as a familiar tragic scene of maternal grief, perfectly at home with patriarchal norms. But Agave's inclination over Pentheus's dead body may be more subversive than that.[25]

Sara Ahmed's own version of inclination, *orientation*, is useful here. Orientation names the demand for rectitude, the straightness that, as Ahmed points out and Cavarero does, too, is the moral geometry of heteronormative sexuality.[26] But the mandated orientation of heteronormativity is vulnerable to "disorientation," Ahmed claims, as she charts a queer path of refusal. Ahmed adds to Cavarero's focus on relationality among persons a focus on our relations to objects (like the table, the philosophers' perennial example) and says, "If we think with and through orientation we might allow the moments of disorientation to gather, almost as if they are bodies around a . . . table. We might, in the gathering, face a different way. Queer objects might take us to the very limits of social gathering, even when they still gather us around. . . . Indeed to live out a politics of disorientation might be to sustain wonder about the very forms of social gathering."[27]

The dead Pentheus, whose body is in pieces, splits the difference between Ahmed and Cavarero. Both an object and a person, he / his corpse / it seems to have the power to do in death what Pentheus could not do in life, though he certainly tried: to reawaken and magnetize Agave's normative maternity. If we see Pentheus's dead body as reinterpellating Agave to maternity, inclination could be seen as buttressing that maternalizing project. In the leaning over him for burial, Agave is in grief once again his mother. But like all dead bodies, as James Martel argues,

Pentheus's corpse also "disrupts and subverts the projections of political authority it is meant to convey."[28] If we allow ourselves to be disoriented by this person/thing, as Ahmed and Martel invite us to be, then we have reason to resist the seeming familiarity of Agave's posture as the inclination of maternal grief. Mindful of how "queer objects might take us to the very limits of social gathering," we may see something else happening in the scene, if only we can sustain wonder at the gathering of the corpse of Pentheus.[29]

What else might Agave's inclination over Pentheus signal, if not maternal grief? Piecing Pentheus back together, Agave laments his death, to be sure. But is that all she does? Let's look at it from the perspective of the bacchants' arc of refusal. Even if we condense the bacchants' large arc of refusal to just one of its points, we may see that this one act of killing the king actually takes place in three steps, and all are on an inclined plane. First, the collective murder of Pentheus by the bacchants; second, their dispersing of the king's body in pieces so widely and far flung they cannot all be found; and finally, third, Agave reattaching Pentheus's head to his dead body for burial. This last inclinational step can be read two ways. It is usually assumed to be grieving restitution for the violence that got out of hand, the nausea that is the price to be paid for the giddiness. But it could also be seen as a tyrannicide's completion of her work: giddiness continued. Agave may just love her son and want to bury him whole, but she may also seek to finish what she started. How so?

Agave is no stranger to the idea that things left out on a field may produce an odd crop. Agave is the daughter of Cadmus, founder of Thebes. Cadmus sowed the teeth of a slain dragon to reap a crop of new men. ("I, Cadmus the great, who sowed the Theban race and reaped that glorious harvest.")[30] One of these men, born of the earth, is Echion, who will go on to marry Agave and father Pentheus. Who would know better than Cadmus and Agave that a regicide that ends with bones and body parts strewn in a field may turn out to be no regicide at all? Is this on Cadmus's mind when he goes out of his way to collect Pentheus, finding, as he puts it, "all I could" and doing his best to reassemble "this gory jigsaw"?[31] It may well be on Agave's mind when she puts Pentheus back together for burial.[32] Burying *all* of him prevents any chance of return. This suggests the inclined burial over her son is part of the regicide, and not its undoing.

But if regicide is what Agave wants, why does she weep over its achievement? Doesn't that weeping, in the posture of maternal inclination, mean she regrets her violence and renounces the regicidal freedom she enjoyed with her sisters? Perhaps. We have reviewed in the Introduction some possible answers to the puzzle, attending to the complexities of the "double bind" (Ahmed) or the "tragic situation" (Williams) in which Agave is enmeshed. And I return to them in a moment. But first, let's note that if we think of Pentheus's dead body as what Ahmed calls a queer object, then we may add another possibility: the queer corpse occasions new social relations and does not just restore everyone to their old ones. As James Martel says of all (un)buried bodies, "unburied bodies represent a general field of struggle that does not readily lend itself to the wishes and power of either side" in a conflict.[33] This means that the killing and the burial are up for grabs as far as their signification is concerned.

We know that during the attack, the young king calls to his mother, begging for his life, but Agave cannot hear him, or will not (should we imagine she has stopped up her ears, like Ulysses?). And in the delight of the sacred hunt, she and her sisters tear the young man limb from limb. When it is all over, Agave carries Pentheus's head home, thinking it is that of an animal. She wants it hung in the palace to mark the women's hunting prowess. Perhaps the feast she calls for will be made of his remains. She calls out for Pentheus to help her, and so we can see that she seems not to realize he is dead. The audience knows what she does not yet: that she will soon suffer because her son is gone and she is responsible. This is the standard reading. Another reading opens up, however, if we recall that these sisters have killed before (recall the sisters' implication in the death of their sister, Semele, mother of Dionysus) and if we think about these final acts of killing and burial *as parts of* the larger arc of the bacchants' refusal to submit to sovereign power.[34] Moreover, if we recall that the creature Agave thinks she has killed is a lion, and recall that the lion then as now symbolizes monarchy, we may begin to "wonder," as Ahmed wants us to, what exactly we are gathering around, what exactly gathers us round, when we now gather with Agave around the corpse of Pentheus, who was king.[35]

The assumption that the women rue the regicide, that they only rue the regicide, exceptionalizes the killing by overlooking the fact that every act performed by the women in this play is regicidal, from the beginning to the end. That is why earlier I referred to it as a slow regicide. When the women refuse work, when they join up with newly arrived bacchants, when they establish an inclinational heterotopia to unlearn old normativities and ground new ones, when they topple and attack a creature who spies on their secret rites, when they return to the city and demand glory, all of these are parts of an uprising: the women rise up and challenge sovereign power. Why, then, should we think that when they finally actually commit the regicide, *that* is when things got out of hand or they went too far? Why not assume this is a political parable? Peter Euben reads the play that way: he sees it as a cautionary tale about the dangers of dispersion and the need to unite the city again. We could follow him and see a parable here, but read it differently: as a parable, yes, but one that teaches the *dangers* of unity and shows the need to dismember sovereignty or patriarchy. The parable teaches the vulnerability of sovereignty to the check of inclination understood not as maternal care, not only, but also as agonistic sororal action in concert.[36]

On such a reading, what jumps out is how difficult it is to kill a king: regicide is not easy. The sisters have to do it over and over before it is done. And even then, as we shall see in Chapter 3, it is not done. Even after Pentheus is gone, Cadmus will still try to put the new genie of gender equality back into the old bottle of patriarchy. In the end, the bacchants' success or failure at transformation will turn on their own powers of fabulation and ours.

We could say, then, that Agave laments her son but not the king. That is a way to distinguish regicide from filicide and attribute ambivalence to Agave and not just regret. But this is too neat, surely, since the king, as it were, is what keeps the son, and mother, in their places. That is to say, filicide and regicide will *always* coincide in patriarchy. This is why Ahmed's "double bind" better captures the problematic than does Williams's tragic situation, which unbinds the knot and shows two discrete threads, forcing a choice between them. Williams's tragic situations, so painful and human, are thus not the problem (as we are invited to assume) but the solution. They displace the deeper problem of the double bind that entraps women in patriarchy in ways beyond the reach of Williams's moral remediations of regret or remorse.

Rather than carve Pentheus up into his distinct roles (two threads), we do better to see how, in its ambiguity, the corpse "disrupts and subverts" that symbolic: hence Cadmus's own late effort to put everything back into its proper place and restore everyone to their proper places in the puzzle. But in finding all he could, Cadmus does not find everything; some remainders escape even his long reach. When he tries to correct for this and to save the Thebes he founded by setting Agave to mourn and bury Pentheus, Cadmus projects his own "political authority" over the body of the king. Why? Cadmus may well hope to bury not just the body of Pentheus but also the tumult sown by Dionysus. If so, Cadmus shows he deserves the punishment that will soon be meted out to him, since he here reperforms and does not undo the very wrong that Dionysus has come to Thebes to correct: the burial of the crime against his mother, Semele, along with her remains.[37] Insofar as Semele's death was the result of sororal violence, what Cadmus sought to bury then and what he seeks to bury now are the same thing—inclination, instanced here by the agonistic power of sororal action in concert, generative and caring, violent and murderous.

Here, an inclination reading of the *Bacchae* highlights the undecidably caring *and* murderous nature of inclination. Cavarero acknowledges that inclination disposes us to both, but in her reading of Leonardo's Madonna she splits them. As I will now argue, a *Bacchae* reading of inclination resists that move.

Leonardo's Madonna: A *Bacchae* Reading of Inclination, I

> A relationality that reflects the everyday experience of the maternal rather than the monumentality of the sacred.
>
> —ADRIANA CAVARERO, *INCLINATIONS*

The *Bacchae* dramatizes inclination as refusal, but the central agency of inclination in the play is not maternity but sorority. This is important for a feminist theory of refusal because the sororal relationship is the more egalitarian of the two.[38] In addition, the mood of inclinational refusal is not per se altruistic, as Cavarero says. It is agonistic: intimate and contestatory. I will argue that sorority and agonism appear alongside or in place of what Cavarero casts as a pure expression of maternity and altruism in her own preferred example of inclination, the painting of the Madonna by Leonardo, which is arguably more Greek, more agonistic and, even, more sororal than it first appears to be. Indeed, a *Bacchae* reading of the painting's inclination highlights details of inclination as a refusal concept that we have not yet recorded.

First, referring back to that image, we see that the two women as Leonardo painted them look more like sisters than like mother and daughter. As art historians have pointed out, Anne does not appear older than her daughter, at least not old enough to be her mother. So we have a suggestion of sorority where Cavarero posits maternity.[39]

Second, if we do treat the women as mother and daughter, in accordance with their names, we see that there are two mothers and two children. Mary is the child of Anne, and she is seated on her mother's lap. Mary's child, Jesus, is on the ground, off his mother's lap. Cavarero says that by taking the child off the mother's lap, Leonardo subverts the norm of representation. As Cavarero also notes, the norm sets "the Christ child [as] not only held by Mary, but seated in her lap with his back turned toward her, facing outward; according to the traditional canon, Mother and Child should not look at one another." But Leonardo, she argues, presents "a mother who is face to face with her child; a child whose head is twisted back to face the one who visibly tilts out to support him."[40] Leonardo does not only subvert the norm (Jesus off Mary's lap, twisting to look at his mother), however; he also cites the norm as Cavarero describes it (Mary is on Anne's lap, facing away from her). Still, his subversion does occasion the inclination that Cavarero calls maternal, showing one mother reaching for the child and the child looking in her direction. But what warrants the assumption that the mother is reaching *for* the child? Moving from Cavarero's inclination reading of the painting to a *Bacchae* reading of the painting's inclination, we may see it is unclear whether it is the infant or the lamb Mary seeks. On Cithaeron, the bacchants would prefer the lamb to the baby after all. Moreover, even if we allow that the child is the center of the mother's attention, the *Bacchae* can also lead us to wonder whether the mother's inclination in the painting is caringly extended *to* the child or abandonment leaning *away* from it.[41] The painting does not decide it for us.

Why does this matter? Because, third, the untraditional distance between Leonardo's Mary and child, the nonholding noted by Cavarero, does not just cite and subvert *maternal* inclination as natal care. It is actually more typical of the gesture between living and dead, and this is instanced most famously in the world of Greek tragedy by Antigone, the sister who inclines toward/over the dead body of Polynices, though also by Agave, the mother inclined over the pieces of Pentheus in mourning. Cavarero has already criticized Elias Canetti, "whose imaginary," she says, "is inhabited by unmistakably masculine figures (such as the warrior over the corpse)."[42] But as the examples of Antigone and Agave suggest, death care reads feminine (sororal and/or maternal), too. Is Leonardo perhaps citing the inclination of death care when he positions Mary inclined to her son? Cavarero herself notes that Leonardo's painting points in this direction: with the baby, Jesus, on the ground, playing with the lamb, we see "a symbol of the passion and the sacrifice that awaits him."[43] Cavarero says the symbolization puts that later violence, Jesus's sacrificial fate, offscreen, as it were. But if inclination is a gesture of death care, then the mother's lean to or away from the baby suggests not just care for—and abandonment of—the living but also care for and abandonment of the dead.

The painting's coupling of care and abandonment brings us to the fourth point. Although Cavarero identifies the mother in Leonardo's painting only with altruistic care, she does acknowledge that the capacity to care comes always also with the possibility of wounding. Inclination, she says, "consists in the alternative between care and wound." This doubled possibility, she explains, is not belied by maternal inclination, for to be maternally inclined is not yet to care or to wound but to be positioned for either of these, poised on the cusp, in response to the call of the exposed other.[44] So far so good: inclination is not now maternal pacifism, as such, but the posing of a question that we must answer. When Cavarero says the "alternative between care and wound, as well as that between love and violence [is] entirely inscribed in inclination as a predisposition to respond," she means to affiliate the posture of inclination with responsiveness as such, leaving open the question of the nature of the response. Nonresponsiveness is "an expression of irresponsibility, which is structurally distinct from evil understood as a violent act."[45]

But then Cavarero posits Leonardo's painting as an inclinational depiction of care and altruism and says we must look *elsewhere* for maternal murderousness, specifically, she says, to Euripides's Medea, a filicidal mother like Agave. "Alongside Leonardo's Madonna lovingly bent over baby Jesus, consider Euripides's Medea, the infanticide. . . . [Medea, who kills her two young sons to avenge wrongs committed against her by their father] reminds us that care is not an automatic or obvious response of maternal inclination."[46] Thus, her term "alongside" notwithstanding, Cavarero splits the caring and the wounding of which she says inclination / maternity is simultaneously capable, by assigning each to a separate work of art: one Christian, one Greek, one representational, one dramatic, one Madonna, one Medea, one caring, one murderous.[47]

Freud, however, saw no need to reach for Medea when Leonardo's Madonna offers the very undecidability Cavarero seeks. For Freud, Mary appears as the secret repository of the verticality that Cavarero sees as indexed only by the lone tree that Leonardo put (safely?) in the background of the two loving women. Cavarero points out the tree, acknowledging it but reassuring us of its distance. In doing so, she establishes the heterotopian quality of the women's scene of inclination. But Freud saw (with the help of Oskar Pfister) something more proximate and possessed of more immediate danger than the tree: the outline of a vulture in the women's dress drapery.

The creature represents the capacity to wound, Freud says. And it marks Leonardo's mother's wounding of her son, evidenced in Leonardo's own recollection of his childhood. As a baby, the artist had dreamed that in his cradle "a vulture came down to me, and opened my mouth with its tail, and struck me many times with its tail against my lips." In his earlier psychobiography of Leonardo, Freud had seen the dream as a screen memory of homosexuality whose repression, Freud said, enabled the flowering of artistic genius. But by way of the Madonna painting and its hidden bird of prey, Freud revises his earlier view and says that Leonardo's mother, "like all unsatisfied mothers, took her son in place of her husband, and by too early maturing his eroticism robbed him of his masculinity."[48] In short, we have here an example of maternal caring *as* wounding, albeit a rather misogynist one.

Cavarero does better when she acknowledges the coincidence of caring and wounding in the figure of maternity but without Freud's misogyny. She says, "To think the maternal merely as care, however, not only risks repeating the stereotype of the self-sacrificing woman; it also, and above all, obscures the ethical valence of inclination, which consists in the alternative between care and wound." Inclination is a "disposition" to provide care. Verticality is "an avoidance of the question." And the stereotype, which helps avoid the question, prepares the ground for misogyny's faulting of women for failing to live up to its ideal.[49] That said, Cavarero's reading of Leonardo's painting seems to insulate the image from the question she wants to make unavoidable.

Leonardo da Vinci, *The Virgin and Child with Saint Anne*, with Vulture Outline.
Louvre Museum. Outline by Matthew Martin

A *Bacchae* reading of inclination better centers "the alternative be-tween care and wound" by treating Leonardo's painting as if it were a detail of the *Bacchae*. The painting depicts two women, who seem to be about the same age, sisters perhaps, at ease in a field with a baby and a lamb, oriented perhaps to the lamb, having just put down the baby. There is also that slightly forbidding-looking tree standing ramrod straight in the background. A *Bacchae* reading of the image suggests it could have been called *In the Fields of Cithaeron*. Or, recalling Agave, Pentheus's (caring and murderous) mother, *Agave with Two Others*.[50] Or even, with Deleuze and Guattari in mind, *One of a Thousand Plateaus*. Were Leon-ardo's painting recast as Greek, not Christian, then the future portended here would be not the sacrifice of the baby (prefigured by the lamb, as Cavarero argues) but the murder that the tall tree in the background would call to the mind of anyone familiar with Euripides's *Bacchae*: Pentheus's hiding spot is at the top of a tree.[51]

Is it too much of a stretch to see the outlines of Euripides's women and their soon-to-be toppled tree in Leonardo's painting? It is no more of a stretch than finding the outline of a vulture in the women's dress drapery surely. And once we have found that vulture, we are already with the Greeks: the Sphinx, in some renderings, is part woman, part *vulture*. But perhaps less outrageously, we may note that this is not, in any case, the first time a Christian-themed work by Leonardo was recast as clas-sical or pagan. Indeed, in the late seventeenth century, Leonardo's orig-inal portrait of Saint John was painted over and made into a Bacchus.[52] Leonardo's *Saint John*, with its "disconcerting, somewhat ambiguous sensuality," was described as "suavely beautiful, youthful and slightly androgynous" and was thought to have "neither devotion, decorum nor similitude."[53] Beneath the baptism lay the bacchanalia. The proof was the ease with which the staff of the Baptist could be changed to a bac-chic thyrsus (the thyrsus is carried by celebrants of Dionysus in the *Bacchae*).[54]

The point here is not uncritically to repeat such historical classiciza-tions of Leonardo's Christian (yet somehow disturbingly pagan) art but rather to use this painting's vulnerability to such a maneuver to perform the political and cultural work of dis/orientation. Singularizing the mother and the maternal gesture, casting maternal violence as "Greek," Cavarero hopes to keep inclination on the cusp of responsiveness but ends up distancing inclination from the agonism it needs if it is to be powerful. By contrast, a *Bacchae* reading of the painting sees inclination in a range of kinship roles and postures in which care and/as murderousness are inextricably intertwined, not just positioned on the cusp between them. How is murderousness caring? When the bacchants kill the king, they release everyone and him, too, from the false idolatry of patriarchal sovereignty. Alongside and in contention with Cavarero's maternal, pacifist inclination, the bacchants offer up a gesture of inclination that is sororal, agonistic, and (figuratively) regicidal.

Procne's Refusal: A *Bacchae* Reading of Inclination, II

> "'Mother, look at me,
> Recognise me, Mother!'
> Agave stares, she blinks, her mouth wide.
> She takes her son's head between her hands
> And rips it from his shoulders.
> She lifts it, like a newborn baby, Her red fingers hooked into the hair
> Letting the blood splash over her face and breasts—
> 'Victory!' she shrieks. 'I've done! I did it!'"
> —TED HUGHES, "BACCHUS AND PENTHEUS," *TALES FROM OVID*

> "Though he calls me mother, why can she not call me sister?"
> —PROCNE

I have suggested in response to Cavarero that inclination should be oriented not primarily in maternity but in sorority, and that we should see its care and murderousness as more inextricably intertwined than she allows. The classical myth of Procne and Philomela furthers the point. Euripides would have known the myth of Procne and may have drawn on it for the *Bacchae*. He certainly knew Sophocles's tragedy, *Tereus*, a prior reworking of the myth now mostly lost to us. Thus, the second *Bacchae* reading of inclination, to which I now turn, enlists the *Bacchae* in the company of Procne.

In the myth of Procne, two sisters conspire to avenge a wrong. Procne is daughter of one king (Pandion of Athens) and wife of another (Tereus of Thrace). In the tale, as we have it from Ovid who recorded it later, the sisters, Procne and Philomela, collaborate to avenge Tereus's violation of Philomela. Sent by Procne to Athens to fetch her sister for a visit, Tereus rapes Philomela when she is under his care, and when she screams in protest, he then (in an ancient version of today's ubiquitous nondisclosure agreements) mutilates her to muteness, confines her in secret to "a lodge in distant woods," and tells Procne that her sister died on the voyage. The mutilation does not stop Philomela, however.[55] "Great trouble is inventive," notes Ovid when he later retells the story, "and ingenuity arises in difficult times." Philomela uses a loom in her captive room to weave the crime into a fabric.[56] The shuttle speaks with the aid of a servant who takes the fabric on Philomela's behalf to Procne, who has believed for a year her husband's lie that Philomela is dead. Thus begins the women's sororal conspiracy. Procne rescues her sister, and the two then seek vengeance for the wrongs done them by Tereus's infidelity, prevarication, and violence. They avenge the violations by murdering Itys, Tereus's young son with Procne. Then the sisters invite the unsuspecting Tereus to a filicidal meal prepared for his delectation. He eats. The cannibalism is horrifying, but the horror is not just in the filicidal meal; it is in the idea that women—a mother even—would prepare such a feast. This seems particularly brutal. But so was the rape. And the mutilation that tried to seal it.[57] Less brutally, we may see the meal as a culinary invocation of a world of sex/gender justice, issued to a king who would never think of it.

Pairing the myth and the *Bacchae* presses on us a new reading of Euripides's bacchants as not mad but knowing (at some level) what they were doing when they took Pentheus down. Procne certainly knew what she was doing when she took Tereus down.[58] When Pentheus shrieks in the *Bacchae*, "Mother, Mother," he rhymes with Itys's "Mater, Mater," in Ovid's account.[59] Procne is not a mad maenad. But she, no less than Agave (for a time), refuses to be shrieked back into maternity.[60] Procne will go about her violence just like Agave but more deliberatively, since Procne actually poses explicitly the question of kinship's conflicting obligations: "Though he calls me mother, why can she not call me sister?"[61] *Why* not? Here, Procne all but anticipates the patriarchal objection that Cadmus will later spring on Agave: that she is daughter, wife, and mother. Sister is missing from Cadmus's list of relevant kin, as we shall see in Chapter 3. The implication is that "sister" does not exist and must not register. And neither should "bacchant." Agave falls for it. Perhaps she is unprepared for it: she and her sisters do not deliberate as Procne does about how to rank the claims of kinship, nor does Agave insist on sorority as kinship too.

"The delusional Agave is a *far cry* from the hyper-conscious Procne," argue Gildenhard and Zissos.[62] But if we focus more on the "cry" and less on the "far," surprising interpretative possibilities open up. In both the tragedy and the myth, the women precommit to violence. The bacchants' worship of Dionysus in Euripides's play *is* the women's precommitment, their Ulyssean tying to the mast. In the myth, we see Procne renewing her resolve. She has no such precommitment in place, and so she undergoes and wrestles with the temptation to abandon her plan. When Itys beseeches her, it works: her "tempestuous anger" on her sister's behalf "is allayed." And so Procne nurses the wound, determined to stay focused on her task.[63]

> And, as by turns surveying both she stood,
> While this fond boy (she said) can thus express
> The moving accents of his fond address;
> Why stands my sister of her tongue bereft,
> Forlorn, and sad, in speechless silence left?

Procne can here be seen to be tempted by her son's final "fond address." She has to steel herself to withstand his entreaties; however, Agave, more like Ulysses, seems not to hear the entreaties at all. We have seen how Agave's terrible mourning of her lost son, Pentheus, is taken to mean she killed him unintentionally. But read with Procne, we may see how even if Agave had recognized Pentheus, she might have killed him anyway and then still mourned the loss. This is what we learn from Procne, who hesitates to kill Itys but then does so. Why? Because she is not just killing Itys. She is killing something else through him. Perhaps it is Tereus. Perhaps it is patriarchy.

Read with Procne and Philomela in mind, the *Bacchae*'s energy is refocused. The bacchants' sororal refusal to be confined to the quiet of the loom is radicalized by Philomela's usurpation of the loom for her loud refusal to be silenced (the former is a suspensive refusal of use, the latter intensive). That same subversive refusal is evident in the women's cooking. In place of the bacchants' regicidal raw and slow food on Cithaeron, a refusal that suspends the labor of cooking, Procne and Philomela cook a splendid feast for the male head of household, doing what women in the city do. But their cooking is a refusal that intensifies and subverts their supposedly submissive role. The feast they provide does not please a master or give vital joy: it cannibalizes Tereus's son and aborts the king's future. It is a raw and brutal cooked.

One other detail helps make the case for the myth's illumination of the play. Both take place in the context of Dionysian festival. Procne is able to rescue Philomela from her "fatal lodge," because the festival is being celebrated, and with everyone wearing masks and fawn skins, it is easy for the sisters to disguise themselves without detection.

> From thence, her sister snatching by the hand,
>
> Mask'd like the ranting Bacchanalian band,
>
> Within the limits of the court she drew,
>
> Shading, with ivy green, her outward hue.

Reunited, the sisters begin to plot their vengeance for Tereus's terrible wrongs.

We could emphasize as other commentators do that Procne is not really a bacchant (going back to the "far," not to the "cry"). Procne only feigns what Agave performs for real.[64] Or we could simply note that in both the myth and the play, both sets of sisters find ways to act nonsubmissively because of the wine god's blessings. Either way, it is notable that Ovid reports with empathy the travails and torment of Procne and Philomela and abstains from judgment regarding their murder of Itys, their son and nephew. Ovid does not pathologize; he merely records the actions taken and their consequences. Why not take a similar approach to the *Bacchae*?

Inclination's Heterotopia: In or out of the City?

The *Bacchae* reading of inclination enabled by the myth of Procne helps to secure the *Bacchae*'s key corrective to Cavarero, shifting care and inclination from maternity to sorority, from the ethical cusp to agonism, and as we shall see next in Chapter 3, from heterotopia to the city. When Cavarero proposes inclination as "an imaginary *completely apart* from geometric verticalism," she links it to heterotopia. She does not rule out the kind of gravitational pull that such experiments sometimes exert on others. But by turning to heterotopia, she does insulate inclination from the risk of direct contest with verticality. If we return to the city and the city is not ready, we risk falling into its conceptual clutches, to be judged wanting from its perspective, to be pressed anew to relent to its demands. This is, indeed, the arc of the bacchants' refusal from which we do well to learn. Still, as Bernice Johnson Reagon points out in a speech that became a classic essay, "Coalition Politics," heterotopias are where dissenters or minoritized peoples learn what they want, practice how to be otherwise, and reimagine what the world might be.[65] Reagon has in mind the women's music festival where she spoke, but her observations apply to Cithaeron, too, and as we shall see in Chapter 3, to the fugitive spaces of waywardness explored by Saidiya Hartman. Such heterotopias vivify alternatives to what is. Without their rehearsals of equality, beauty, or joy, we risk losing sight of what is wrong with an unjust society and can become reconciled to it, habituated to our place in it.[66] Reagon counsels her audience to go further and take home the new practices and perspectives honed in heterotopian settings. Relive every day the festive form of life, she says; practice its virtues and refine its commitments so that you wake up "every day and find yourself alive."[67]

In defense of Cavarero on this point, we might well note that in the *Bacchae*, the breadth of the women's promise is narrowed when they set their sights on toppling a king. The women defend their right to *klinē* and they succeed to some extent, but they do not win. Cavarero is alert to how subversive movements or actions can be undone by being drawn into the violences and agitations they want to oppose. This is the problem of mimetic aggression we noted earlier. That is a risk of agonism: hence, surely, Agamben's preference for the cleaner if less efficacious operations of suspensive inoperativity. But suspensive festivals and inclinational heterotopias have their own risks. To leave verticality aside and build elsewhere is to leave the vertical empowered to do its work: that tall tree, still there, offers not only shade but also judgment and a platform for surveillance. My own view, born in part of reading the *Bacchae* as a feminist parable of refusal, inoperativity, and inclinational care, is that when they succeed for a time, heterotopias valuably serve as spaces or times of rehearsal where alternative forms of life can be tried out and explored. They may inspire others who cannot envision change without the actualization of empirical inspiration and the reassurance of possibility. The bacchants teach the importance of that experience as rehearsal and example when they complete the arc of their refusal by returning to the city to claim it. At that point, it is up to the city: is it ready to receive them?

3   Fabulation and the Right to the City
Hartman with Arendt

We have reread Euripides's *Bacchae* through the lenses of inoperativity (Chapter 1) and inclination (Chapter 2), and we have rethought inoperativity and inclination through the lenses of Euripides's *Bacchae* as well as other *Bacchaes*. The aim has been to recover inoperativity and inclination for a feminist theory of refusal. I turn now in this final chapter to fabulation, the counter-narrating "method of refusal" that animates Saidiya Hartman's *Wayward Lives, Beautiful Experiments: Intimate Histories of Social Upheaval*.

Hartman's book is a *Bacchae*. Her book does not refer to Euripides' play by name nor to Greek tragedy, as such, but I will suggest it is a *Bacchae* all the same. With its desiring women audaciously seeking freedom and its three choruses protesting injustice, making their own way, and singing sorrow songs, *Wayward Lives* adheres to the tragic form while channeling the pains and pleasures of freedom-seeking women. Hartman's wayward women know the odds are against them but they, like the bacchants, are tragically hopeful under constraint. Hartman retells their stories to conjure freedom from the past for the future. This puts *Wayward Lives* very much in the tradition of Toni Morrison, who famously said she felt "at home" reading Greek tragedy because of its similarity to "Afro-American communal structures (the function of song and chorus, the heroic struggle between the claims of community and individual hubris)."[1]

Telling stories to inspire freedom is the aim of Hannah Arendt's work, as well. Stories of human action in concert give meaning to the world and ground new possibilities. As we shall see, Arendt emphasizes the role of the city and the archive (history) in holding such stories and transmitting them to future generations. Attuned to how the city holds the archive, however, Arendt does not look into how the archive holds (back) the city. The latter question is Hartman's. Responding to the archive's profound erasure of Black life, Hartman takes what the archive has to offer and fabulates the rest. Her fabulation refuses the authority of the archive, contests its moral judgments, and defies the positivism in which it has historically been wrapped.

Hartman's fabulation rescues her wayward women from careless cruel obscurity by individuating them, offering to each an indelible individuality and the shelter of tender memory. Fabulation as she practices it incorporates inoperativity as intensified use and inclination as sororal care. If we recall that in the ancient world, storytellers were sometimes called "song-stitchers," it will make sense that the image Hartman's practice of fabulation calls to my mind is that of Cee, in Toni Morrison's *Home*. Cee stitches tattered rags into a quilt that will become a shroud for a man murdered long ago. With her brother, Cee gathers the man's remains into her hand-stitched fabric and together they rebury him with dignity.[2] It is possible his ghost tips his hat in thanks as he dances away. This is a figure for Hartman's work in *Wayward Lives* on behalf of women whose stories we can never truly know. Finding in the archive the tattered traces of discarded lives, Hartman gathers up their remains to wrap them lovingly in hand-stitched fabulations that record their joy, pleasures, and dreams.

But Hartman's stories, especially in the first two thirds of *Wayward Lives*, are of momentary triumphs. Her wayward women carve out spaces of refuge in the city, but rarely succeed in claiming for themselves anything larger than stolen time or temporary space. Her characters seem more Icarus than Agave, or more Agave as she is conventionally read than as she is read here.³ Can fabulation also collectivize or politicize? In the end, Hartman offers her wayward women what Agave sought out for herself: membership in a chorus. But unlike Agave, Hartman's chorus members do not return to the city to claim it on behalf of their people.

In this chapter, by way of two *Bacchae* readings of Hartman's fabulation, I ask whether this is a limitation of Hartman's approach. The first tracks Hartman's turn to the chorus as a solution to the problem of individuation (individuation is itself her solution to the archive's erasures). The chorus offers collectivity, but in the ancient world it was likely a conservative institution, a temporary solution to the problem of female desire, in which chorus members experience some sexual freedom but are soon recruited back to patriarchy's enclosures. This happens as well to the women in *Wayward Lives*. The escape and collectivity offered by the chorus are short-lived. Hartman's turn to the chorus links her wayward women to classical tragedy and offers shape to their story, but does it also limit their reach?

The second *Bacchae* reading of fabulation highlights the difference between Hartman's arc of refusal and that of the bacchants. There is no collective effort to claim or transform the city in Hartman's book. I read that absence as a refusal, Hartman's way to register the limitations of the city, in particular its unreadiness to receive and welcome Black joy. This helps reopen conventional assessments of the bacchants' exile at the end of Euripides' play. The exile is assumed to be—it is presented as—the bacchants' deserved punishment. But, with Hartman, we are able to appreciate exile as also an expression of a city's limits, a confession of its unpreparedness to respond to challenges, and evidence of its incapacity for transformation.

I close this chapter with a discussion of Annette Gordon-Reed's review of *Wayward Lives*. In her criticisms of Hartman's fabulation, I find reason to think that Hartman herself (if not her wayward women) can be read as claiming the city after all. Fabulation claims a right to the archives. Hartman seeks to hold and distort the archives on behalf of a future, rather than allow them endlessly to hold us in relation to a distorted past. Gordon-Reed sees danger in this route. Her critique highlights how Hartman, like Agave, is engaged in an agon of fabulation. That agon, in spite of everything, postulates an attachment to the city, I conclude. Recovered for a feminist theory of refusal, fabulation attaches us to the city that refuses to acknowledge us and it commits us to return again and again, though we may fail.[4]

I begin though with a bit more detail on Hartman's book, *Wayward Lives, Beautiful Experiments*. I then turn to a fabulation reading of the *Bacchae*, focused on the play's neglected agon between Agave and Cadmus. The agon is one of fabulation. At stake is how the women's story should be told: fabulation opens the scene to a new reading.

Wayward Lives, Fabulation's Stories

I want to be free. Hold on.
—SAIDIYA HARTMAN, *WAYWARD LIVES, BEAUTIFUL EXPERIMENTS*

Linking arms.
—JUDITH BUTLER, *NOTES TOWARD A PERFORMATIVE THEORY OF ASSEMBLY*

Hartman turns to fabulation to tell the stories of Black girls and women in New York and Philadelphia between 1890 and 1930. Most of these are women we know about because they were caught up by an intrusion, precisely the sort of "observation" against which the bacchants fought. In the case of Hartman's wayward women, the intrusions take the form of a peeping camera lens, a police report, a sociologist's diagnosis, or an employer's complaint. The intrusions are preserved in images and reports of so-called deviant demeanor or behavior that Hartman assembles into an archive. From that archive, Hartman fabulates the possible lives of some of those "deemed unfit for history," Black women who lived free.[5] "I have crafted a counternarrative," Hartman explains, drawing on documents of deviance "liberated from the judgment and classification that subjected young Black women to surveillance, arrest, punishment, and confinement."[6]

Hartman fabulates women who worked hard, idled, trained, partied, gossiped, flirted, deviated, danced, or experimented with desire, notwithstanding the racism, homophobia, and sexism that limited their movements and constrained their possibilities. The strongest or most resistant of the women embraced their so-called deviance rather than yield to stigmatization. "Sexual modernists, free lovers, radicals and anarchists," Hartman's women lived bacchant lives, waywardly loving and beautifully experimenting in the interstices of urban life and outside its bounds, too.[7] They elasticized kinship and rebelled against reform in acts of "open rebellion" like those Robin D. G. Kelley calls infrapolitical.[8]

When Hartman says, "I have crafted a counternarrative," she embraces the "method of refusal" she calls fabulation.[9] If fabulation is a method of refusal, that is because it rejects the archive's normative judgments, which render insignificant the lives of Black women, especially those who are sexually minoritized. Fabulation is also a good term for the depathologizing work done here for the bacchants in Euripides's fifth-century tragedy, the *Bacchae*, and for the many bacchants before and since from Procne and Philomela to Toni in *The Fits*. Like Hartman, who draws on documents of deviance, I have crafted a counternarrative, too, following the documentations of deviance provided in the *Bacchae* but releasing the bacchants from the normative judgments in which they may be wrapped by Euripides and by centuries of interpreters since.

As we saw in Chapters 1 and 2, a feminist theory of refusal draws on (1) inoperativity's idleness, which rejects use and on (2) inclination's care, which (on Cavarero's account) is lavished by the mother on the child and grounds a radical ethics of mutuality. We recovered both: inoperativity into intensified use and inclination into an agonistic sorority of care. But this does not wash away the history in which these virtues were perverted: in the U.S., idleness has historically been criminalized for some as vagrancy or loitering, and care treated as part of a one-way extractivist economy of domestic work that supports kinship for some and violates it for others.[10]

Hartman documents all of this. When she tells the stories of wayward women, she shows how inoperativity and inclination operate as refusal practices for Black women otherwise treated as objects for use or spectacle.[11] Work refusal and renegade care practices are staples of wayward living. But Hartman's technique of depathologization goes further to locate idleness, care, and abandon in the context of fugitive forms of life, and this may be its own kind of recovery.[12] Fabulation allows Hartman to give new and joyful meaning to idleness and care, erasing for a while the history that scripts these postures and pastimes as deviant when not leashed to subservience. In her fugitive settings, inoperativity and inclination signify differently, as moves in an infrapolitical practice. As her book's title indicates, even beauty is altered, turned from something to be seen to something to be done. It becomes a trait of experimentation, as indeed it is for the bacchants on Cithaeron. Thus, Hartman's fabulation models respect both for the archive's overlooked and for the too much looked at, preserving but never showing them in the same old ways, turning their beauty into something to be enjoyed without being made into a thing for others' viewing pleasure or a commodity for consumption.[13]

I turn now to a fabulation reading of the *Bacchae*, which focuses on the agon between Cadmus and Agave. At stake is how the bacchants will be remembered. As gloriously free? Or tragically duped? A fabulation reading of the *Bacchae* highlights the dependence of the women's action on the capacity to tell it as a tale of refusal. Otherwise, that tree they felled in the woods—the one holding King Pentheus, whom the women bring down—will not make a sound. It will be drowned out by the roar of the archive's official stories.

The *Bacchae*'s Other Agon: A Fabulation Reading of the *Bacchae*

> The price of enfranchisement is [for some] living through pathologization.
>
> —JUDITH BUTLER, *NOTES TOWARD A PERFORMATIVE THEORY OF ASSEMBLY*

The bacchants of Euripides seem poised for success. Early on, they exert a gravitational pull on the world: when they ran, "the world ran with them." When they are exiled at the end of the play, though, they seem, like Hartman's wayward women, to be fated to a fugitivity that leaves the world of the city unaltered.[14] In the *Bacchae*, the hinge between these two possible fates is the agon between Cadmus and Agave. Agave wants to celebrate what Cadmus will want to condemn, to mythologize what Cadmus will pathologize, and to emplot as jubilee what Cadmus sees only as mournful tragedy. It is an agon of fabulation. From the perspective of a feminist theory of refusal, this agon is far more important than the one between Pentheus and Dionysus, which captures the attention of most commentators.[15]

When Agave returns to Thebes, Cithaeron's new partition of the sensible clashes directly with the old one of Thebes. Agave calls for her father to come see what she has brought home, evidence of the exploits of the women she led to victory against a wild creature who dared to spy on them.

> "Father you have the right to make the proudest boast, for you have sired the bravest daughters in the world. And of us all, I am the foremost: leaving the shuttle and loom for bigger things—hunting animals with my bare hands. . . . Here father . . . share the glory of my kill and invite your friends to a feast of triumph. You are blessed, blessed by my accomplishments."[16]

A *feast?* We noted in Chapter 1 that Agave's call for a feast can be seen as signifying her awareness that moving back to the city means giving up the raw for the cooked. But now that we have reviewed the myth of Procne at the end of Chapter 2, we may consider another possibility. In Agave's proud boasts of hunting prowess and in her call for a feast, Cadmus may hear a certain "culinary invocation" echoing the one that ended with a king's future cannibalized.[17] He does not want to be made a Tereus! Is that Agave's plan?

We know why Procne brings Philomela to the palace: to save her from Tereus and to plot, as sisters, the revenge he deserves. But do we know why Agave returns to Thebes? Is recognition what Agave seeks when she returns, boasting about her accomplishments and crowing about the unthinkable things women have done? She certainly proclaims the women's powers loudly and calls attention especially to her own. She led the bacchants in an attack against a wild creature. The women are better hunters than the men. The men use tools and weapons, whereas the women use only "these pale blades," by which Agave means their bare hands. Agave wants the head of their kill to be displayed in the palace. "I caught it without traps or snares," she says.[18] Agave boasts of the women's "triumph" while holding in her hands the proof of their achievement. When she asks the Asian chorus if she has done well, they approve. But she wants Cadmus to take pride in her and her sisters, too.

This may sound like a bid for recognition. But the play's resonances with the myth of Procne and the sheer audacity of Agave's demands suggest the return to the city cannot be merely that. Recognition is a mechanism that incorporates a potential challenger to the status quo. Sometimes the status quo is altered a bit, sometimes not.[19] What Agave demands is more radical than recognition: no less than a radical repartitioning of the city's arrangements of gender, sexuality, and power. Rather than give up Cithaeron, she seeks to bring it to Thebes. True, her move from the slow food of Cithaeron to the fast feast of the city suggests she is willing to compromise; or this may just be a concession to the slow time of transition. Sometimes change requires baby steps.

Her father understands the stakes of Agave's proclamations and the potential power of her fabulation, which tells of the women's bravery and asks for glory. His response is to buttress the old familiar order against the proposed new one, shoring up the virtues of productivity and verticality against the new glories of inoperativity and inclination. To this end, Cadmus does not argue with Agave; he reinterpellates her into the world as he knows it and wants it to be. He does not extend himself to her; he reformats the situation to suit himself.[20] With a series of questions to his daughter, Cadmus carefully shifts Agave from a proud revolutionary woman to a mourning mother. That is to say, in Arendtian terms, Cadmus robs Agave of *who* she is and returns her to *what* she is. He offers her not the transformative power and glory she craves but the homogenization of the social and restoration to her proper place in the structural map of kinship. Here is how he goes about it:

> "Can you hear me?" he says
> "I'm sorry Father; I can't remember: what were we talking about?"
> "Into which house did you marry?"
> "I married Echion, One of the Sown men they say."
> "And the name of the son you bore your husband?"
> "Our son is Pentheus"
> "And whose head do you hold in your hands?"
> "A lion's . . ."
> "Look at it properly"
> "Ah, No! No! I see the greatest sorrow!"
> "Does it still look like a lion?"
> "No! No. It is . . . Oh gods. It is Pentheus' head I hold."[21]

"Look at it *properly*." Martha Nussbaum says that with this series of questions, Cadmus returns Agave to the real world of moral reasoning. Another commentator calls it "therapy by words."[22] But neither quite captures the reformatting that Cadmus here engineers.

One by one, Cadmus's questions reimpress Agave into the roles she left behind and out of the one kinship role she prizes: "Can you hear me?" means: I am your father, you are my daughter. "Into which house did you marry?" means: who is your husband, to whom are you wife? And "Who is your son?" means: you are a mother. Cadmus's periperformative ("and to whom were you married?") works like the conventional performative ("I now pronounce you"), and returns Agave to the patriarchal fold.[23] His invocations of patriarchy's kinship roles—Father. Husband. Son.—reposition her as Daughter. Wife. Mother. These traits or roles are emplotted as the unalterable chronology of a woman's life. Sister is nowhere to be heard.

"Yes," says Cadmus when Agave agrees to his interpellations, "and whose head do you hold in your hands?"[24] Agave will now see that the head she holds belongs to Pentheus and she will grieve accordingly. Having taken the final restorative step, she is no longer a bacchant. No longer a sister. Once again daughter, wife, mother, she belongs once again to father, husband, son.[25] To say that she can now see properly is to say she has been reentered into the order of proper seeing. Pentheus's remains signify differently to a daughter, wife, and mother than they do to a revolutionary leader of a tribe of women. The severed head is no longer a trophy to be hung with pride; it has become an uncanny thing of horror.

But Agave, too, has been dismembered and reassembled, and this for a reason. When Cadmus turns her from an ecstatic revolutionary leader, proud sister to other tribe leaders, into a static mourning mother who is a member of a male-headed household, he displaces the women's regicide. The only crime now open to view is the tragic filicide that calls for mourning. Obscured from view, regicide is now en route to becoming once again an unthinkable act. By comparison with Cadmus's, then, Pentheus's efforts to domesticate the women pale. Pentheus opposed the women through force. He claimed they were wild, but he was not persuasive. The herdsman resists the king's claims.[26] So does Agave. But Cadmus does not engage with claims. He does not counter or argue with Agave. He simply dissolves her refusal. In just a few lines, Agave is repatriated to patriarchy, "the everyday and reiterated manner of producing and fomenting separation between women, again and again establishing some type of masculine mediation between one woman and another and, thus, between each woman and the world."[27]

Why call Agave revolutionary, though, if the women, thinking they have killed a lion, seem not to realize what they have done?[28] Is this not fabulation gone wild? Let's return to the scene: the messenger reports how Pentheus sat high in a tree and then "out of the sky a voice—Dionysus, I suppose," says the messenger, "pealed forth: Women, here is *the man* who made a mock of you, And me, and of my holy rites."[29] Agave then calls the bacchants or maenads to "catch this climbing *beast*." The "beast" is later called a lion when Agave carries home the head of her kill, "the head of a young mountain lion," the messenger says.[30] When Agave in Thebes tells her own version of what happened, she says that she and her sisters brought down a "beast," then caught their "prey." Then she mentions a lion cub. Then, after Cadmus speaks with her, she calls it Pentheus. So we have here: Man, Beast, Lion, Pentheus. As we saw in Chapter 2, the queer corpse is a screen for all sorts of projections.[31]

One projection in particular stands out, though, and argues for regicide. It is important that the lion then as now symbolizes monarchy. Agave's quite horrified recognition that it is Pentheus the bacchants have killed does not nullify the significance of this symbolization. When Agave mistakenly believes she holds in her hands a lion's head, she may know, without knowing, indeed she may say without saying, that the women have killed the king. When the "hopeless head" she holds becomes Pentheus, her horror can be seen not as illumination where there was blindness but as a brutal recognition of the *costs* of the women's regicide. Her son is lost, and this was a cost not reckoned with until now. She must now confront the implications of patriarchy's double bind. It is simply not possible to kill the king without losing the son, not just because of the circumstantial fact that her son Pentheus is also the king, but more fundamentally because killing the king means killing patriarchy, the structure of kinship to which the position of "son" belongs.

When Cadmus relocates Agave from leader of the women on Cithaeron into daughter, wife, mother, Agave loses hold of her power to fabulate. This is what returning to normal means. Nussbaum approves it, probably because the alternative is violence, it seems. But there is violence both ways. (And, in any case, this is a play; we may talk in terms of figuration and metaphor when we talk about killing kings.) When Cadmus denies Agave her proclaimed identity as a "who"—a powerful huntress—in favor of her identity as a "what"—daughter, wife, and mother—he kills a world.[32] Agave is now simply and only the mourning mother of a tragically dead king. The leader of a chorus of free women is dead. She has been put back in her place.

Usually, in classics, political theory, and philosophy, the figure of the mourning mother is assumed to be radical, not conservative, a danger to the city and not a vehicle of its restoration. Indeed, from Pericles in Athens to Hegel in *Phenomenology* to today, women's laments are seen as dangerous because they unsettle the state's capacity to arm itself by drafting young men, mothers' sons, to put their lives on the line in battle. But, we may see now, those dangerous mourning mothers are not just disturbing; they are also comforting. They may be dangerous because they are mourning, but at least they are *mothers*, and not maenads. This is why Cadmus maternalizes Agave. It works. He persuades centuries of commentators but also, within the play, Agave herself, who falters as a result. She loses hold of her story and becomes a lamenting mother in his.[33] Early in their exchange, Agave says to Cadmus that she is coming to her senses; however, they are his senses she is coming to. As for Cadmus, by the end of this agon, the world is an even sadder place, but at least it is once again legible to him.[34]

The wonderful thing about the *Bacchae*, though, is that it seems to anticipate such outcomes and to resist them by itself staging the question of narrative (un)reliability, plural perspective, and the contested politics of fabulation. This is not mere theatrical reflexivity, which some critics are impressed to find in the fifth century.[35] It is more important than that because it undoes what much of the commentary on the play claims to find. Euripides's script does not only pass judgment on the women. In the play's telling of the wild before it is tamed there is evidence of the play's openness to alternative fabulations. Just like the documents of deviance on which Hartman draws, Euripides conveys a renegade view of the women—there was a time when we were free and powerful—but unlike the archive, Euripides shows *how* the women are made renegade by Cadmus's delicate engineering: those women were crazy, so crazy that one mother killed her own son without even realizing what she had done! The *Bacchae* thus presses us to think of fabulation as an agonistic practice, a contest over meaning. Indeed, the play records many discrepancies between official stories and dissident or minoritized perspectives.

For example, as we saw earlier in the Introduction, the *Bacchae* begins with Dionysus contesting Thebes's official story, demanding the city face the truth about his mother's death, rupturing Thebes's reality: the true story of his origins rejects the official version of the story that falsely declares him a stranger to the city. Instead, he charges the women of the ruling family, his aunts, with causing his own mother's death. Thus, he contests what to Thebans seems obvious and makes clear the power of plural perspectives to decenter the dominant one, while highlighting the full force of the grip that buried pasts can have on the present. That grip is so powerful it might take a god to loosen it. Or a band (or two or three bands) of women. Or a blind prophet. In fact, it is Tiresias who contests Dionysus's narrative most directly, noting, as we saw earlier, that the story of Dionysus's origins is actually quite murky and confused: "Instead of saying 'Zeus showed her the sky' it was garbled over the years to 'sewed in the thigh.'"[36] We are living in a game of broken telephone. We should laugh at the nonsense it produces, but sometimes we worship its outputs as sacred truths.

As for the women's refusal, the play offers various descriptions of it, too, from multiple perspectives, and it leaves unclear whose version is credible.[37] The agon between Cadmus and Agave can now be seen to be one locus of narrative contestation. Another is when Pentheus says the women are licentious, and the herdsman who saw them with his own eyes says to the king that the women were not "as you say." Everything is opened to agonistic contestation, if the king can be wrong. Where the king and the herdsman see either wild madness or calm joy, the bacchants offer a third perspective: revolutionary worship, the jubilation of jubilee, and the collective power of the chorus.

Hartman's Three Choruses: A *Bacchae* Reading of Fabulation, I

[Euripides] explores from the inside the vicissitudes of fortune and desire
that threaten . . . the woman's successful transition from girlhood into
marriage and motherhood.

—SHEILA MURNAGHAN, "THE DAUGHTERS OF CADMUS"

Hartman says of one of her wayward women: she "carried on as if she
were free and in the eyes of the world that was no different from acting
wild."[38] That sentence could have been written about the *Bacchae*'s Agave
or any of the bacchants leaving "the shuttle and the loom for bigger
things."[39] But there is an important difference between them. Where the
bacchants mostly act in concert, the wayward women fabulated by
Hartman in *Wayward Lives* seem disinclined or unable to join together
politically or to make common cause. Hartman's fabulations through the
first two-thirds of her book are, for the most part, more Nietzsche's self
as a work of art than Arendt's world building by way of action in concert.

There are some exceptions: early in the book, there is an intimation
of power more collective than individual. We see it through the eyes of
Helen Parrish, white, landlord, rent collector, moral improver, and
journal keeper, who fears the power of concerted action in the Philadelphia tenement she runs. The women were "too much together, too much
at home, and they loved to talk and gossip. [Helen] found knots of women in
the yard, and whatever she did was sure to bring about some discussion—
alone they were amenable, but en masse far from it."[40] Here, in the phrase
"alone they were amenable, but en masse far from it," is a suggestion of
the power of Arendt's in-between, not only "social" but also potentially
political.[41]

Later in the book, another of Hartman's wayward women is shocked
and delighted to find herself in a salon of sexual inquiry.[42] The salon releases her from judgment, offers acceptance, and opens the way to a
potential community, though that doesn't last long. Another intimation:
a woman walking the city streets is said to pass right by Emma Goldman,
the best known of the anarchist walkers celebrated by political theorist

Kathy Ferguson.[43] Recording a near miss of what might have been, is this fabulation also an invitation to stop and talk next time?

Amidst the missed opportunities, intrusive surveillance, moral improvement, and frightening arrests are the joyous freedoms that are movingly recorded but seem never to gather much collective steam. Hartman suggests nonetheless that there is something collective, or at least collected, going on when she characterizes the flight of her wayward women to the city and their resistance to normative judgments as a general strike. In *Black Reconstruction*, Du Bois used that same term— general strike—to describe the actions of enslaved men fleeing the plantations to fight in the Civil War.[44] Two years before the publication of *Wayward Lives*, Hartman criticized Du Bois for focusing only on the men, noting "Black women, too, refused the conditions of work on the plantation." Du Bois knew that. He saw the women "among the 'army of fugitives' rushing away from the fields. Yet," Hartman says, "in the shift from the fugitive to the striking worker, the female slave becomes a minor figure. Neither 'the potentialities for the future' represented by the fugitive nor the text engendered by flight and refusal and furnished for abolition idealists embraced her labors."[45] Using the term general strike for her wayward women, Hartman not only fabulates for them a collective agency; she repairs the wrong of Du Bois's erasure.

But it is not until Hartman turns to the chorus, in the last third of the book, that she fully conjures collectivity. She actually fabulates *three* choruses; and as it happens, the *Bacchae* has three choruses, too ("I saw three companies of women's khoroi, one of which Autonoe led, the second your mother Agave, and the third khoros, Ino," says the messenger).[46] Her turn to the choruses recalls Morrison's singling out tragedy's "song and chorus," as well as "the heroic struggle between the claims of community and individual hubris." But Hartman attenuates the distinction between tragedy's radical individuals and the collectivity of the chorus as she moves her wayward women in and out of choral embrace.

The first of Hartman's three choruses is made up of young women whose "sonic riot" at the Bedford Hills reformatory occurred in 1919 and

1920 (preceded by earlier riots in 1917 and 1918).[47] Their rage of refusal is so loud that it finally reaches beyond the doors of their confinement. "Exiled to the country for moral reform," the rioters protested their brutal living conditions and formed "a wailing, shrieking chorus" that "screamed through the night. They sang. They yelled. . . . Each voice blended with others in a common tongue."[48] It was the *New York Times* that described the "upheaval and resistance of Lowell Cottage as a 'noise strike,'" noting "the 'din of an infernal chorus,'" which they also called a "jazz chorus."[49] Hartman follows the lead of the archive but revaluing the normative judgments of the newspaper of record and staying focused on the Black women mostly ignored: "it was resistance as music," she says of the riot at the reformatory school whose brutal methods of discipline extended outside its walls as well.[50] The riot may have "spoken with one voice," as Hartman says, but as she also reports, the women at Bedford Hills were partitioned by race both inside the school and out: "Ruth Carter and Stella Kramer and Maizie Rice were the names that appeared in the newspapers."[51] They were white. Loretta Michie was "the only colored girl quoted in the newspaper article," and Hartman can only wonder why an exception was made for her.[52]

The second chorus is a chorus line of dancers in Harlem in the 1920s, one of whose members, Mabel Hampton, is so talented that for a time it seems she might break out of the confines of her "station," only to fall like Icarus to her social death. This chorus seemed to promise talented young women like Hampton a way out of poverty and the demands of straight respectability. Mabel "moved to Harlem to escape the marriage plot," Hartman says, but would later find herself a character in a story not her own.[53] The chorus must have seemed to Mabel Hampton a promising heterotopia. But its refuge turns out to be temporary, at best a reprieve. For most chorines, the domestic servitude or marriage they seek to escape does arrive in the end, just a bit later, suggesting that life in the chorus might itself be a *part* of the marriage plot, a stage in the story rather than an escape from it.[54] If so, then the chorus manages women's desire at a delicate point of transition only to return them to the fold, leaving the chorine with a fond memory to which, later in life, the mind can wander while dishes are washed and kitchens scrubbed clean. "Sweep her narrow shoes, / From the closet floor," ends the Edna St. Vincent Millay poem, "The Chorus," in a note of resignation.

And so, recalling the bold and vital Toni, star of *The Fits*, we may ask: must all chorines get "Cadmused" in the end? Toni is a chorine, member of a dance team like the women in Hartman's second chorus. Does Hartman's Mabel Hampton offer a glimpse of Toni's future? Commenting on the ancient chorus, Sheila Murnaghan says the chorus was the site at which the troublesome transition of women to marriage could be managed and non-normative desires vented until the women could be returned to the business of reproduction. This is what we see Cadmus doing to Agave, a chorus leader, when he repatriates her to patriarchy.

Unlike Murnaghan, Hartman treats the chorus as emancipatory, not ambivalent, while nonetheless charting its failure to save those who turn to it. She notes that as a chorus member, Mabel Hampton experienced a sense of "the beauty of becoming with seven other girls, which unfolded in public under the pressure and encouragement of the gaze of strangers."[55] The "pressure and encouragement of the gaze of strangers" is the gift of the theater, which is both the domain of Dionysus and one of Hannah Arendt's models for the public space of political action.[56] In such spaces, Hartman wagers, something eventful could occur: "Dancing and singing fueled the radical hope of living otherwise." (The same might be said for Euripides's bacchants on Cithaeron, rehearsing an alternative form of life.) Choreography, which taught collaboration and coordination, was "another elaboration of the general strike."[57] Then the second collaborative chorus starts to slip into the more futural third: in the chorus's choreography, Mabel "knew that she was slipping into another arrangement of the possible."[58]

The third and final chorus is said to "open the way." This chorus "makes a plan, they draft a blueprint: move, escape, rush to the city, quit the job and run away" and invites us to "dare believe another world was possible."[59] This last chorus is neither riot nor fugitivity but futurity. It melts away all remaining individuation: "One girl can stand in for any of them."[60] And the chorus's "collective moment points toward what awaits us. . . . So everything depends on them and not [on] the hero occupying center stage, preening and sovereign." This third chorus, Hartman says, "envision[s] things otherwise. . . . To not be defeated by defeat." It bears the sorrows of life and gives form to tragedy.[61]

These three choruses—the no of the sonic riot (Bedford Hills), the chorus line that collaboratively rehearses the pleasures of non-normative belonging, and the futurity of the third chorus—are, in my view, three points on an arc of refusal in which each presupposes and requires the others. The no of riot is on behalf of a future; the rehearsals of the chorus line exemplify the preparation needed to be ready when the time comes ("Each dance was a rehearsal for escape"); the possibility of futural action motivates our readiness to say no, loudly and collectively, to temptations or coercions along the way.

Hartman never mentions the *Bacchae* (though she does draw on recent work in classics when she conjures a chorus), nor does she theorize an arc of refusal, but her three choruses, and Euripides's, may be seen as convergent points on the bacchants' arc of refusal.[62] Hartman's first chorus, the sonic riot, parallels the bacchants' work refusal (for which they are imprisoned and then riotously break out) and the chorus line parallels the bacchants' collective dance on Cithaeron. This seems to leave us to pair—in spite of their differences—Hartman's futural, tragic chorus and the bacchant sisters' going off into exile at the end of Euripides's play. That exile is usually read as a tragic lamentable fate with no future. But another option presents itself when we read the *Bacchae* with Hartman: might the final exile of the bacchant choruses' leaders "open the way," as in Hartman, to something new if not yet possible? Surely, the bacchants, like Hartman's wayward women, have "a will to unsettle, destroy, and remake."[63] Why should we assume, then, that the bacchants, once so eager to leave the city, are now distraught to find their punishment is that . . . they must leave the city? Might not Agave and her sisters experience the divinely ordered exile not just as tragic punishment (the conventional reading) but also as a kind of emancipation to waywardness, perhaps even a wilderness ritual?[64]

Granted, in the ancient Greek context, leaving the polis meant becoming vulnerable to enslavement and violence beyond the city's walls, so there are good reasons for Agave and her sisters to be distraught. Still, we may wonder whether the women are not *only* distraught. Read in light of the closing line of Hartman's book—*"How can I live? I want to be free. Hold on"*—we notice that when Agave and her sisters depart from Thebes, they may hold hands, and we may see in the moment some promise alongside the despair.[65] "Guessing at the world and seizing at chance," Hartman says, the chorine "eludes the law and transforms the terms of the possible."[66] When Dionysus exiles the women, is he perhaps again true to form? Has he given the women what they secretly desire?

Thinking about the connections between Hartman's three choruses and the three points of the bacchants' arc of refusal calls attention to another of her refusals. When Hartman fabulates three choruses and not just one, she pluralizes the chorus, differentiating each from the others. Might this lessen the chorus's power to recruit us back to tragedy's familiar terrain (as Murnaghan leads us to expect it should)? If a single chorus whispers tragedy, then three together may just sing jubilee. If a single chorus only ventilates desire to serve the marriage plot, three together may upend it. In their polyphony, they may provide the plurality that is, for Hannah Arendt, a necessary condition of action in concert and worldliness.

But there is yet one more way to be guided in our reading of Euripides by Hartman's third chorus, and one more angle from which to consider the limitations of waywardness as a politics: not to pair the third futural chorus with the exile at the end of the *Bacchae* but instead with the bacchants' return to the city to which Agave tries to claim the right. I turn now to elaborate this detail, which will alter not only our reading of the *Bacchae* but also of *Wayward Lives.*

The No, the Chant, the Return, the Exile: A *Bacchae* Reading of Fabulation, II

The Chorus threatened to steal the show.

—SAIDIYA HARTMAN, *WAYWARD LIVES, BEAUTIFUL EXPERIMENTS*

Scheherazade does not tell her first story to the sultan, but rather to her sister. [The sultan] is still not the explicit addressee of a tale that is requested by him, but rather only a listener knowingly seduced by the narrative art and her strategy of suspension.

—ADRIANA CAVARERO, *RELATING NARRATIVES*

In *The Human Condition*, Hannah Arendt fabulates a beautiful thought that we might treat as a peek into the perspective of Agave and a motivation for her return to Thebes. Noting that the walled polis created the conditions for the "organized remembrance" of action, Arendt muses (actually, leaping over a gap of hundreds of years, she *fabulates*), "not historically, of course, but speaking metaphorically and theoretically, it is as though the men who returned from the Trojan War had wished to make permanent the space of action which had arisen from their deeds and sufferings, to prevent its perishing with their dispersal and return to their isolated homesteads."[67] It is as if, realizing their stories and their glory depended on it, the men built the polis so that their exploits could be sung and preserved.[68]

In light of this fabulation, let us reconsider Agave's return to Thebes. We have already seen that she returns not for recognition but for transformation, but we have not yet explored all the details of the scene. They are revealing. When she arrives from Cithaeron, Agave calls first to the Asian bacchants in the city, a fourth chorus, and then to the men of Thebes and only after that to her family, which is to say, her father and son. First: "Bacchae of Asia . . . I bring this sprig, newly cut, from the mountain. The hunting was good." To which the chorus responds: "we see you and welcome you, fellow reveler." They see and recognize her. But she wants more: "share in the feast," says Agave to the chorus. And then, starting to think of the others, Agave says (in a periperformative utterance, beginning to bring in the men but addressing them only sideways, as it were), "Soon the men of Thebes"—"and Pentheus your son," interjects the chorus (beginning the maternalization that Cadmus will soon complete)—"will," Agave goes on, "praise the mother who caught the whelp and brought him home." The chorus then says, in effect, don't just share this with us, "show the citizens what you caught," and so Agave turns and says directly now: "Look at this, men of Thebes, citizens of this towered city, look at the prize!" And then to a subset of those citizens: "you armed hunters" (but why are you armed? we can almost hear her musing, mocking; *we* killed *our* prey with our bare hands) and then the fateful third and fourth addresses: "But where is my father, Cadmus? He should be here. And where is my boy, Pentheus?"[69]

Addressing the city, Agave signals she does not intend to come home. Calling first to the Asian bacchants, she tries to constitute a new public. Calling to the men second, she indicates her desire to unify what has been riven. Calling to her natal and conjugal families next, she lets them know that all is forgiven and it is time for repair in a context of civic renewal. The king may be dead, but that need not mean their loved ones also need to be given up. Does it?

Not so fast, Cadmus will say. He will call for restoration instead. Don't you know what you are? he will say. But what he really means is, Just who do you think you are?

Thinking with and against Arendt and Hartman, we may refabulate the Theban bacchants' story as follows: The women led by Agave and her sisters reject confinement to work and labor. They seek more than freedom-intimating moments such as those stolen in a yard out back. They want something more, so they flee the city. But they want more than flight, too, something more lasting, so they seek out an alternative. They join a chorus! They leave the city for Cithaeron, where they learn to collaborate and they rehearse new ways of being, exploring forbidden pleasures, learning their powers. They press their bodies into new non(re)productive uses. They chant. They experience a shared enjoyment in nature's embrace. The earth shares its bounty without demanding their efforts. Food and drink appear magically before them. Water, wine, milk, and honey: the women want for nothing. They nap, nurse and care for wild animals in the field, suckling wolves and playing with snakes, freed from anthropocentric restriction and from reproductive time. When necessary, they fight off interlopers and protect their space from intrusion. They achieve the limited but splendid freedom of fugitivity and something approximating the jubilation of jubilee. But something was missing. It all felt somehow unreal and maybe also temporary. What was missing was a fabulation that Hartman does not talk about, what Arendt says was missing for the Trojan War's heroes: the fabulation provided by the polis of remembrance. Arendt says that "to be deprived of it means to be deprived of reality . . . the reality of the world is guaranteed by the presence of others, by its appearing to all."[70]

If, in Arendt's fabulation, the men of the Trojan War look to the city to preserve their war stories, then the women of the *Bacchae*, who want stories told of their courageous equality, look to the city, too. Agave aims to establish the equality of women in the polis as its norm and not just outside it for an exceptional moment. It is, we may say using Arendt's words, as though the women who returned from Cithaeron "had wished to make permanent the space of action which had arisen from their deeds and sufferings, to prevent its perishing with their dispersal and return to their isolated" households.[71] They want to be real.

Were the women successfully to claim the right to the city, the effect would be a repartitioning of the sensible. ("The freedom to make and remake ourselves and our cities" is, David Harvey says, "one of the most precious yet most neglected of our human rights."[72]) Everything would be up for grabs including, especially, the sexual contract into which Agave is reentered by Cadmus. If the ancient chorus, as Sheila Murnaghan argues, was the site at which the troublesome transition of women to marriage could be managed by the city, we might say here that in the *Bacchae*, the women's reentry to the city is managed by marriage. This is the task taken up by Cadmus.

In the end, however, Cadmus's effort to restore Agave to her patriar-
chally required social roles is no more successful than is Agave's claim
to the city. Cadmus' effort to return the women to the household is
interrupted by Dionysus, who orders them all into exile. For Dionysus,
exiling Cadmus, his wife (as snakes), and separately, their daughters,
Agave and her sisters (in human form), is punishment for crimes against
his mother and himself. I have suggested the exile grants the bacchants
their secret wish of waywardness, though exile is also their greatest fear.
But there is yet another way to read the exile: as a judgment about the
unreadiness of the polis to receive the bacchants.

The polis is unprepared to sing the bacchants' praises. The women
are undeserving of praise from the city's still regnant perspective. Cadmus
arguably speaks for the city when he tries to domesticate the bacchants
via (re)marriage. Dionysus's response is to make the women wayward
again. Instead of the hoped-for songs in their honor, which build public
memory, these women will sing the sorrow songs of exile, which make
the burden bearable. But we must not let the much focused-upon un-
bearableness of exile occlude from view the extent to which return to
the household would also have been unbearable.

Attending to the unreadiness of the city calls attention to the importance to refusal of rehearsal and prefiguration. And good timing matters,
too. If Hartman opts for fugitivity over the city, that is because she believes the city is not ready for the wayward and has reason to doubt it
will ever be. The question is, can we nonetheless say we must ready the
city? Commit ourselves to it? This would mean impressing ourselves into
the full arc of the bacchants' refusal. Arguably, this is a theme of the *Bacchae* in which the women of the *Bacchae* come back too soon. Their
sojourn on Cithaeron is interrupted. Pentheus's intrusion and the ensuing
violence redirect the women's course. If the murder of the king/lion un-
seated the women from Cithaeron prematurely, then the women are
unready to return, and the city is unready to receive them. That they are
unready for each other is allegorized by the capacity of each one to look
at the same object and see something entirely different: the city sees a

king; the Theban women see a lion. In the end, both will decide to see Pentheus.

That the women are unready shows in Agave's vulnerability to Cadmus's easy maternalization, her incapacity to refuse the tragedy of remarriage into which he conscripts her. That the women are, however, *almost* ready shows in Agave's call *first* to the bacchants of Asia and only after that to the men of Thebes and her natal family. She is in the grip of sorority.

Unready, both—the women and the city to which they want to claim their right. Still, what the *Bacchae* offers a feminist theory of refusal is this aspiration and orientation: the idea that fabulation solicits those who leave the city to return, both to make their freedom permanent in Arendt's sense, and for the sake of those left behind, still partitioned by old divisions into silence or powerlessness, left (at best) to interstitial joy but deprived of public affirmation. Agave fulfills that obligation and stakes a claim to the city as she envisions it might be: a polyglot place of foreign bacchants, free women, men of the city, and natal and conjugal kin, together in inoperativity, inclination, and fabulation.[73] If refusal is to be a politics, and fabulation part of a feminist theory of refusal, then returning to the city to claim it is key.[74] It is from the perspective of Agave's effort to do so that the *Bacchae* can be seen not as a tragedy of the women, as in the conventional readings of the play, but as a tragedy of the city.

A return to the city is what started all this. The *Bacchae* begins when Dionysus himself returns to Thebes. I have been suggesting that such a move has the power to inaugurate a politics. It is an Arendtian idea, but Arendt would surely not connect her ideas to the *Bacchae*. And yet, there is a surprisingly Dionysian moment in Hannah Arendt's *On Revolution* when she describes the political action she values as a kind of intoxication. She notes Robespierre's worry "that the end of revolutionary power and the beginning of constitutional government would spell the end of 'public liberty'" (what in the U.S. was called "public happiness"). Robespierre's fear, Arendt says, was that "the new public space would wither away after it had suddenly burst into life and *intoxicated them all with the wine of action* which, as a matter of fact, is the same as *the wine of freedom*."[75] The question for Robespierre, the regicide, and for the French revolutionaries more generally, Arendt says, was, in effect, how to preserve the drunkenness of public happiness under the sobriety of "constitutional government" or, Arendt continues, "whether the revolution should be declared in permanence."[76] Constitutional government terminates public freedom to "guarantee civil liberties and rights," she explains. It seems we are left with a choice: between Government saying "Go home, Revolution, you're drunk," and Revolution saying, "Government, you're no fun—too sober."

Figuring action in concert as intoxication, Arendt invites us to think, with Agave, of the women's drunkenness "metaphorically and theoretically"; of how, like the heroes of the Trojan wars whom Arendt admired for precisely this, and yet unlike them, the bacchants, too, were intoxicated by action in concert and they, too, wanted to secure their exhilarating experience. The city preserved the men's war stories. The women want the same. Only if their stories of skill and courage were preserved would their freedom be real and their equality lasting.

When Agave returns to Thebes, she does not give up on the gifts and powers of the polis. She completes a quest that first took her out of the city—to Cithaeron where new forms of life could be rehearsed and explored—but then returns her to it. We know from Chapter 2 the power of heterotopias like Cithaeron to subvert conventional ways of doing and knowing. And we now know from Cadmus's example how the conventional center holds on to power in the face of such challenges when they come home: by turning such heterotopias into sites of madness or exception and reinserting wayward women into their proper locations in the structural map of patriarchal kinship. Agave's appeal to her father is a misstep, a concession, even, to his authority. Her vulnerability to his reinterpellation is poignant. Back among the men of the polis, the women in the *Bacchae* lose their way. It is unsurprising. Creating counters to patriarchy requires more than a few days in the woods. But, recalling Du Bois' term in *Black Reconstruction*, a "splendid failure," we may speculate whether the splendidness of the women's failure can itself have the power to generate new readings of the sisters' return from Cithaeron to Thebes (as a claim to the city) as well as of their exile from the city at the end of the play (as the gift of waywardness).

Euripides—who wrote for the Dionysia outside the city—puts Agave's quest on the page, and there it remains for us to revisit. With Hartman's help, we may now see the play's plural choruses as polyphonous. With its plural choruses and clashing perspectives, the *Bacchae* exceeds the moralism by way of which it has until now mostly been received, and it demands new hearings and new fabulations. Fugitivity will not be its satisfaction. Fabulation will be its fuel.[77]

Between Archive and Imagination

> Perhaps the achievement of paradise was premature.
> —TONI MORRISON, NOBEL LECTURE (ABOUT THE BIBLE'S TOWER OF BABEL)

> "I'm both a pessimist and a wild dreamer"
> —SAIDIYA HARTMAN (*NEW YORKER* INTERVIEW, OCT. 2020)

I have argued that a fabulation reading of the *Bacchae*, together with two *Bacchae* readings of fabulation, highlight the classical, tragic motifs of *Wayward Lives* while also confronting its author with an arc of refusal that postulates a return to the city before possible exile. Moreover, I have suggested that if, as Arendt says, the city is the site of public remembrance and the archive the keeper of its values and houser of its vernacular, then fabulation presupposes and requires a right to the city: this means a right to retake its archive and maybe even transform the city. Like all new rights, this one demands a response from those who may not be ready for the claim, and so it may or may not succeed.[78] I have suggested that this is a right Hartman's wayward women do not seek collectively and that the bacchants do seek but fail to win. Still, reading *Wayward Lives* alongside the *Bacchae*, it is hard not to hear Hartman's wayward women call joyously for a feast to celebrate their (fabulated) return. And yet their agency is not conceived of as political. Their world building is not by way of the kind of action in concert that battles to make the city live up to the promise of justice and equality. The women Hartman fabulates are policed but not political in Arendt's sense.

I want now to suggest that, although Hartman's wayward women do not, as it were, return to the city to claim it, we may see Hartman as doing precisely that. Since the archive is her point of departure and the target of her method of refusal, we may see Hartman's book as a refusal *in* the city and not *of* the city after all. I conclude this chapter by pushing this reconsideration further in light of a recent review of *Wayward Lives* by Annette Gordon-Reed. Gordon-Reed reproaches Hartman for the liberties she takes with the archive. The reproach is gentle but firm. In the course of it Gordon-Reed worries the line between archive and imagination, and in the worrying there is the suggestion that Hartman herself, unlike her wayward women, does not just evade the city's reach but knocks rather brusquely on its door.

When Hartman's women build worlds by building non-normative lives in the shadows, alleys, and interstices of the city, this is compatible with her embrace of refusal and fugitivity as scenes and scenarios of Black joy and freedom. But there is a *politics* in her counter-archival practice, which tells the stories that haunt the archive and resist its erasures.[79] The stakes of it all are clear when Gordon-Reed questions Hartman's inference from the archive—the arrests, commitments, and debts recorded there—that the women in question lived admirably free and transgressive lives, fully embracing and hotly pursuing them. Gordon-Reed presses on Hartman the idea that the women whose pathologized traces are found in the archives could just as well be seen as ambivalent about—or even desiring of—the normative bourgeois life that would not have them. Nothing in the archive licenses the idea that these women are only and loudly seeking freedom from such, and the critique of bourgeois values so central to our contemporary understanding had not yet taken hold early in the twentieth century, she says.

Gordon-Reed, who in her own more positivist archival work has made the archive speak of those thought to be forever lost, wants to preserve the archive. Presumably she believes it still has gifts to offer. For her, the issue is the survival of the archive as part of a truth-telling infrastructure, though she knows the archive, which hands down the perspectives of the masters but not the enslaved, certainly has to be wrestled with. Though she concedes that authors should write the books they want to write, she registers a wrong when she asks, nonetheless, why Hartman would not write her work as fiction?

Gordon-Reed notes Hartman's own aperçu about Du Bois, so judgmental of young Black girls in his Philadelphia study, but capable nonetheless when he wrote literature of transforming "a ruined girl who grew up in a brothel into a heroine." Citing Hartman's judgment of Du Bois— "literature was better able to grapple with the role of chance in human action and to illuminate the possibility and the promise of the errant path"—Gordon Reed asks the same question of Hartman: "Why a book of nonfiction and not a novel?" In effect, Gordon-Reed asks Hartman to take these lives off the register of refusal and out of the reach of fabulation, and return them to the "discipline" of history. Choose: either History or Literature, Gordon-Reed all but says. She concedes, "of course, people should write the books they want to write." But that concession is part of Gordon-Reed's construction of an opposition between archive and imagination that Hartman's fabulation is precisely out to trouble. Fabulation, which works with the archive, is after all not just imaginative but in the middle: between archive (History) and imagination (Literature).[80]

We can anticipate a similar set of concerns playing out with reference to the radical rereading of the *Bacchae* proposed in these pages. To depathologize the women of the *Bacchae* on behalf of errancy is to risk being seen as errant, or charged with errant (erroneous, even) reading. It is to risk becoming hardly different from the bacchants in the eyes of the reader. It is to encounter resistance from the archive, the history of classical scholarship. Why not just say: they can have the *Bacchae* and we can have its better versions, such as *Wayward Lives*? Why bother with Euripides? Because to leave the archive where it is and build elsewhere is to be pressed into fugitivity's path. Leaving the archive alone, we abet its reproduction of the same. This is the choice. In my view, agonism is the answer. Both Gordon-Reed and Hartman exemplify it, in their very different ways.

It was, after all, from the archive that Gordon-Reed managed to summon Sally Hemings and the children of hers that Thomas Jefferson fathered but did not acknowledge.[81] The result of Gordon-Reed's work was a kind of toppling of the hero, a long overdue reconsideration of that Founding Father. By contrast, in Hartman's hands, a different hero-toppling occurs.[82] Jefferson is unmentioned, and women descended from those he enslaved are pressed to the foreground. When Hartman conjures their Black joy from the archive of white oppression, she offers an alternative to Jefferson's American idea of "public happiness." Black joy is shared and conjugated in Hartman's pages; every life she retells is enfolded in its embrace. Does Black joy just fill a lack by countering the pathologization of Black life? Or does it—might it—reoccupy the city, disorient its so-called "public" happiness, and disturb its reproduction of the same? There is now no avoiding the agonism of joy and fabulation. Reading Hartman in this way, we might just get to see what happens, finally, when the invitation of a feminist theory of refusal is accepted and a politics of refusal comes home to stay.

Conclusion
Sister Is an Anagram for Resist

SHALL WE DANCE THEM AGAIN, THE NIGHTLONG DANCES?
DANCE AGAIN WITH BARE FEET IN THE DEW?
SHALL I TOSS MY HEAD AND SKIP THROUGH THE OPEN FIELDS
AS A FAWN SLIPPED FREE OF THE HUNT AND THE HUNTERS,
LEAPING THEIR NETS, OUTRUNNING THEIR HOUNDS?
—EURIPIDES, *BACCHAE*

THESE FESTIVAL WEEKENDS ARE PLACES OF CRISIS AND YOU CAN DO
WONDERFUL THINGS IN A CRISIS. . . . YOU GO BEYOND YOURSELF ANYWAY
AND YOU TALK ABOUT IT FOR YEARS. . . . YOU GO WISHING EVERY DAY WAS
LIKE THAT. EVERY DAY AIN'T LIKE THAT AND WHAT REALLY COUNTS IS NOT
WHAT YOU DO THIS WEEKEND, BUT TAKE WHAT THIS WEEKEND HAS
MEANT—TRY TO DIGEST IT. AND . . . BEFORE TWENTY-FOUR HOURS GO
AROUND, APPLY IT. AND THEN DO IT EVERY DAY YOU GET UP AND FIND
YOURSELF ALIVE.

—BERNICE JOHNSON REAGON, "COALITION POLITICS"

In Chapter 1, I recovered inoperativity as an agonistic feminist practice of intensification that slows time and doubles down on use, rather than suspend time and seek a purist escape from use. In Chapter 2, I recovered inclination, shifting it from a feminist, pacifist, maternal orientation of care to a feminist, sororal practice of peaceful and violent mutuality and care. In Chapter 3, fabulation became a meaning-making practice that postulates the return to the city that Hartman's wayward women may not (for good reasons) embrace but the bacchants do risk (and Hartman herself may risk as well). *A Feminist Theory of Refusal* builds on these three concepts, casting them as concepts of refusal, learning from each of them, and then critically recovering each one. Why these three? I conclude now by recalling their connections and the specific reasons for their centrality to a feminist theory of refusal.

Inoperativity is important to a feminist theory of refusal for its critique of use, since use is a particular mode of subjection imposed on women and other minoritized peoples historically and to this day in modern liberal democracies. But a feminist theory of refusal cannot enlist inoperativity as we find it because it generates no assembly and seems to abjure power. We need to move inoperativity from the suspension of use to its intensification so that we work through it. This is necessary to remedy the problematic purism of Agamben's inoperativity, which does not take inspiration from women's experience (quite the opposite in fact).[1] But even a recovered inoperativity falls short of refusal's needs because it does not by itself press action into concert with others. This is where the *Bacchae*, subversively reread as a tale of slow regicide, is so, well, useful.

So we moved on to *inclination*, not to replace inoperativity but to partner the recovered inoperativity with the ambivalent mutuality of a recovered version of inclination. Inclination corrects for any (over-)rejection of use because it is a register in which we seek to make ourselves useful to others. As a feminist refusal concept, Cavarero's inclination is a disposition toward another, hopefully oriented to pacifism, mutuality, and care but faced with a choice because carelessness, harm, or abandonment are also always possibilities or temptations within its ethical universe. As we saw, this refusal concept has to be recovered, too, shifted from maternalism to sorority, which is the more egalitarian kin relation, and from being on the cusp of pacifism *or* violence to being in the dirt, practicing a kind of care and power that seek peace but risk implication in violence, too.

If we end, finally, with *fabulation*, it is because, without what Hartman calls her method of refusal, the work of inoperativity and inclination (which means rejecting the reduction of life to use and practicing the "being useful" of care) will always be vulnerable to reabsorption into the dominant frames that silence or exceptionalize feminist agencies. Powerful examples are lost, women's actions pathologized, the histories of minoritized peoples erased. Those who care for others are seen as devoted or subservient when in fact they are likely either exploited or freely giving. Women like the bacchants, who rise in rebellion against a king, are remembered as drunk or mad and therefore worthless, even while men's political action in concert is celebrated as its own kind of intoxication and their ensuing deaths or exiles are commemorated as glorious: poignant, tragic, honorable, and worthy. As we saw, the bacchants claim glory just like men had done before. Is the women's claim too mimetic? Perhaps so. But demanding glory they also claim the right to the city, and that is a claim to political power.

Contra Arendt, who seems to suggest we need stories for memory, fabulation shows how we need stories for survival and for the power to guide action by telling ourselves what we are doing in the doing of it. Fabulation is agonistic. This is what we learn from the *Bacchae*'s agon between Agave and Cadmus and from the agon over fabulation instanced by Gordon-Reed's review of Hartman's *Wayward Lives*. Fabulation refuses the habits and assumptions of the archive (it sides with Agave, not Cadmus). But, as an agonistic practice, fabulation also postulates the city, whose walls in the ancient world held the story for all to share, retell, or contest. That was true then, now, and in the future. We have to hold our stories. Recovered for a feminist theory of refusal, fabulation adamantly claims the city that is always at stake in the contest over meaning. The city may be a different constellation of relations now than it was then. And it is certainly a more plural entity with lots of new subdivisions. But still, without its housing, refusal is ephemeral. The risk of the return to the city is absorption into the city's conflicts and the loss of our bearings. It is against that that we rehearse.

Importantly, in the *Bacchae*, inoperativity, inclination, and fabulation together make up an *arc of refusal*. The arc is not teleological but phenomenological, stretching from the women's flight from the city, to their heterotopian rehearsal on Cithaeron of skills and relations needed for a new form of life to their return to the city. The idea of refusal as an arc and not an act is a central feature of the feminist theory of refusal developed here. In her above-referenced speech, published as "Coalition Politics," Bernice Johnson Reagon tells an audience at a women's music festival that refuge may be a necessary *moment* in the politics of refusal, but in the end we all have to go home, back to the proverbial city, where we have to deal with each other and make others deal with us. Reagon was claiming the women's music festival for a more intersectional feminism than many had yet embraced. But she was also illustrating what I have here called the arc of refusal: leave, suspend use in festival, hide out, rehearse some new moves, corporealize different habits, intensify use, try out a new world, imagine it, make it real, join up with others, fight with each other, care for each other, come back and claim your right to the city, too. You have the right to leave, the right to build elsewhere, but you also have an obligation to return because we are all depending on each other. We may succeed or fail. But we are in it together. This commitment is not for everyone all the time. But it is part of the promise of refusal as a world-building practice, and this makes of refusal a politics far larger than political theory's old debates about civil disobedience and more daunting even than the heroic politics to which we build monuments.

As I write, many monuments in the United States, and around the world, have been brought down by protesters, and others will follow. One of my favorite topplings, however, has left the monument in place for now. It is the statue of Robert E. Lee in Richmond, Virginia. Rather than bring it down, protesters covered it with expressive graffiti after the police killing of George Floyd. Then they projected in deep colors of blue the image of Harriet Tubman on the side of the pedestal. Above her head is a quote: "Slavery is the next thing to hell." And above that, the horse on which Lee still sits astride. But screened onto the horse and calling to itself all the attention that is left are three letters: BLM, for Black Lives Matter. Lee is still there, but with all that is now going on, one does not notice him. He has gone from hero to screen. And that seems to me to be a great way to topple a hero (as Page duBois advises us to do in our readings of Greek tragedy). Some statues must be toppled but if others are to be left where they are, we need not cede the scene to the hero. In the protesters' layering of statuary and illumination, they relegate the men some want revered into sad irrelevance. This is the agon of fabulation.

In the 1960s and 1970s, political theorists, including John Rawls, Michael Walzer, and Hannah Arendt, debated the validity of civil disobedience and conscientious objection, but they did not think about the gender politics of dissidence, nor did they look into refusal, except to distinguish legitimate expressions of dissent from illegitimate ones. They were interested in normative justification and the kind of theoretical specifications that would lend their weight to political stability. For example, all three specified the contours of dissent in such a way as to put what they called rioting outside the bounds of proper political participation.[2]

There were other exclusions as well. Although she was writing in 1970, Arendt made no mention of Muhammad Ali, who was at that very moment engaged in costly civil disobedience against the Vietnam War. She focused on Thoreau and Socrates and argued that "good men become manifest only in emergencies" ("they suddenly appear as if from nowhere in all social strata"), but the "good citizen [is always] conspicuous."[3] Ali was at the time conspicuous, to say the least. Arendt must have seen his story more than once on the front page of the newspapers. He was the disobedient of the day. For refusing the draft, he was tried and convicted in June 1967, by an all-white jury in Houston, of violating Selective Service laws. His conviction was approved by the Court of Appeals in May 1968. The World Boxing Association stripped him of his title, and other state-level boxing associations suspended his boxing license and refused to allow him to box under their purview. He was exiled from his sport at the prime of his career. What followed was a years-long battle to defend himself, ended ultimately by a decision in his favor from the US Supreme Court in 1971.

Legally, Ali claimed conscientious objection to the draft, but in his pursuit of justice he practiced a broader politics of refusal that combined elements of inoperativity, inclination, and fabulation. In his case, the three concepts of refusal are less an arc and more a repertoire. He was a fabulator from the beginning, and this drove his critique of use and the charm of his inclination. I discuss his example in more detail in the Appendix. His story closes this book. He was no feminist, but he played with the codes of gender in ways that resonate with feminism's later third wave and with the bacchants' much earlier rebellion.

For now, I note briefly: he refused to be made use of for imperial purposes (inoperativity), he inclined toward his fellows similarly drafted but less powerfully positioned to refuse (inclination), and he set an example, fabulating his experience so that it might alter the perspective of others, also endangered by the draft, as well as reach those Americans who were insulated from the danger (fabulation). Ali's draft refusal was part of his forceful criticism of the Vietnam War as an imperial war that put soldiers in places they had no real (nongeopolitical) reason to be and then provided them with "self-defense" as a justification for the violence they committed against the local population.[4] His draft refusal was part of his broader refusal of American white supremacy and empire. His conduct throughout this long episode dramatized the kind of individuality and concertedness presupposed and produced by the determination to refuse injustice even when (precisely because) its powers are manifold.

Arendt's failure to acknowledge Ali in the context of theorizing civil disobedience and conscientious objection in 1970 is itself an argument in favor of a new approach. Given her awareness of the Dionysian dimensions of participatory democratic life, it is sometimes surprising to find Arendt drawing such sober lines around the properly political. The participation she valued is actually vivified and inspired by larger experiments in refusal. Theorizing feminist refusal through inoperativity, inclination, and fabulation helps break the grip of the old debates and categories of civil disobedience and conscientious objection. These debates and categories are attenuated by the march of events from 1970 to 2020, and by the wide array of new political theory responses that follow.[5] Foregrounding these three concepts of refusal, highlighting the gendered erasures that screened them from view, a feminist theory of refusal introduces a feminist swerve into the Arendtian approach.

Indeed, it is striking to me, looking back over these chapters, how the three refusal concepts revisit Arendtian categories and concerns. Inoperativity, for example, can be seen as an expression of her own well-known antipathy to use and to the instrumentalization and acceleration of everything in conditions of modernity. However, in spite of her use of Adam and Eve to show how both genders labor, Arendt does not attend to the social constructs that actually identify one gender with reproductive labor and the other with a class that labors. Next, inclination, in a way, shares Arendt's commitment to the concertedness of action and to the plurality that is its necessary, worldly condition, though it does risk the figurations of kinship that she criticized (for her, it was "fraternity") on behalf of a feminism of chosen kinship, performative sorority, which is the result and not just the condition of acting together against misogynistic sovereignty. And as I argued in Chapter 3, fabulation draws for its recovery on Arendt's well-known commitments to stories as the energizers of action, storehouses of memory, and threads of the fabric that binds a community together and gives it shape and maybe a future.[6] Fabulation's stories, however, unlike Arendt's, center not on the archives' heroes but on the marginalized, the forgotten, the feminized. This refuses and interrupts the values of the archive on behalf of the world as it might be. Refusal is generative. Thus, refusal, as an arc and even (as in the case of Ali) a repertoire, pushes us beyond Arendt to the gendered politics of refusal and to the more bacchic possibilities she entertained from time to time but mostly set aside.

I opened this book with brief mention of Occupy Wall Street. I want to close here with a different occupation. As I write, a few streets in Seattle have been taken over by protesters. Called Chaz, Seattle's Capitol Hill Autonomous Zone, or CHOP, the Capitol Hill Occupied Protest, the zone is not quite a Cithaeron of their own, nor is it a women's space. It is barricaded, but residences are accessible and businesses are operating: "at a barricade on the eastern side, activists even painted some makeshift parking spaces for liquor store customers. Those businesses and residents—as well as CHOP occupants—still use electricity and water. And unlike any actual autonomous zone, people move freely in or out."⁷ The president cries melodramatically that the city has been kidnapped, and the mayor responds sanguinely that it is only a few blocks. In a strange way, both are right. Because something is going on, but it is not clear yet what: when inoperativity and inclination are unleashed, the contest of fabulation will follow. Is CHAZ/CHOP a "failed experiment" or "a new sort of utopia"? Either way, it is a vivid example of what life could be, and it takes shape on the ground.⁸ "Walking around CHOP," Jane C. Hu reports, "I saw countless mutual aid booths. When I'd been in the same area the week before, back when it was just a regular old protest space, activists had already established similar booths, but their size and sophistication had grown." As on Cithaeron, there is plenty: "The 'No Cop Co-Op' had piles of bread, jam, oats, and peanut butter, with a sign encouraging people to avail themselves. The extreme abundance of food I saw is noteworthy," says Hu, citing the sign outside the co-op, which says: "Do not take one granola bar—take the whole box. Take an entire case of pop. You do you. Just stop looking and start shopping."

There is no mention of gender equity or transformation so far in the coverage of this refusal. But the right to the city is claimed, a parapolitics of inoperativity and inclination is practiced, and an alternative to what was the everyday, before COVID-19, is vivified. That all this takes place in a street that houses a now-evacuated police station resonates beautifully with (though it is not violent like) the bacchants' murderous regicide on Cithaeron.⁹ From the perspective of a feminist theory of refusal, there is promise in this example, though the community was finally dispersed and many of its defenders arrested. The police returned.

Keeping the experiment going would have been wonderful. But we can still struggle against such policed enclosures and proliferate alternatives to them. And then, when the occupation ends, as they tend to do, it is important then, to answer Bernice Johnson Reagon's call—it is a kind of chorus in this book: to "take what this [occupation/Cithaeron] has meant—try to digest it. And . . . before twenty-four hours go around, apply it [call for a feast!]." If we "do it every day," we might just find ourselves alive.¹⁰ And maybe our cities will, too.

Appendix

Recalling Chapter 1's critical engagement with Agamben's glorious body, I note here that the Appendix is the least useful of human organs, and yet once in a while it announces itself and maybe even ruptures the body's routine in a kind of refusal. So, as part of this book's critique of use, it is perhaps doubly appropriate to locate here some final thoughts, by way of four reflections: on a classic film (*Modern Times*), a new play (*A Map of Virtue*), a recent film (*What Is Democracy?*), and an iconic life (Muhammad Ali). The hope is that these vivify further for readers the interpretative promise of a feminist theory of refusal. The first three illustrate the recovered versions of inoperativity, inclination, and fabulation, in that order. And finally last, in the example of Ali, already discussed briefly in the conclusion, we see in more detail how these three concepts of refusal might operate not only as an arc, as in the *Bacchae*, but also as a repertoire, one on which Ali drew throughout his life and career.

Inoperativity in Chaplin's *Modern Times*

In Melville's "Bartleby, the Scrivener," Bartleby, famous for his "I prefer not to," is mostly resistant to but also a carrier of employers' demand for a total workday. Even before he takes up residence at the office, Bartleby eats the little he eats at his desk, prefiguring the effort by Henry Ford, just a few decades later, to dispense with workers' lunch break. As Corey Robin notes, Henry Ford engaged in a "never-ending quest for control of the workplace." He "confronted many foes, but none as wily or rebellious as the human digestive tract," which Ford "called the body's 'disassembly line.'" Hoping to solve the problem of metabolic inefficiencies,

Charlie Chaplin as Maenad. Still from *Sunnyside,* Charlie Chaplin, First National Pictures, 1922

Ford provided sandwiches to workers in his Highland Park, Michigan plant, and gave them ten minutes to eat them. "So industrialized was ingestion at the plant that workers growled about their 'Ford stomach,'" notes Robin.[1] The Ford stomach stands for a larger, embodied, refusal of industrialization's demands even when workers may also try to comply with them, by keeping up with the accelerations of the assembly line, for example.

Ford's ambitions for the workplace are powerfully satirized by Charlie Chaplin in *Modern Times,* released in 1936, not long before the Flint, Michigan sit-down strike, which led to the unionization of GM auto workers in 1937 and, later, of Ford auto workers in 1941.[2] In the film, Chaplin's Tramp—a comic Bartleby—is selected to test a new feeding machine that promises to feed workers efficiently, to minimize the time of the midday break.

The scene of the Tramp's selection recalls the "primal scene" of Taylorism, described by Gabriel Winant, who draws on Taylor's *The Principles of Scientific Management* (1911) to recount the history: "Employed at Bethlehem Steel for $1.15 a day, and known among workmates for his physical vigor and thriftiness," Henry Noll was asked by Taylor to take part in an experiment: "'Are you a high-priced man?'" The response was, "Vell, I don't know vat you mean." After a few more such go-rounds, Taylor explained, "'What I want to find out is whether you are a high-priced man or one of these cheap fellows here. What I want to find out is whether you want to earn $1.85 a day or whether you are satisfied with $1.15, just the same as all those cheap fellows are getting.' . . . Then," notes Winant, came "the rub: 'You see that pile of pig iron?' Taylor explained that a high-priced man did exactly as told, 'from morning till night.'" From then on, Noll "'worked when he was told to work, and rested when he was told to rest.' [His] output increased from twelve tons of pig iron moved every day to 47."[3]

In Chaplin's version of the scene, things go less smoothly. The Tramp seems happily compliant. He puts down his half-eaten apple (symbol of innocence betrayed?) when called to test the feeding machine, which is placed over the stopped assembly line belt, with workers seated nearby

Still from *Modern Times*, Charlie Chaplin,
United Artists, 1936

on their lunch break. The Tramp is strapped in and given instructions by a white-coated representative of the new discipline of scientific management. But the machine is soon rendered inoperative by its own glitches, which innervate the Tramp's recalcitrant body (and vice versa).[4]

A Bartleby-figure, the Tramp simply cannot conform to the machine's demands. His body "prefers not to," though he appears as willing as Noll was when he was summoned by Taylor. As the machine's pace accelerates, the Tramp cannot keep up. The experts that accompany the machine are outdone, too. The machine breaks down, sparking and smoking, and when it releases the Tramp suddenly from its cold embrace, the factory boss announces, "It's no good—it's not practical," and the Taylorites are sent away. The impracticality of the machine, not its inhumanity, is the reason it is rejected.[5]

The feeding machine vivifies fantasies, like Ford's, to have total control of the workday which, in our own time, involves diapering workers to prevent the need for bathroom breaks. This, too, is anticipated by Chaplin who is ousted from the bathroom and sent back to work by a surveillant boss who personally monitors workers' movements from a screen on the bathroom wall. Winant highlights not the power but the impotence of the moment: "The boss may have an all-seeing panopticon, but the prehistory of every strike begins when one worker catches another's eye."[6] It is notable, then, that the feeding machine in *Modern Times* harnesses the worker the way blinders fix a horse's gaze. No such sideways looking is possible in the apparatus, but then, the apparatus is rejected.

The feeding machine may fail to feed, but it succeeds in recalling the force-feeding routinely used against hunger strikers in the 1910s. When Taylor was revolutionizing work, rechoreographing the human body into ever-greater efficiencies, English prisons were force-feeding Suffragettes to stop them hungering in protest. (In Ireland, Republicans were treated similarly.) Mechanisms of control travel from one disciplinary institution (prison, where force-feeding goes on to this day) to the next (workplace).[7] *Modern Times'* feeding machine scene goes even further to invite us to imagine a dystopic line of workers being machine-fed, turned from workers on an assembly line whose bodies disassemble the line, as Ford said, to themselves become the products of an assembly line tasked with producing the fed worker of a new biopolitical economy.[8]

Chaplin's film invites us to imagine the dystopia while also, however, featuring several escapes from it. Moreover, *Modern Times* enacts a refusal of its own when it evades then-popular and technological demands for sound in the wake of the first talkie, *The Jazz Singer*, released just a few years earlier. Enlisting something like Bartleby's "queer" formula, Chaplin's film offers up the miracle of sound but without acceding to the demands of communicative language when he has the Tramp sing audibly a song that makes no sense, now known as the nonsense song.

The performance of the nonsense song is funny because of Chaplin's intensified bodily gestures, the very gestures of which, Agamben says elegiacally, the Western bourgeoisie were dispossessed by cinema (avant la lettre) in the nineteenth century. After the release of *The Jazz Singer*, those gestures were eulogized as casualties of a new sound technology that rendered them redundant and silent film moot. As we saw in Chapter 1, *The Fits* contests that claim. So did *Modern Times*, whose nonsense song, first succeeds quite well in entertaining the on-screen audience, suggesting the possibility, finally, of commercial success for the otherwise relentlessly unproductive and unsuccessful Tramp. But then his ill-fittedness asserts itself again, and the performance that entertained devolves into chaos.

This is Chaplin's critique of the inevitablization of progress. His refusal of the new technology is rooted in awareness of technology's suitedness to exploitation. And so Chaplin's Tramp is freed for his own "queer escape." When we last see him, he is with his love interest, the Gamin, ambling waywardly away from the city down a dirt road lined by what appear to be telephone poles but with no wires visibly connecting them. His arc of refusal ends here, on a path of inoperativity, powered by a song that makes no sense, calling out to us to do the same.

Inclination in Erin Courtney's *A Map of Virtue*

Erin Courtney's award-winning play *A Map of Virtue*, described by the *New York Times* (2012 production) as "a delicate gem" and "a resonant tale of loss," is built around a list of noble virtues: curiosity, loyalty, empathy, honesty, integrity, love, and intuition.[9] Refusal is missing from the list, even though it is the key to the play, the one virtue that underwrites the other seven.

Critics are struck by *A Map of Virtue*'s formal elements, especially its symmetry: it has seven actors, seven scenes, and seven virtues; the same virtues recur in reverse order in the second half. Courtney, the playwright, says, "I think the play is a little bit of a formal adventure, because it's symmetrical,"[10] and a critic notes that the play's scenes "are arranged in a symmetrical pattern, designed to mirror each other on either side of a central event, like a bird's wings."[11] Birdwings are a recurring motif of the play, which is narrated by a stone-carved meadowlark. (Notably, there are seven kinds of meadowlark.)

However, attention to the play's symmetries, its stylized formalism, distracts attention from its throbbing heart: its exploration of relationships among privileged, damaged white people as refracted expressions of the disavowed genocide on which their presentist history is built. *A Map of Virtue*'s experiment in form offers up (perhaps inadvertently) a haunting forensic analysis of how violence is transmitted, reproduced, inherited, and erased. It charts the inescapability of cruel history in a land where every footstep meets with the blood of the dispossessed. The play is not only a map of virtues; it is also a map to the places where the bodies are buried, though they cannot be found. The virtues listed are built on unmarked graves.

The play's narrator, that stone bird carving, tells us it was purchased in New Mexico by a young boy on an annual family road trip. The boy was sexually abused and grows up to become a school headmaster who forces young students to engage in sex acts while he watches. In his office is a collection of bird carvings, purchased over the years on family trips through New Mexico. One of the students, Mark, steals one, but this small vengeance becomes also a daily reminder of what he suffered. So, one day, years later, he leaves the stone bird on a bench, where a young woman, Sarah, finds it and is inspired by it. Sarah becomes a seer, first, of the carving itself, which she paints so strikingly that when Mark happens upon one of her paintings in a gallery, he is so unsettled by the image that he compulsively attacks it with a penknife. Later, Sarah will see other things that others can't or won't see. (Mark will not. Victor, talking about Mark, says, "Yeah he told me about the headmaster's office. He had told me but it's not something he wanted to talk about too much. He kept that experience in a little box. Separate.")[12]

After Mark attacks her art, Sarah stops painting. She seems lost. Impulsively, one night at a social gathering, she accepts a stranger's invitation to a party and she brings along Mark, whom she has come to know, and her husband, Nate. The three are driven to the country in a windowless van and then find themselves held hostage by the stranger, a woman named June, and a henchman named Ray, who dons a bird mask, and is then called You when June orders him to threaten or harm their hostages. (In fact, her orders interpellate anyone who hears them: "You!") This gothic plot twist comes out of nowhere: one critic describes it as "melodramatic, like something from one of those horror movies in which terrible things happen to urban dwellers when they go to rural places."[13]

But rather than the rural as a site of horror, the play's gothic country prison teems with meaning for those aware of the history of residential schools. June and You hand Mark a note of gibberish and tell him to make quick sense of it and explain it, or he will die. June and You also force the three captives to hold in their outstretched left arms buckets full of water. The hostages are told that the first to move their arm or drop their bucket will be killed or will be forced to kill one of the others by drowning.[14] These scenes recall the experience of Native children in residential schools in Canada and the United States, many kidnapped, then "educated"—told to make sense of strange letters on a page and subjected to sadistic and capricious punishments. The threat of drowning resonates with what their "educators" saw as the beautiful baptismal promise of white education. Richard Henry Pratt, founder of the Carlisle Indian Industrial School, called himself "a Baptist, because," he said, "I believe in immersing the Indian in our civilization and when we get them under, holding them there until they are thoroughly soaked."[15]

Only Sarah seems aware of the proximity of the past. Peering out a window of their locked room, she catches sight of a figure dancing in the fire. Is that a child? she asks Nate and Mark. More likely just smoke, says Nate. Later, after they have been rescued by Mark's partner, Victor, and are safely in his car speeding away, Sarah suddenly worries: What will happen to the children? She screams, "STOP the car!! Stop the car; stop the car. Go back!!"[16] When they return, the house where they were held captive has been burned down by June who, police say, poured the gasoline and lit the match. She and You are dead. There is no sign of children anywhere. But Sarah, who heard the call of the stone-carved bird, cannot stop hearing and seeing the children. She is now haunted by the girl who danced in the fire. She cannot stop the tug of inclination from pulling on her. She is trapped in responsiveness.

"They have not found any remains of children. If there had been children, they would have found the remains," says Nate later. "If they do find that there were children there . . . Well if that turns out to be true, then it still won't be her fault." He finds refuge in a familiar methodological individualism that shelters the privileged from history: "She didn't light the match, you know. She didn't kidnap those kids."[17] But Sarah is not soothed by Nate's words. Perhaps she is tuned in to a different set of facts, no less real, of forced marches and residential schools.[18]

Nate notes Sarah's refusal to give up on those children in the fire: "After all, there are some things that we can never know, but my wife has become obsessed with the girl she believes she saw in the bonfire. She spends her free time checking out lists of missing children to see if she can find her. To prove that she existed. To apologize to the parents.

She remembers the girl in detail. Brown, curly hair and about four foot one. She had round cheeks and big bones and she liked to dance. According to my wife."[19] But it is not just this one girl. Sarah sees many things that Nate does not.[20] She once had two birds tattooed on her chest: swallows. Later, she comes to feel they are not rightfully hers. She had copied them from a clipping. But her husband disagrees with her. Of course you earned them; he says. "You paid for them; I was there." But to Sarah, payment is neither vindication nor justification, and she has already begun the painful process of removing them. "I just feel like I stole them, that's all. . . . I just feel like I want to start over."[21] Perhaps she does not want to swallow any more.

This is her refusal. It is an eighth virtue, unnamed, unlisted, unmapped in the play, but it is silently and absolutely necessary to all the others. Curiosity, loyalty, empathy, honesty, integrity, love, and intuition, the named virtues of this play, all postulate the capacity to refuse the official stories of cultural innocence, to question the seeming self-evidence of proclaimed facticity, and to resist mandated adherence to practices and boundaries that delimit what can be seen, felt, and known. You paid for them; they are yours!

A feminist theory of refusal asks: Are they, though? Should they be?

In the myth of Procne, the three major protagonists in the end become birds. Perhaps this metamorphosis is also part of Sarah's story. Removing her tattoos, Sarah acknowledges the harms of appropriation, the violent processes of assimilation or erasure that background it and get under our skin, and the terrible painful difficulty of trying to refuse it all. It may be that the knot of borrowing / theft / citation / inhabitation / (in)fidelity is one of the things meant to be avoided by the recent embrace of formalism in literature and drama. But like many such attempted avoidances, A Map of Virtue just lands us right back in it. The bird statue gives the game away when it says: "I finally got my wish. To be changed! I am something else entirely now."[22] In Ovid's telling of the myth of Procne and Philomela, people become birds and their metamorphosis reveals a truth. In America, all too often, metamorphosis becomes mere reinvention, and a long history of avoidance continues undisturbed.

Fabulation in Astra Taylor's *What Is Democracy?*

Astra Taylor's *What Is Democracy?* opens with Taylor, the film's director, and Silvia Federici in Siena, Italy, commenting on *The Allegory of Good and Bad Government*, a series of three frescoes painted by Ambrogio Lorenzetti in 1338–1339.[23] In one part of the painting, we see a woman sawing something. "I think she is sawing the social body," says Federici. "The saw is the sign of division." Astra Taylor replies, "It's a good metaphor, I think, for our problems today; the social body being sawed apart."[24]

Sometimes, though, sawing things apart may be a *good* thing, if it allows for them to be put back together in a more just way. Then we have not necessarily ruination but possibly betterment, as the bacchants of Euripides might attest. Indeed, we might liken the woman Federici lights on in the painting to the women in the *Bacchae* who dismember Pentheus and then later put him back together for burial. In the film, Greek classicist Efimia Karakantza comments in this spirit on the politics of dismembering then re-membering: "We live in a shattered dismembered society and this society has been dismembered because of extreme economical inequality; and what we are faced with is the need to re-member this dismembered society."

One such dismemberer and re-memberer is Cleisthenes, an aristocrat who in 508 B.C. broke up the clans of sixth-century Athens and established randomized demes in their place. But before Cleisthenes introduced his reforms, Karakantza notes, "There was a riot. I love this idea. There was a riot of the citizens." She does not return to the detail. It is merely a prelude to her account of Cleisthenes, during which Karakantza kneels and lowers her arm to the ground. Stick in hand, she draws in the gravelly, dusty dirt lines to represent the three zones of Athens at the time, calling them the coast, the urban place, and the countryside. "So the idea of Cleisthenes was to break down and abolish completely all the local centers of power, which were created around a powerful aristocrat and the clientele around him." With the stick in her hand, she now draws lines crosswise through the three zones. She explains, "He takes these zones and he mixes up everybody to create a new collectivity. It's completely arbitrary, but the new political space is now based on this new division. . . . It's a community of citizens," not of friends or kin who will have their "little interests," she says. "No, you have to support somebody whom you've never seen in your life, and work together to support your polis."[25]

Focused on the power of design, Karakantza never returns to the tantalizing detail with which she began: "There was a riot." Attending to the riot opens up the contingency of the moment, precisely what technocratic, design-based solutions avoid. The film does not cover it, but we know about the riot from the work of Josiah Ober who sees the riot as a refusal. Ober explains in "'I Besieged That Man': Democracy's Revolutionary Start," that by this time, late in the sixth century B.C., "the ordinary Athenian male was no longer a politically passive client of a great house. He had begun to view himself as a citizen rather than as a subject."[26] So the democratization that Cleisthenes is said to introduce had already begun. When one of Cleisthenes's rivals for power in Athens tried to dissolve the assembly, "the councilmen refused to obey the dissolution order," and the rest of the Athenians "rose up in arms." The uprising of Athenians is the "riot" that recalled Cleisthenes from exile, and it was then that he "immediately set about instituting the promised changes in the constitutional order."[27] In Ober's version of the story, it is not technocracy's design but democracy's mobilization that is the prime mover of events.[28]

Attending to the riot places the history of democracy in the dirt. That is democracy's spatiality, we may say. But it also has temporalities, one of which is on the verge, that moment between riot and response, where possibilities are plural and contingency reigns: it is not clear who—if anyone—will rise to the occasion or be crushed by it. Later, the history will be written in a way that makes sense of it all; causes and conditions will take the edge off the wild uncertainty that suffuses such moments in the present. This, Arendt says, is how natality dies. But it is also how we try to preserve it: by telling the story of natal political action and by memorializing it in images, art, and sculpture that last and even take on lives of their own.

As it happens, that temporality of being on the verge is a unique development in Italian sculpture and painting that occurs not long after Lorenzetti painted those frescoes with which Taylor's film opens and closes. The moment of anticipation is depicted in Leonardo's *Last Supper* in Milan and in Michelangelo's *David* in Florence. The *Last Supper* depicts the moment before Jesus tells his followers about Judas's betrayal of him. He knows at this moment, but they do not yet. Other depictions of the scene until then had shown the moment after, as the terrible wrong dawns on the company. Similarly, Michelangelo's *David* shows the hero not in the moment of his triumph, holding Goliath's severed head, but in the apprehensive moment before battle, resolute but on the verge, knowing what he was about to do but not knowing yet how it might come out. The hope, fear, and vulnerability of not-yet are palpable when we are on the verge, which is the temporality of riot and of refusal, too.

Taylor's film *What Is Democracy?* is a eulogy for the time when we were on the verge of democracy. But that time is now and has been for a while. In July 2019, in Puerto Rico there was an uprising so spontaneous that it was undeclared and then it forced the governor out of office. And then the next would-be governor and the next named one, too. And then, retroactively, the people being in the streets was called a general strike, which was a (Du Boisian) way to make sense of it. Not quite a year later, the Movement for Black Lives took to the streets, too, throughout the United States. A would-be president tried to call their protests riots. Many saw refusal, an uprising for equality, long denied. We are still on the verge.

Muhammad Ali's Repertoire of Refusal[29]

> Like a dancer, a boxer "is" his body.
> —JOYCE CAROL OATES, *ON BOXING*

> To enter into the ring near-naked and to risk one's life . . . is to risk and sometimes to realize the agony of which *agon* (Greek "contest") is the root.
> —JOYCE CAROL OATES, *ON BOXING*

Muhammad Ali is a Dionysian figure who refused the draft (inoperativity), boxed inclinationally, and understood the dependence of refusal on the powers of fabulation.[30] Like Euripides's Dionysus in the *Bacchae*, Ali was also exiled and returned, played with conventional gender expectations, used trickster techniques to defeat opponents while charming almost everyone else, told the truth about a violent past and present that no one wanted to confront, and demanded to be worshipped. He "brought to the deadly-serious sport of boxing an unexpected ecstatic joy," says Joyce Carol Oates, who also notes his doubleness: Ali even has two names—"There has always been something enigmatic about Clay/Ali, a doubleness."[31] Oates cites Hugh McIlvanney's observation that "the young boxer seemed to see his life as a 'strange ritualistic play' in which his hysterical rantings were required by 'the script that goes with his destiny.'"[32] Doubleness is a Dionysian trait, and "strange ritualistic play" conjures this god more than any other. Norman Mailer cites Ali's taunting of his opponents with words that recall powerfully those said by Dionysus to Pentheus in Euripides's play. Says Mailer, quoting Ali, "'Come and get me, fool,' he says. 'You can't, 'cause you don't know who I am. You don't know *where* I am. I am human intelligence and you don't even know if I am good or evil.'"[33]

More than any other sports figure in the modern era, Muhammad Ali claimed glory, calling himself the "greatest" ("I am the greatest! I shook up the world! I'm the greatest thing that ever lived! . . . I'm the prettiest thing that ever lived. I shook up the world. I want justice"). He talked himself and everyone else into it, even as he worked and trained and fought his way into it, too. He understood the importance of fabulation and its power. So did Toni Morrison, who as an editor at Random House first suggested Ali write an autobiography. And even though he clearly enjoyed celebrity (every car ride was for him a "parade," Roger Ebert noted), Ali knew that fabulation involved something different and more powerful: a worldly, world-making story that would outlive him but that, even during his lifetime, could be a mighty force.[34]

For Ali, inoperativity, inclination, and fabulation did not form an arc, as they do in the *Bacchae*. They were part of a repertoire of refusal that includes his 1966 draft refusal (inoperativity, refusing to be used against others); his introduction of dance to the heavyweights' ring via the "Ali shuffle" combined with his unusual, backward-leaning comportment in the ring, with his hands down (inclination); and his demand to be recognized as the greatest, as he brilliantly negotiated the various and contradictory representations of his refusals and the contests over whether he would be granted the glory he had earned (fabulation).[35]

Inoperativity

In 1966, Ali refused as a conscientious objector to serve in the US military during the Vietnam War. He was tried and convicted in twenty minutes by an all-white jury in Houston, but he stayed out of jail while appealing his conviction all the way to the Supreme Court. That took over three years. Ali's draft refusal was part of a larger practice of radical refusal that was later domesticated and even obscured by his commercialization and then by the illness that ultimately silenced him.[36]

Ali's draft refusal was on religious grounds. He had converted to Islam in 1964 and was a member of the Nation of Islam. Some of his critics charged he was just following orders from the Nation of Islam's Elijah Muhammad and suggested Ali lacked the masculinist autonomy that moralizes a man.[37] Convicted and then denied a license to box in almost every state when he was at the height of his powers (from age twenty-five to twenty-nine), Ali "faced the prospect of abiding his best years behind bars" until finally his conviction was overturned by the US Supreme Court in 1971.[38] Time lost. Records lost. Skills lost. Certainly, a great deal of money lost. Ali *paid* for his refusal.

And yet, when he was asked whether he regretted what he had lost and was still losing (the Supreme Court had not yet sided with him at the time), Ali said he was at peace with his choice and fabulated it as follows: "I would like to say to those of the press and those of the people who think that I lost so much by not taking this step, I would like to say that I did not lose a thing up until this very moment, I haven't lost one thing," he said. "I have gained a lot. Number one, I have gained a peace of mind. I have gained a peace of heart."[39] He objected to the tragic frame of the media's version of the story: "I strongly object to the fact that so many newspapers have given the American public and the world the impression that I have only two alternatives in this stand—either I go to jail or go to the Army. There is another alternative, and that alternative is justice. If justice prevails, if my constitutional rights are upheld, I will be forced to go neither to the Army nor jail. In the end, I am confident that justice will come my way, for the truth must eventually prevail."[40] The idea of a third alternative where there seem only to be two is a rather Dionysian idea.

Inclination

Ali was also accused of being unmanly *in* the ring because of his unusual posture. When he first came to be known in professional boxing (he was then Cassius Clay), he was criticized for his unorthodox, unmanly, or unprofessional style. He did not stand straight up to address his opponents in the ring, he wove and danced his way through the early rounds, "dropping his hands and leaning back from punches," leaving his opponents confused and exhausted: off balance.[41] Only then would he go in for the kill. For example, in his gold medal round in the 1960 Olympics, Clay's opponent (from Poland) "finished the three-round bout helpless and out on his feet" but, A. J. Liebling complained, "he had just run out of puff chasing Clay, who had then cut him to pieces."[42] This recalls, rather sharply, the shadowboxing with Dionysus that precedes the demise of Pentheus, and the dismemberment into pieces that results.

"What kind of boxing *is* this?" sports reporters asked. Beneath that question lurked another: What kind of masculinity was this? Critics were puzzled by Ali's "refusal to exchange punches with his opponent in the traditional manly fashion, his way of dancing, circling an opponent, flashing lacerating jabs that came lashing from the hip . . . this was not proper, somehow." Why would he not keep his hands up, "come to the center of the ring and fight like a *real* man?"[43] Float like a butterfly, sting like a bee. Why subject his pretty face to unnecessary blows? he would joke in his soft whispery voice. The day after he won his second fight against British boxer Henry Cooper in 1966, Ali appeared on the *Eamonn Andrews Show,* and Lucille Ball, another guest, marveled, "You haven't got a mark on you." Ali smiled and said, "Hit and run away and live to fight another day."[44] Ali was not the first Black man to play with heteronormative gender codes, nor even the first boxer to do so. But he was the first heavyweight boxer to do so.

"Hit and run away and live to fight another day" was also the motto of Charlie Chaplin's character in *City Lights:* lured into the ring and determined not to be hit, he dances to stay behind the referee. He mirrors his opponent's movements, keeping the referee between them, and makes it impossible for his opponent to lay a glove on him. Ali's way of moving in the ring recalls Chaplin's spoof.[45] But Chaplin's spoof *embraces* the feminization with which Ali's sportswriter critics thought they could embarrass the boxer. Ali was beyond their reach, though, as he so often was beyond the reach of his opponents in the ring. Years since, a new consensus has emerged about Ali: "Ali, in fact, was a beautiful boxer, changing rhythms and speeds as smoothly as a jazzman, cracking jabs, digging hook to the ribs, sliding away with a shuffle to survey the damage he'd done, and then cracking more jabs. He turned violence into craft like no heavyweight before or since."[46]

By the time he was returned to the sport after his period of exile, seeking to reclaim the championship taken from him, Ali could no longer dance to fatigue his opponents, waiting until they tired themselves out. His power to dance like that was lost to time, and so he adopted a different Dionysian technique: he took his opponents' blows in the ring—his own theater—just as he had done outside of it. Rope-a-dope, he called it. He had "to train to take, and not exclusively give, punishment."[47] It was a bit like a tragic hero absorbing the blows of fate, but Ali was more trickster than tragic. Oates calls him a "trickster-as-athlete."[48] He sometimes feigned fatigue, leaned into the ropes, and when his opponents, tired from punching him, dropped their guard, he came alive.[49]

Inclination, as we saw in Chapter 2, cannot survive verticality's hegemony without seeking out occasionally fugitivity's refuge. Notably, Ali's inclinational powers were first learned and nourished in a fugitive setting, later honed in another. First, his Black coach Fred Summers, to whose gym in Louisville Ali turned to balance out in the evenings what he learned elsewhere in the day. Later, when Ali returned to boxing after his exile, he reprised that structure, when he bought land and had a training camp built outside the city in Deer Lake, Pennsylvania.[50] We know a fair amount about that first heterotopia, in Louisville, which may have prepared the stage for the second. Ali disclosed on an episode of *This Is Your Life* that he had two boyhood trainers: one, Joe Martin was white and the other, Fred Summers, was Black. Ali trained all day at Martin's gym, but he would routinely then head over to Summers's. Louisville wasn't integrated then, Ali explained, and although Martin had a television show featuring amateur boxers, Summers was training Golden Glove winners. Notably, it was at Summers's gym that Ali was taught "not to stand still," to keep moving. Was this boxing's version of Hartman's waywardness? To slip by, evade the blow? Summers also had, Ali joked, "the connection and the complexion to get the protection." It was an early education in dance and inclination, and a lesson in the power of heterotopia.[51]

Fabulation

In 2017, GQ magazine put Colin Kaepernick on the cover and depicted him as a contemporary Ali. They wanted, they said, to "connect" Kaepernick to Ali, to "a crusade that stretches back decades."[52] It was not a bad idea. But the term *crusade* is troubling. Ali refused the military draft on grounds of conscience as a Muslim. This is why, in the midst of the travails that followed Ali's draft refusal, Bill Russell said of Ali that he envied him because of his Muslim faith: "He has something I have never been able to attain and something very few people I know possess," Russell wrote. "He has an absolute and sincere faith. . . . He is better equipped than anyone I know to withstand the trials in store for him."[53] And yet Ali's story, referred to in 2018 by GQ as a "crusade," was also, even early on, emplotted as Christian. As early as 1967, *Esquire* magazine depicted the boxer as Saint Sebastian and called the image "The Passion of Muhammad Ali."[54] Saint Sebastian is the patron saint of soldiers, athletes, and gay men, and Esquire depicted Ali like the martyr, with six arrows appearing to pierce his body, blood seeming to leak from the wounds.[55] That is to say, Ali was, in effect, depicted as the glorious body of Giorgio Agamben, discussed in Chapter 1. Recall, the "glorious body" became for Agamben, as in Christian iconography, an aesthetic object for contemplation rather than an organism of appetites and desires that might nourish a more vital, not-merely Bartlebyian politics of refusal.

Not for these reasons but for other good ones, Ali initially objected to the shoot: as a Muslim, he could not be depicted as a Christian saint, he said. He only agreed to go along after George Lois, the shoot director (and the man on whom *Mad Men*'s Don Draper is modeled), cleared it with Elijah Muhammad in a phone call about the political theology of the situation. But Ali also took matters into his own hands. He detheologized and politicized his so-called martyrdom when, during the photo shoot, he named the arrows that seemed to pierce his body. Pointing to each one, he named them for the men responsible for his plight: "Lyndon Johnson, General Westmoreland, Robert McNamara, Dean Rusk, Carl

Muhammad Ali, *Esquire* magazine photoshoot, 1967. Photograph by Carl Fischer

Clifford, Hubert Humphrey."[56] Ali wanted to stake his claim to the city and to use the magazine cover to do so. But on his own terms.

He would not be martyred, especially not for a presumed belief in Christ, by nameless Romans and their emperor. Ali was up against anti-Black agents of American empire and he refused the effort to Christianize his refusal. Naming the arrows, Ali subverts the power of Sebastian and claims it for himself. Notably, Sebastian survived the arrows; so would Ali.

Was Ali the man of conscience, the civil disobedient, and the critic of sovereignty Hannah Arendt was looking for when she wrote in 1970 about the distinction between civil disobedience and conscientious objection?[57] At that moment, Ali's draft refusal and his pending Supreme

Muhammad Ali, *Esquire* magazine photoshoot, 1967. This photograph appeared on the cover of *Esquire* magazine, April 1968. Photograph by Carl Fischer

Court appeal were frequently referenced in the national newspapers. But Arendt never mentions him, training her eye on Socrates and Thoreau.[58]

Ali may not have come in the guise *she* expected, a boxer, a Black man, a Muslim, a speaker in rhymes, a philanderer—but prophets rarely do. And Ali knew it, too: "I am America. I am the part you won't recognize. But get used to me—black, confident, cocky; my name, not yours; my religion, not yours; my goals, my own. Get used to me." Did I say he was Dionysian? Lest there be any doubt, he said this, too: "I've wrestled with alligators. I've tussled with a whale. I done handcuffed lightning. And throw thunder in jail."

Writing in the exact period of his draft refusal, as his case moved its way up to the Supreme Court, Arendt fabulated a "tradition" of refusal precisely by not ennobling Ali alongside Socrates and Thoreau whom she found wanting for their nonpoliticality but whom she admired nonetheless. Arendt was surely part of reproducing the official archive against which Ali fought with his signature demand: "Say my name!"[59]

As the years went on, the contest of fabulation continued, most noticeably in the Rocky film franchise, which took its inspiration from one of Ali's fights. After Ali beat George Foreman in 1974's Rumble in the Jungle, Ali, now the heavyweight champion again, fought Chuck Wepner, a fighter from New Jersey who managed to knock Ali off his feet in the ninth round (by stepping on his foot) and dreamed for those few seconds that he might be the next heavyweight champion. Ali got up, kept fighting, and then knocked Wepner out in the fifteenth round. The fight, which had been promoted with the tagline "Give the white guy a break," did in fact give Wepner quite a break: what he lost in reality he went on to win in film.[60]

Wepner was the inspiration for Sylvester Stallone's *Rocky* (which also paid tribute to Rocky Marciano). In *Rocky*, the first film of what went on to be a huge franchise, Rocky fights Apollo Creed, who is modeled on Ali, to the fifteenth round and the fight is awarded, by a split decision, to

Ron Kuntz Collection / Diamond Images / Getty Images

Creed. For Rocky, an unknown, it is a moral victory. In the second film of the franchise, Rocky wins. Roger Ebert watched *Rocky II* with Ali, by then retired. Ali liked the film but noted it was not surprising that Creed would lose this time: "For the black man to come out superior," Ali said, "would be against America's teachings. I have been so great in boxing they had to create an image like Rocky, a white image on the screen, to counteract my image in the ring. America has to have its white images."[61]

Joe Frazier's family and neighbors know it. The Philly boxer was finally memorialized by his hometown with a statue only in 2015, four years after Frazier's death and over thirty years after the twelve feet eight bronze statue of the fictional white boxer "Rocky" was erected in that city. The Rocky statue, commissioned by Sylvester Stallone for *Rocky III*, was left in place as a gift to the city.[62] "It always seemed strange that Philadelphia chose to exhibit a statue of a celluloid heavyweight champion and overlooked one of its own who had been an authentic one."[63] Strange is one word for it. In the city, the contest of fabulation goes on.

Notes

PREFACE

1. Bonnie Honig, *Antigone, Interrupted* (Cambridge: Cambridge University Press, 2013).

2. Yopie Prins, *Ladies' Greek: Victorian Translations of Tragedy* (Princeton, NJ: Princeton University Press, 2017), 226.

3. Patricia Yaeger says that "in women's writing the incorporation of a second language can function . . . as a subversive gesture representing an alternative form of speech that can disrupt the repressions of authoritative discourse and still welcome or shelter themes that have not yet found a voice in the text's primary language." *Eta Bakkae*, which melds *logos* and *phone* in its chant and is instituted by the arrival of foreign bacchants, harbors its own doubleness and serves as something like what Yaeger has in mind in "Honey-Mad Women: Charlotte Brontë's Bilingual Heroines," *Browning Institute Studies*, Vol. 14, The Victorian Threshold (1986), pp. 11–35 (p. 16). On the blending of phone and logos, see *Antigone, Interrupted*, Chapter 5.

4. The ambition here differs from my earlier work on *Antigone*. In *Antigone, Interrupted*, I turned to classics for the history that might help decenter political theory's mythology of Antigone, finding in fifth-century norms and changing laws about women's lamentation the resources to develop a counter-reading of the play and then, with that, to interrupt its legacy of lamentational politics today. Here, I enlist the *Bacchae* as an exemplary illustration of the arc of refusal, chart the erasure in the play of the women's refusal, and, with the play, think about what rises to the register of refusal and what doesn't, and why. Since there is no political theory mythology of Agave to dethrone, I work not historically but conceptually, recovering the play for an archive of refusal, critically assessing some of the key contemporary concepts of refusal in the company of this drama. For those interested in historical contexts, see Barbara Goff, *Citizen Bacchae: Women's Ritual Practice in Ancient Greece* (Berkeley: University of California Press, 2004), esp. 271–287.

INTRODUCTION

1. Why argue for a return to the city for a politics in which the problem is that the city keeps falsely claiming jurisdiction and title over you and your land? Exemplary here is Glen Coulthard's powerful argument in *Red Skin, White Masks*:

Rejecting the Colonial Politics of Recognition (Minneapolis: University of Minnesota Press, 2014). Refusal's entry in recent years into the lexicon of political theory comes from Indigenous thinkers, such as Glen Coulthard and Audra Simpson, who draw on Fanon and others to position refusal as not just privative withdrawal or a course corrector for liberal democracies but also as an active politics of dissensus from settler colonialism. These Indigenous thinkers depathologize anger, silence, resentment, and refusal, seeing these emotions or affects as legitimate responses to white supremacy, settler colonial enclosure, and extractivist appropriation. Others who theorize refusal, working on race, environmentalism, gender, and class politics, also locate refusal outside the contours of mainstream politics. Many have turned in recent years to fugitivity as a historical and contemporary expression of the desire to experience freedom collectively or idiosyncratically outside statist, patriarchal, or settler colonial structures.

2.   The bacchants' arc of refusal is occluded when, as Yulia Ustinova notes, Euripides splits the bacchants: the Asian bacchants at the end of the play are described "as *komos*, 'band of revelers,' rather than *thiasos*, the term [Euripides] applied to the raging Theban maenads" (*Divine Mania: Alteration of Consciousness in Ancient Greece* [New York: Routledge, 2017], 189). Revel and rage may be two sides of the same refusal coin, however.

3.   The idea that heterotopia is a space/time of rehearsal is closer to how Adriana Cavarero conceives of it, as we will see in Chapter 2. The term *heterotopia* will call to mind Michel Foucault's famous essay "Of Other Spaces" (*Diacritics* 16 [Spring 1986]: 25.) One of Foucault's examples is honeymooners who go away for the period of first sexual intimacy, then return to the city, ready for dispassionate domesticity. The honeymoon is a kind of ventilation, a space where desires and pleasures forbidden in the city can be more or less safely explored outside of it. The bacchants' time on Cithaeron is often seen in such familiar terms, as a transgression that may be permitted or punished. But, notwithstanding the honeymoon example, Foucault claims heterotopias are "capable of juxtaposing in a single real place several spaces, several sites that are in themselves incompatible." And that way of thinking about heterotopia is closer to the *Bacchae*, as I read it. For another reading of heteropia as political critique, see Lisa Diedrich, "The Cruise Ship as Disease Heterotopia," (May 5, 2020), https://nursingclio.org/2020/05/05/the-cruise-ship-as-disease-heterotopia/.

4.   Juxtaposing classical and contemporary materials does not deny their many differences; it risks what may look like such a denial to see how they illuminate and test each other. On juxtaposition as method in a different context, see Juliet Hooker, *Theorizing Race in the Americas: Douglass, Sarmiento, Du Bois, and Vasconcelos* (New York: Oxford University Press, 2017). See also recent work in the area of Critical Antiquity Studies.

5.   Robin Robertson, introduction to *Bacchae*, by Euripides, trans. Robin Robertson (New York: Harper Collins, 2014), xxviii. See also Judith Butler: "The agon of the play is between two cousins, Pentheus and Dionysis, both of whom

are vying for control over the women" ("Breaks in the Bond: Reflections on Kinship Trouble," Housman Lecture, UCL, London, 2017). I note here that I draw on various translations of the play in this book so as not to promote any particular one. Because I pluralize the sources, citations are to Greek line numbers. I am very grateful to Clare Kearns for her help in checking and tracking citations to the play.

6.   M. Gorup summarizes Du Bois's view in *Black Reconstruction* as follows: "The stunning example of black citizenship that Reconstruction unleashed upon the world-stage—the very essence of its 'splendidness'—ensured that in the following decades ambiguity would remain about who could legitimately claim membership in the polity." Reconstruction may have failed, but Du Bois took no small satisfaction from knowing that its splendidness would haunt those who witnessed the "stunning example of black citizenship." See M. Gorup, "The Strange Fruit of the Tree of Liberty: Lynch Law and Popular Sovereignty in the United States," *Perspectives on Politics*, May 2020, 1–16.

7.   Euripides, *Bacchae*, Perseus Digital Library, trans. T. A. Buckley (London: Henry C. Bohn, 1850); *Philologic*, 275–283.

8.   Euripides, *Bacchae*, trans. Buckley, 421–423. Dionysus is also the god of theater. This last trait matters given the play's several metatheatrical allusions. Spectatorship, costuming, gesture, and direction are all thematized in the play.

9.   "As time passed, men confused the words of the story. Instead of saying 'Zeus showed her the sky' it was garbled over the years to 'sewed in the thigh.' And so, a myth is made." Euripides, *Bacchae*, trans. Robertson, 294–297.

10.   Indeed, Cadmus makes this similarity between mother and son clear when he says to Agave about Pentheus, "He turned out similar to you, not revering the god." See *Bacchae*, trans. Richard Seaford (Liverpool: Liverpool University Press, 1996), 1302.

11.   Euripides, *Bacchae*, trans. Buckley, 443–448.

12.   Euripides, *Bacchae*, trans. Margaret Behr and Robert Banks Foster (Kaslo, BC: Eva Nova Press, 2019), 447–448.

13.   Euripides, *Bacchae*, trans. Robertson 726–727.

14.   Later the women will also tear Pentheus limb from limb, *perhaps* thinking he is an animal. I return to that "perhaps."

15.   Euripides, *Bacchae*, trans. Robertson, 721–764. This reference to divine guidance may seem evidence of Dionysian manipulation. Dionysus even claims the women are his pawns: "I have driven these sisters mad," he boasts. This is why Judith Butler ("Breaks in the Bond") observes: "this is not a story about women's liberation." For her, the women are manipulated by Dionysus, who boasts about his powers of manipulation, and so the women cannot be said to know what they are doing. But many of the ancient Greek heroes—Oedipus, Ajax, Hercules, Achilles, for example—are credited with agency even though they act with limited knowledge and are manipulated by the gods. Another reason to think the *Bacchae* is not a story of women's liberation is the women's failure. But, I will argue, before they fail and

maybe even after, they experience something liberatory. For Hannah Arendt, liberation fells the old oppressive powers, while freedom requires inaugural institutionalization and maintenance. The bacchants succeed at Arendtian liberation; it is the more permanent Arendtian freedom that may elude them.

16.   This is true of nearly all classical tragedies. I am grateful to Des Manderson for this formulation.

17.   Euripides, *Bacchae*, trans. Robertson, 827, 455–459.

18.   Euripides, *Bacchae*, trans. Robertson, 925–926. For Sheila Murnaghan, this joins Pentheus to the women's chorus *and* to the women on Cithaeron. See "The Daughters of Cadmus: Chorus and Characters in Euripides' Bacchae and Ion," *Bulletin of the Institute of Classical Studies, Supplement, Greek Drama III: Essays in Honour of Kevin Lee* 87 (2006): 99–112. I return to her account of the ancient chorus in detail in Chapter 3.

19.   See Eric Csapo, "Riding the Phallus for Dionysus: Iconology, Ritual, and Gender-Role De / Construction," *Phoenix* 51, no. 3 / 4 (October 1997): 253–305.

20.   Euripides, *Bacchae*, trans. Robertson, 1095–1120

21.   Though what hand-holding means is open to question. Nancy Worman's claims in "Electra, Orestes, and the Sibling Hand" are summarized by Sarah Nooter: "The haptic is always highlighting the tragic part of tragedy," especially in the case of "familial touching," which tends to "push or pull, attack or protect. . . . In almost every case, violence wins over affection, erotics, or security. Even the affectionate touching of Sophocles' Electra and Orestes takes on a minatory tone." See Sarah Nooter, "Review of *The Materialities of Greek Tragedy: Objects and Affect in Aeschylus, Sophocles, and Euripides*," *Bryn Mawr Classical Review*, November 3, 2019, https://bmcr.brynmawr.edu/2019/2019.11.03.

22.   Euripides, *Bacchae*, trans. Buckley, 310–320.

23.   Butler, "Breaks in the Bond."

24.   I draw here on Lisa Diedrich's "Articulating Double Binds: Between a Rhetoricity of Rights and Vulnerabilities (Relation, Pedagogy, Care)," *South Atlantic Quarterly* 118, no. 3 (July 2019): 573–594. Diedrich focuses on the double binds of race and disability (double binds are "rhetorical structures that expand or limit the frames of reference in which a person can live and act upon the world" [580]), drawing on Sara Ahmed, *Queer Phenomenology* (in which "a double bind might be considered a kind of disorientation device that then potentially engenders new articulations" [575]) and Patricia Williams, *Alchemy of Race and Rights*.

25.   See Williams's contribution to *Utilitarianism: For and Against*, by J. J. C. Smart and Williams (New York: Cambridge University Press, 1973). For a longer account of my view of Williams, see Bonnie Honig, *Emergency Politics* (Princeton, NJ: Princeton University Press, 2009).

I thank Lori Marso for discussion of the wrenching loss of love and connection that feminist politics may require. Although I was once drawn to Williams's notion of the tragic situation, I have come to think feminism is better approached via double binds than conflicting oughts, especially when considering women's agency in patriarchy. I refer to my use of Williams here as "loose" because I doubt he would categorize regicide as an "ought." With this formulation, I take liberties.

26.   This is not to justify the bacchants' violence; it is a play, and their violence is part of a parable of what can happen to refusal over the course of its arc. Or, better, we could draw on Michel Foucault here, who says regicide is at bottom the crime that underlies all crimes in an absolutist regime: "every crime constituted as it were a rebellion against the law," and made of every lawbreaker "an enemy of the prince" (Michel Foucault, *Discipline and Punish: The Birth of the Prison*, trans. Alan Sheridan [New York: Vintage Books, 1995], 50).

27.   Diedrich says in the context of pedagogy that the kind of teaching (or performance) she promotes should be done "not as mimetic but as prismatic, through which knowledge is multiplied rather than reproduced." The aim here, she says, is about "seeing simultaneously, yet differently. . . . Slowing things down [she says, about de-escalation training, but the point has a larger implication] is also about giving a person the space [and time!] to see a situation multiply." This is a good analogy for the work of fabulation. Diedrich, "Articulating Double Binds," 583–584.

28.   For a reading of the dismemberment scene as a parable of membership, see Peter Euben, "Membership and 'Dismembership' in the *Bacchae*," in *The Tragedy of Political Theory: The Road Not Taken* (Princeton, NJ: Princeton University Press, 1990), 130–166.

1. INOPERATIVITY AND THE POWER OF ASSEMBLY

1.   On the refusal of Non Una di Meno, see Enrica Rigo and Francesca De Masi, "Fighting Violence across Borders: From Victimhood to Feminist Struggles," *South Atlantic Quarterly* 118, no. 3 (July 2019): 670–677.

2.   Agamben's account of impotentiality echoes Arendt's account of the "hiatus" that occurs in the whir of willing and nilling and is sometimes evident in moments of (in)action, which I think Agamben does not credit. What kicks us into action, according to Arendt, and out of the hiatus, is action itself. The will does not possess a capacity to end its endless nilling and willing; it is credited in retrospect. See Hannah Arendt, *The Life of the Mind*, vol. 2 (New York: Harcourt, 1978), 207. For a more detailed reading of the will in Arendt, see my "Arendt, Identity, Difference," *Political Theory* 16, no. 1 (February 1988): 77–98.

3.   My early reservations about Bartleby's impact on the "Bartleby left" appear in my response to Eric Santner in *The Weight of All Flesh: On the Subject-Matter of Political Economy* (Oxford: Oxford University Press, 2016). Elsewhere, I criticize those who affiliate aestheticization as such with fascism and poststructuralism. See Bonnie Honig, "The Politics of Agonism: A Critical Response to 'Beyond Good and Evil: Arendt, Nietzsche, and the Aestheticization of Political Action' by Dana R. Villa," *Political Theory* 21, no. 3 (August 1993): 528–533. Here, I criticize Agamben's particular aestheticization as a depoliticizing purism.

4.   Michael Levitin, "The Triumph of Occupy Wall Street," *The Atlantic*, June 10, 2015. Occupy's less than radical gender politics were noted and criticized at the time. See Karen McVeigh, "Occupy Wall Street's Women Struggle to Make their Voices Heard," *The Guardian*, November 30, 2011.

5.   Giorgio Agamben, "Notes on Gesture," in *Infancy and History: the Destruction of Experience* (London: Verso. 2007), 135–140.

6.   Turning now to "a queer escape" from interpellation: "As much as recognition seems to be a precondition of liveable life, it can serve the purposes of *scrutiny, surveillance, and normalization* from which a queer escape may prove necessary precisely to achieve liveability outside its terms." See Judith Butler, *Notes toward a Performative Theory of Assembly* (Cambridge, MA: Harvard University Press, 2015), 62.

7.   Giorgio Agamben, "Bartleby; Or, on Contingency," in *Potentialities* (Stanford, CA: Stanford University Press, 1999), 250.

8.   It is worth noting that "performativity," a key term in Butler's thinking and my own, actually began life as "operativity." Performative utterance is J. L. Austin's term for the practice and effect of linguistic inauguration or reinscription (the appearance of something new in and through speech acts), but Austin originally called it "operativity." See J. Hillis Miller, *For Derrida* (New York: Fordham University Press, 2009), 151. This detail shows how, for many of us, Agamben's *in*operativity is directed right at the heart of practices of resignification central to the last thirty years of feminist and queer scholarship, pitched not on the verge but in the mix: "Sometimes," Butler says, it is "a question of acting and in the activity laying claim to the power one requires." Or, we might add, *generating* the power, as Arendt would say, by the very act of claiming it (I called this "taking" in *Democracy and the Foreigner* [Princeton, NJ: Princeton University Press, 2001]). "This," Butler says, "is performativity as I understand it." See Butler, *Notes toward a Performative Theory of Assembly*, 58.

9.   Thanks to Jacques Khalip, whose labeling of the office as "postwork," encouraged me as I developed the reading offered here.

10.   In "Bartleby; or, The Formula," Gilles Deleuze notes that the formula is occasionally altered and features an occasional "would" ("I would prefer not to"). One effect of the alteration is it underlines Bartleby's free will, a possibility called to mind by Melville's reference in the story to debates about free will by Joseph Priestley and Jonathan Edwards. With no change in the formula, Bartleby might have appeared as merely robotic. Another way to read the imperfect repetition is as an example of what Deleuze calls the "stutter" of language (not *in* it). See Gilles Deleuze, "He Stuttered," in *Essays Critical and Clinical*, trans. Daniel W. Smith and Michael A. Greco (Minneapolis: University of Minnesota Press, 1997), 107–114.

11.   Uncommunicative and compelled to repeat a gesture (copying) but also adamant in refusing any interruption of his compulsion, one could see Bartleby as autistic or neuro-atypical. Such medicalization is also a political move, however, which insulates us from the inoperative. Agamben notes how some examples of in-

operativity, like the ancient rite that involved the hunger of an ox, are medicalized now: for example, what was once ritualized hungering is now a medicalized *anorexia*. See Giorgio Agamben, "Hunger of an Ox," in *Nudities*, trans. David Kishik and Stefan Pedatella (Stanford, CA: Stanford University Press, 2010), 104–112. Erin Manning offers a nonmedicalized approach to autism via Gilles Deleuze and Félix Guattari in "In a Minor Key," in *The Minor Gesture* (Durham, NC: Duke University Press, 2016), 1–25. I note Bartleby's neuro-atypicality alongside that of Rawls's grass counter in *A Theory of Justice*, and others in "What Is Agonism?" included in "The 'Agonistic Turn': *Political Theory and the Displacement of Politics* in New Contexts," *Contemporary Political Theory* 18, no. 4 (December 2019): 640–672.

12.   Bartleby's "I prefer not to" is not just a no *in* language but also a no *to* language: repeated, it becomes an a-linguistic, formulaic "No." For Deleuze, this is the power of Bartleby's phrase. It is a speech act that is also "an inarticulate block." A "grammatically correct" utterance that "has the same force, the same role as an *ungrammatical formula*." See Gilles Deleuze, "Bartleby; or, The Formula," in *Essays Critical and Clinical*, trans. Daniel W. Smith and Michael A. Greco (Minneapolis: University of Minnesota Press, 1997), 68, italics original.

13.   Is this the "refrain" of Deleuze and Guattari's *A Thousand Plateaus*, enabling the formation of new territories or deterritorializations? As I write this note (Fall 2019), Chileans protesting neoliberalism in Santiago sing in public, after martial curfew, the Victor Jara song, "The Right to Live in Peace," brought by it into proximity with each other in the daylit streets and also in the dark. As I do the final revisions on this manuscript, a similar thing is happening in Verona and Siena in response to COVID-19 shut down. See my "In the Streets a Serenade: Siena Under Lockdown," in *Shell Shocked: Feminist Criticism after Trump* (New York: Fordham University Press, 2021).

14.   Butler, *Notes toward a Performative Theory of Assembly*, 90.

15.   Butler, *Notes toward a Performative Theory of Assembly*, 90.

16.   If Michael Rogin is right, that may be because the story lampoons Thoreau and is not actually to be taken seriously as a refusal but rather as a critique of Thoreau's withdrawalism. See Michael Rogin, *Subversive Genealogy: The Politics and Art of Herman Melville* (Berkeley: University of California Press, 1983).

17.   Arendt makes a particular point that violence defies the instrumentality that is often used to justify it. Once unleashed, its impact cannot be controlled. See Hannah Arendt, *On Violence* (New York: Harcourt Brace, 1969).

18.   Agamben, "Hunger of an Ox," 112. He also says "new—or more ancient" uses (Agamben, "Hunger of an Ox," 112). For a more detailed account of Agamben on new use, see my "Is Man a 'Sabbatical Animal?' Agamben, Rosenzweig, Heschel, Arendt," *Political Theology* 20, no. 1 (2019): 1–23. It occurs to me that my criticism here of Agamben on festival as exception (on behalf of something more emergent and quotidian which festival both expresses and disseminates) is in a way an iteration of my Rosenzweigian critique of Agamben on emergency (Bonnie Honig, *Emergency Politics* [Princeton, NJ: Princeton University Press, 2009]).

19.   For a different reading of Agamben, see James Martel, *Unburied Bodies: Subversive Corpses and the Authority of the Dead* (Amherst, MA: Amherst College Press, 2018), on *homo sacer* and the inoperative. Martel's critique of Agamben is that he is a processual thinker (formal, I would say), hence Martel's rejection of the "inoperative," arguing that the dead body "operates" (34). Agamben would call these operations inoperativity, Martel notes, but this is the perspective of the state on things, while Walter Benjamin, says Martel, offers a nonstate perspective that problematizes the state. In sum, we might say, Agamben's account is infected by the *homo sacer* whose status is defined by its (non)relation to the state.

20.   Highlighting a suggestion by Freud that "organic life makes us pacifists," Butler argues that "vacating the received human form, a new kind of ethical relationality becomes possible" (16). Without it, we are doomed to destruction: "Destroying destruction, however, only fortifies and augments destruction unless its second instance swerves from the first and refuses to replicate its logic—in another queer turn from the straight path." See Judith Butler, "Solidarity/Susceptibility," *Social Text* 36, no. 4 (2018): 1–20.

21.   There will be other gendered examples of inoperativity as well since there are many *"Bacchaes."* *The Fits* is one, and as I will argue in Chapter 3, so is Saidiya Hartman's *Wayward Lives.*

22.   Grounded normativity is Glen Coulthard's term.

23.   See Guillermina Seri, "Giorgio Agamben's *The Open:* Man and Animal," *Politics and Culture* (May 7, 2005), https://politicsandculture.org/2005/05/07/giorgio-agambens-the-open-man-and-animal/.

24.   Victoria Wohl, "Beyond Sexual Difference: Becoming-Woman in Euripides' *Bacchae,*" in *The Soul of Tragedy,* ed. Victoria Pedrick and Steven M. Oberhelman (Chicago: University of Chicago, 2006), 150. In a different article, Segal introduces a distinction between myth and tragedy that seems to render inoperative the binaries that structure his reading of the *Bacchae:* "If one of the functions of myth is to mediate contradictions, myth as recast by tragedy calls into question the stable mediations implied in the social structures and reflected in the myths" (Charles Segal, "Euripides' *Bacchae:* Conflict and Mediation," *Ramus* 6, no. 2 [1977], 103). Myth binarizes, but tragedy is its undoing.

25.   Wohl, "Beyond Sexual Difference," 149.

26.   Wohl, "Beyond Sexual Difference," 143–147.

27.   Borrowing the term from Artaud. It is interesting, though, that return to proper kinship places is in this play instanced rather explicitly when Cadmus leads Agave from bacchant back to her "self" by reinterpellating her into her roles as mother, daughter, and wife. This is an oedipalization, via father to daughter, which I discuss in detail in Chapters 2 and 3. Oedipalizers of the play might note that Mount Cithaeron, the *Bacchae's* "killing ground," is where Oedipus's parents sent him to die "when he was a newborn child and years later he wandered the same slopes, old, self-blinded, and mad with grief" (Euripides, *Bacchae,* trans. Robin Robertson [New York: Harper Collins, 2014], xxiv). For Wohl, Cithaeron is a site of

Deleuzean desiring, consistent with Dionysus having been born not out of "the loving union of man and woman—two becoming one—but instead is understood as a series of unexpected and transitory conjunctions" (Wohl, "Beyond Sexual Difference," 148). Butler, for her part, notes that since Zeus birthed Dionysus from his own thigh/womb, Dionysus had two mothers—Zeus and Semele: both wombed him (Judith Butler, "Breaks in the Bond: Reflections on Kinship Trouble," Housman Lecture, UCL, London, 2017).

28.   Wohl, "Beyond Sexual Difference," 150.

29.   Charles Segal, *Interpreting Greek Tragedy: Myth, Poetry, Text* (Ithaca, NY: Cornell University Press, 1986), 25. Segal sees the play as an exploration of tensions between (grand)fathers and sons, like Cadmus and Pentheus, who clash over their desires for the mother before everyone returns to their proper kinship position. "The two scenes at the center of the play (defeat of hoplites by Maenads and clothing of king as a Bacchant) . . . [show] the limits and boundaries which constitute as well as defend the ordered life of the polis with its values of male supremacy, reason, discipline's martial force, dissolve at the touch of a figure [Dionysus] who embodies marginality in every sense" (Segal, "Conflict and Mediation," 107).

30.   Wohl's reading is in keeping with Deleuze's warning, in a different context, that "the dangers of a 'society without fathers' have been pointed out, but the only real danger is the return of the father" (Deleuze, "Bartley; or, The Formula," 68). This return is engineered, almost successfully, by Cadmus, as we shall see in Chapter 3.

31.   In sum, the play is well illuminated by a Deleuzean focus on intensities like Wohl's. But the Deleuzean lens also obscures some things, like the intense temporality of Cithaeron, which is not all "whirling" and "yelling" but also slow, doldrum-like (Wohl, "Beyond Sexual Difference," 149). Because Wohl is focused on assemblage (Deleuze) not assembly (Butler's book comes later), the possibility of seeing in the *Bacchae* a specifically feminist inoperativity does not come up.

32.   Euripides, *Bacchae*, trans. Robertson, 683–688.

33.   Butler, *Notes toward a Performative Theory of Assembly*, 89–90. We can add sleeping at the wrong time (in the day) to Butler's account of sleeping in the wrong place: in public. "Sleeping" in public, she says, is "a way to put the body on the line . . . overcoming the distinction between public and private for the time of revolution" (98). Notably, the horizontal here may align with the inclinational, discussed in the next chapter. For development of the interesting notion of a "right to sleep," building on and past Jonathan Crary's *24/7: Late Capitalism and the Ends of Sleep* (New York: Verso, 2013), see Jonathan Goldberg-Hiller, "Is There a Right to Sleep?" *Theory and Event* 22, no. 4 (October 2019): 951–983. Says Goldberg-Hiller, "The concept of a civil sleep brings back into legal thought an affirmative sociality of the flesh that mortality does not. This idea of a civil sleep is in many ways uncontrollable"; and that is in its favor (972).

34.   Euripides, Bacchae, trans. Robertson, 690.

35.   Euripides, Bacchae, trans. Robertson, 724.

36.   Euripides, Bacchae, trans. Robertson, 692–702.

37.   The use of slow motion will be important when we turn to *The Fits*. The "doldrums" is D. W. Winnicott's term to note the importance to human development of time spent not doing or achieving anything; like a sailboat, its loosened sails luffing or its taut sails caught windless. Time in the doldrums resists the association of one's worth with achievement, progress, and work. Time in the doldrums is slow time. Its agency is nonsovereign (if the wind is not blowing, we do not move), though it may birth or nurture new sovereignties in the future. Out of the experience of nonsovereignty, we may regroup into new forms of sovereign self-governance. Winnicott's "doldrums" are necessary to all of us but particularly necessary to adolescents (see Bonnie Honig, "Lecture Two: Care and Concern: Arendt with Winnicott," in *Public Things: Democracy in Disrepair* [New York: Fordham University Press, 2017]). Winnicott chides those who perceive youth as lazy and, hoping to keep them out of trouble, keep them always busy and productive. Like all of us, adolescents need not always be pulled taut, like sails moving fast; they need room to luff. Although I focus here on the women's experience of relaxation in the *Bacchae*, I have elsewhere explored, with Winnicott's help, evidence that the *Bacchae's* Theban king, Pentheus, also desires the doldrums (Bonnie Honig, "'Out like a Lion': *Melancholia* with Euripides and Winnicott," in *Politics, Theory, Film: Critical Encounters with Lars von Trier*, ed. Bonnie Honig and Lori J. Marso [New York: Oxford University Press, 2016], 356–388).

38.   Euripides, *Bacchae*, trans. T. A. Buckley (London: Henry G. Bohn, 1850), Perseus Digital Library, 142–143.

39.   The bacchants are "honey-mad women." Patricia Yaeger's "Honey-Mad Women: Charlotte Brontë's Bilingual Heroines" builds on the description, by Lévi-Strauss in *Mythologiques*, of "an exotically defiant figure—the Honey-Mad Woman—who eats honey in bizarre amounts, who feeds on it wildly and to excess. She consumes honey rather than plantains or meat because honey, as Lévi-Strauss explains, delineates the ambiguous border between culture and nature, they border where—in primitive societies—woman herself is asked to reside. As a prearticulated, predigested substance, honey is at once raw and cooked, processed and unprocessed; in consuming it in great quantities, the honey-mad woman becomes an archetype of sexual as well as gustatory defiance. Breaking the rules of politic eating, she covertly defies the system in which women are exchanged by men, for the ostensible purpose of containing women's 'natural' disorder and fecundity. An inhabitant, then, of the agonistic border between nature and culture that societies erect to protect themselves from ideological collapse, woman is the unwitting dupe, the strange symbol, the wild card in a primitive metaphysic. But in consuming honey so avidly, the honey-mad woman preempts this symbolization, for by consuming a substance like herself, she usurps her society's right to consume her" (11). See Patricia S. Yaeger, "Honey-Mad Women: Charlotte Brontë's Bilingual Heroines," *Browning Institute Studies* 14 (1986): 11–35.

40.   Norman Bryson, *Looking at the Overlooked: Four Essays on Still Life Painting* (London: Reaktion Books, 1990), 22, emphasis added.

41.   Noting Philostratus's third-century A.D. commentary on two still-life paintings, Bryson reads Philostratus's *Xenia I* and *Xenia II*: the first, featuring figs, and the second, featuring game, represent the raw and the cooked, which are also the effortless and the artful (we might say the inoperative and the useful). In the first, food is "simultaneous plenitude," as on Cithaeron, but in the second, "food is structured temporally, as a series of dishes," as in a city like Thebes. In *Xenia II*, "the ease of the natural world gives way to effort and irritation." The dessert will not be honey, as in *Xenia I*'s "raw food par excellence," but rather *"palathé*, a delicacy or sweetmeat." Likewise, *Xenia I*'s "'self-opening' chestnuts" become in *Xenia II* difficult-to-open medlars and acorns, and *Xenia I*'s vital sparrow "perched on a fig" becomes, in *Xenia II*, "the heap of waterfowls ready for the oven." Thus, "*Xenia II* repaints *Xenia I* in terms of the transformation of nature into culture, item by item" (27). See Norman Bryson, *Looking at the Overlooked: Four Essays on Still Life Painting* (London: Reaktion Books, 1990). Or we might say this is a juxtaposition of fermentation's bioculture and civilization's agriculture. For Segal, notably, Dionysus "confounds the nature-culture polarity from below, as it were, bringing the human worshippers from the 'cooked' to the 'raw'" (Segal, "Conflict and Mediation," 110). Barbara Goff notes that eating "cooked as opposed to raw meat" was "fundamental to Greek identity" in *Citizen Bacchae*, 272.

42.   See Véronica Gago, *Eight Theses on the Feminist Revolution: The Women's Strike Assembly* (October 30, 2019), https://www.mixcloud.com/avaradio/veronica -gago-eight-theses-on-the-feminist-revolution/?fbclid=IwAR1QyrFy5O86wohe0vQ HcgHebVprKKmcjW3KeyszWIYyApBMcIbgNKaQZo4. Given the centrality to Cithaeron of slow time, it is worth noting with Gago that the time of the women's strike is a "double temporality. . . . We strike for a few hours in our workplaces *and* for the whole day we remove ourselves from the gender roles that assign us the task of care. We strike and we make time for ourselves. . . . We organized ourselves to be able to dispose our time, to free ourselves from the daily obligations and open up a time."

43.   On yeast as a lens onto US racial politics in the nineteenth century, see Kyla Wazana Tompkins's *Racial Indigestion: Eating Bodies in the 19th Century* (New York: New York University Press, 2012). On fermentation's powers (suggesting Dionysus is god of fermentation), see "Fermentation as Metaphor: An Interview with Sandor Katz," *Emergence Magazine*, https://emergencemagazine .org/story/fermentation-as-metaphor/.

44.   The slow time of fermentation is different from the human-powered time of shuttle and loom. In counting on the anti-oedipal for contestation, does Wohl place herself on the side of the former in each of the listed binaries? For her, there is either the "epidemic" or "the Penthean resistance to it, reinscribing antithesis as the paradoxical yet inevitable structure of the world" (Wohl, "Beyond Sexual

Difference," 150). By way of inoperativity as intensification, I am seeking not to avoid that agon but to pluralize its contenders.

45.   See Shiri Pasternak, *Grounded Authority: The Algonquins of Barriere Lake against the State* (Minneapolis: University of Minnesota Press, 2017) for a great account of an Indigenous tribe's relation to land as one of temporality, focused on nonextractivist ways of finding nourishment. This may be, in fabled form, what the plenty of Cithaeron is also meant to suggest: the plenty of land that comes from being on intimate terms with it.

46.   In *A Thousand Plateaus*, the various plateaus are "planes of intensity" made up of "intensive" processes. Chapter 10 treats "intensive experimentation" as a becoming that shades into assemblage. Intensification, my term, is probably still too subject-centered to pass muster with Deleuze and Guattari. In "The Case against Agamben's Impotence," Ricardo Sanín-Restrepo offers a similar critique of Agamben to the one developed here, working out the details through Agamben's reading of Aristotle, not Bartleby, to explain why Agamben clings to the liminal via inoperativity. In brief, the answer is because he assumes actualization betrays inoperativity. He will not risk impurity for politics. Neither would Bartleby. But the bacchants will. Agamben, Sanín-Restrepo explains, takes "refuge in impotence. In the face of what he deems the collapse of potentia, Agamben rushes to preserve its power in full passivity, in the passion of impotence." He adds, "What Giorgio Agamben sees in the actualization of potentia is the irreversible loss of contingency and hence the utmost frustration of there being anything new. The sheer death of politics." See Ricardo Sanín-Restrepo, "The Case against Agamben's Impotence," *Critical Legal Thinking* (September 30, 2019), http://criticallegalthinking.com/2019/09/30/the-case-against-agambens-impotence/. Similarly, Banu Bargu criticizes Agamben for his "passive refusal" and his "passive contemplation" and argues that "Agamben's theory takes away the counterpower that Foucault grants to every subject" (*Starve and Immolate: The Politics of Human Weapons* [New York: Columbia University Press, 2014], 77).

47.   Wohl, "Beyond Sexual Difference," 149. The miracle of plenitude is now demanded by women precisely as a way to free time; hence recent women's strike demands for a universal basic income. See Marina Montanelli and Michael Hardt, "The Unforeseen Subject of the Feminist Strike," *South Atlantic Quarterly* 117, no. 3 (July 2018): 702–703.

48.   Butler, *Notes toward a Performative Theory of Assembly*, 183.

49.   If Butler's performative theory of assembly wants to ask "how bodies will be supported in the world," Cithaeron's answer is its assembly's unique "culinary invocation" to the slow time that is the postulate of its miraculous plenty (Butler, *Notes toward a Performative Theory of Assembly*, 72).

50.   Giorgio Agamben, "The Glorious Body," in *Nudities*, trans. David Kishik and Stefan Pedatella (Stanford, CA: Stanford University Press, 2010), 91–103. Agamben assumes walking is prior to dance, though this essentializes the quotidian (walking) and treats the festive as its exception, when in fact most babies dance first

and only later learn walking. I discuss this point in "Is Man a Sabbatical Animal? Agamben, Rosenzweig, Heschel, Arendt"" *Political Theology* 20, no. 1 (2018): 1–23.

51.   Agamben, "Hunger of an Ox," in *Nudities*, 112. It is the same in his "Notes on Gesture," *Infancy and History: On the Destruction of Experience*, trans. Liz Heron (New York: Verso, 1993), 155), which I discuss below. An analogous observation is made by Benjamin Noys, whose essay in *Cinema and Agamben* (along with others) highlights, as reviewer Nico Baumbach puts it, "the concern that Agamben leaves little room for conceiving of cinema politically as a common practice, restricting it to 'the realm of the avant-garde or the rarity of the aesthetic judgment'" (98). See Nico Baumbach, "Cinema and Agamben: Ethics, Biopolitics, and the Moving Image," *New Review of Film and Television Studies* 13, no. 2 (2015): 211–230.

52.   Agamben, "The Glorious Body." 98.

53.   Agamben, "The Glorious Body," 98.

54.   But ostension and display have their own uses and executions. As I note in Chapter 3, Pentheus's seemingly inoperative body is made useful when Cadmus turns it into a device of maternalization. The "Mother, mother" that failed Pentheus in life will be gifted with new perlocutionary force, postmortem.

55.   The problem, says Agamben, is that "discovering another use of the body," a new use, "which this separation" of organ and function "allows us to glimpse—has remained unexplored. In its place we find glory . . ." ("The Glorious Body," 100). For him, glory not only preserves inoperativity so that we become aware of it; it also isolates inoperativity so that it cannot be unleashed or enjoyed. "In this way what was merely a threshold that granted access to new use is transformed into a permanent condition." For Arendt, by contrast, whose account of glory in *The Human Condition* draws on Greek rather than Christian sources, glory enters us into the world; it does not suspend us on its brink.

56.   Ernesto Londoño, "'A Caricature of the Patriarchy': Argentine Feminists Remake Tango," *New York Times*, October 5, 2019. The *New York Times* article ends with a nonbacchic move away from desire, but the reporter records a reservation, marked by the word *still*: "'We've perhaps broadened it into something that is fraternal and not necessarily sensual,' she said. Still, watching her and her patrons dance under dim red lights while a live band played, it was easy to drift into something approaching a hypnotic state."

57.   The literature on the tango suggests a profound diversity that the *New York Times* does not. See, for example, Erin Manning's description of tango as a "pact between strangers that 'guarantees nothing but a listening,'" noted by Debra Cash in "Should a Feminist Dance Tango?" *Women's Review of Books* 32, no. 6 (November/December 2015) and new work on Tango Queer.

58.   However, it is more of a listening-in than a direct seeing, since the events on Cithaeron are reported rather than exhibited. Still, the oral stokes the imagination, too.

59.   Euripides, *Bacchae*, trans. Robertson, 932–934.

60.   I think the play can be read as expressing this sensorial preference, or at least politicizing it, but I note Wohl's claim, in the context of a reading of Euripides's *Troades* and new materialism, that sometimes one sense alone will not do. "Scholars debate whether the force of ἐκγελᾷ ['it laughs out' from Tro. 1176: 'slaughter laughs out'] is visual or auditory." But "it is fully neither: more impression than expression, more affective than constative, it provokes sensation precisely through its opacity of sense" (Victoria Wohl, "Stone into Smoke: Metaphor and Materiality in Euripides' *Troades*," in *The Materialities of Greek Tragedy: Objects and Affect in Aeschylus, Sophocles, and Euripides*, ed. Mario Telò and Melissa Mueller [London: Bloomsbury Academic, 2018], 25).

61.   Butler emphasizes the power of assembly as prefigurative; Davina Cooper uses that term, too, in *Feeling like a State: Desire, Denial, and the Recasting of Authority* (Durham, NC: Duke University Press, 2019). See also Davina Cooper, "Towards an Adventurous Institutional Politics: The Prefigurative 'as if' and the Reposing of What's Real," *The Sociological Review* 68, no. 5 (2020): 893–916). This is what Butler calls the protestors' performativity and I want to call also rehearsal.

62.   I build here on Agamben's *Nudities*, but his later *The Use of Bodies* does not significantly alter his account of inoperativity. It is worth noting that his framing example in the later work on "use" is that of master-slave, a move for which he has been criticized. By contrast, Arendt, in *The Human Condition*, draws on two exemplary instances of bodily use: master/slave and, a different couple, Adam and Eve, thus coupling the labor of production with the *labor of reproduction*. Why start with the slave's labor, which puts the slave to use, and not with the mother's, which puts her body to use? When the originating image of a reflection on use is the master-slave dyad, unpaired with the mother-child dyad, it is perhaps unsurprising that being against use means favoring destituent rather than constituent power, and concluding in favor of contemplation (the free play of the mind, unleashed to care for the world), rather than action. Thanks to Tristan Bradshaw for discussion of these and related issues.

63.   A bacchanalia appears on the cover of Agamben's *The Use of Bodies*, as Tristan Bradshaw pointed out to me. That one is in mixed company, though, and a woman's glorious body, as it were, is on full display in the foreground of the image, as spectacle. The cover of *Nudities* also features a possible *Bacchae*, but the grouped women are too robotic to be mistaken for bacchants.

64.   Euripides, *Bacchae*, trans. Robertson, 951.

65.   Agamben, *Nymphs*, trans. Kevin McLaughlin and Amanda Minervini (Chicago: University of Chicago Press, 2013), 1.

66.   Lynne Huffer argues that Agamben's account of nymphs relies on a "unifying, heterosexual description of image making, cast in the same terms through which the Enlightenment conceived of masculine artistic enthusiasm." She has in mind the Enlightenment fable of Pygmalion in which male artists remake women to their liking and cast themselves in the birth-giving role that discomfits them in

women. Huffer finds in Lars von Trier's film *Nymphomaniac* a radical refusal of that model, quite specifically a refusal of "the recuperative terms of Agamben's heterosexual conception of the image" (Lynne Huffer, "The Nymph Shoots Back: Agamben and the Feel of the Agon," in Honig and Marso, *Politics, Theory, Film*, 101). See also Lori Marso's discussion of Simone de Beauvoir on nymphs as simultaneously "the mythical and beautiful maiden" and "the immature form of an insect" (*Politics with Beauvoir: Freedom in the Encounter* [Durham, NC: Duke University Press, 2017], 170) and her reading of von Trier's *Antichrist* ("Must We Burn Lars von Trier?: Simone de Beauvoir's Body Politics in *Antichrist*," in Honig and Marso, *Politics, Theory, Film*, 45–70), which in effect finds a politics of feminist feeling in what has otherwise been seen merely as horror.

67.   *The Fits*, directed by Anna Rose Holmer (2015; New York: Oscilloscope Laboratories, 2016). We return to the archive of Black girl studies in Chapter 3 via Saidiya Hartman's *Wayward Lives*.

68.   White has a great reading of *The Fits* to which I return below. See Patricia White, "Bodies that Matter: Black Girlhood in *The Fits*," *Film Quarterly* (Spring 2017): 23–31.

69.   Patricia White says, "Toni's sexuality remains submerged" ("Bodies that Matter," 29). I think it is less submerged than performed in all of its ambivalence, on which White also comments, noting the "clear trajectory toward normative gender assimilation into the performance style of the dance team" (29). White sees how Toni's bodily movement in dance "has been shaped by the differently coded bodily discipline of boxing. Where the girls move en masse, all angles, curves, and hair, Toni is declared 'straight as a rail' when fitted for her costume, and she throws punches with targeted precision. She also occupies or attends to thresholds in the space of the school: she wipes glitter from the window looking into the Lionesses' practice room with her finger as if trying to decode this elusive substance; from inside the comfort of the boxing gym she sees Legs and Karisma watching the boys practice from the other side of the window; she lingers in a bathroom stall to watch them at the mirror" (29).

70.   In doing so, it meditates on what Kevin Quashie calls the "sovereignty of quiet" in his book by that name. See Kevin Quashie, *The Sovereignty of Quiet: Beyond Resistance in Black Culture* (New Brunswick, NJ: Rutgers University Press, 2012).

71.   Rizvana Bradley, "Black Cinematic Gesture and the Aesthetics of Contagion," *The Drama Review* 62, no. 1 (Spring 2018): 15, emphasis added. Kafka says, "Cinema lends the restlessness of its own movement to what is seen, the calm gaze seems to be more important" (quoted in Benjamin Noys, "Film-of-life: Agamben's Profanation of the Image," in *Cinema and Agamben: Ethics, Biopolitics and the Moving Image*, ed. Henrik Gustafsson and Asbjørn Grønstad [New York: Bloomsbury, 2014], 91). *The Fits* scrambles these terms to offer up a cinema of the calm gaze. Bradley says, "Holmer's evocative view of Toni tracks not a returned look, but a determined stare that takes possession of, just as it dispossesses, the spectator's line

of sight. To be beheld by Toni is to be held within the *affective intensity* of her unbroken stare. Paradoxically, the film's intimate framing of Toni offers a critique of the 'arrest of the frame' (Moten 2003:108). We are invited into Toni's world via Holmer's framing, but Toni's stare glimpses a world outside the boundaries of the film's frame. Her introspective urgency is embedded in the context of a wider sociality of black female adolescence, of black female artistic and physical labor, and a longer history of resistance to that sociality" (15).

72.   The use of slow motion here could be seen as a pedestrian invocation of the culinary temporality of Cithaeron. It seems to be the time of daytime slumber. When we do finally see her face, during her fit and after she has left the hallway, Toni's eyes are closed. Has she been sleepwalking?

73.   Gesture and gait, the subjects of Tourette's interest in his two studies and the focus of Agamben's attention in this essay, are the subjects of the two chapters that follow. Inclination is a gesture and fabulation's waywardness a gait.

74.   Giorgio Agamben, "Notes on Gesture," in *Infancy and History: On the Destruction of Experience*, trans. Liz Heron (New York: Verso, 1993), 150.

75.   Agamben, "Notes on Gesture," 149–150. For what is in effect a radical critique of this "footprint method," see Kathy Ferguson, "Anarchist Women and the Politics of Walking," *Political Research Quarterly* 70, no. 4 (2017): 708–719. Citing *The Practice of Everyday Life*, Ferguson notes that Michel de Certeau calls a footstep a distinct "kinesthetic appropriation" (97), a compound of exertions and adjustments that add up (ideally) to a rhythmic appearance but *"cannot be reduced to their graphic trail"* (Michel de Certeau, *The Practice of Everyday Life*, trans. Steven Rendall [Berkeley: University of California Press, 1984], 99, emphasis added).

76.   In *Modern Times*, Charlie Chaplin experiences a "tic" (instigated by a fly) and (to borrow Creon's words from *Antigone*) "routs the line": the assembly line of the factory, that is. He is swallowed by the factory machine and emerges as a body out of control. This might have been recorded by Tourette as a tic disorder, but Chaplin casts it as a side effect of factory work. The connection between "what Agamben describes as the bourgeoisie's dispossession of gesture," says Deborah Levitt, is part of a history in which, on Agamben's account, "gesture is expropriated by biopower; the former then becomes the focus of an aesthetic attempt to reclaim it" ("Notes on Media and Biopolitics: 'Notes on Gesture,'" in *The Work of Giorgio Agamben: Law, Literature, Life*, ed. Justin Clemens, Nicholas Heron, and Alex Murray (Edinburgh: Edinburgh University Press, 2008), 195. But some more than others are allowed to own their gestures, and some more than others are divested of theirs.

77.   Agamben, "Notes on Gesture," 149. In *Modern Times*, I argue in the appendix, Chaplin satirized Henry Ford's ambition to feed his workers like / with machines. Similarly, we may say, *The Fits* satirizes Tourette, whose syndrome is conceived of as only neurological, not political, cultural, or spiritual, and who devoted himself to disciplined walking, just forty years after Thoreau celebrated walking as a practice of refusal. The satire is in the hands of Toni, whose ticless,

unblinking gaze grips the viewer and whose steps are taken in the shadow of Tourette's and all the other step studies. We could also say that *all* the experiments in walking from *flâneurs* and *flâneuses* (like the bacchants) to Kathy Ferguson's anarchist walking women, to *The Fits*, refuse Tourette's discipline. On the further political possibilities of walking, in particular, public walking and its "tactical transgressions" as raced, classed, and gendered, see Mona Domosh, "Those 'Gorgeous Incongruities': Polite Politics and Public Space on the Streets of Nineteenth-Century New York City," *Annals of the Association of American Geographers* 88, no. 2 (June 1998): 209–226.

78.   Pasi Väliaho, "Biopolitics of Gesture: Cinema and the Neurological Body," in *Cinema and Agamben: Ethics, Biopolitics and the Moving Image*, ed. Henrik Gustafsson and Asbjørn Grønstad (New York: Bloomsbury, 2014), 116.

79.   He cites Pinocchio elsewhere, but Peter Pan's loss of his shadow could be seen in connection with the so-called loss of gesture recorded by Agamben in his quasi-Benjaminian way. I note that when Wendy repairs the rupture by sewing the boy and his shadow back together, she joins a tradition of corporeal suturing to which the *Bacchae*'s Agave also belongs. Agave will reassemble Pentheus toward the end of the play.

80.   Agamben, "Notes on Gesture," 151. The elegy has a Benjaminian flavor but lacks the revolutionary commandeering of the apparatus appreciated by Benjamin in both his "Work of Art" essay and "The Author as Producer."

81.   The film does not explicitly mention politics either. But its expressed worries about whether there is lead in the water resonate with more general concerns about disinvestment in public things in minority and poor neighborhoods. Bradley lists a three-point critique of Agamben, also noting the importance of race, gender, and class to the film: "The film's dance sequences, which feature various representations of black girls dance team cultures, including line formations, majorette, step, and drill (White 2017:27), emphasize the significance of [a] break between gesture and the body as a disjointedness that" is not simply a deprivation of the bourgeoisie but also "serves as the condition of possibility for the expressive potentiality of black girlhood" (Bradley, "Black Cinematic Gesture," 22). Deborah Levitt's work is also relevant. The connection between "what Agamben describes as the bourgeoisie's dispossession of gesture," says Levitt, is part of a history in which, Agamben says, "gesture is expropriated by biopower; the former then becomes the focus of an aesthetic attempt to reclaim it" (Levitt, "Notes on Media and Biopolitics," 195). But the anxiety about the bourgeoisie's loss of gesture occludes the fact that for some, but not all equally, the theft of gestic vocabulary is part of a larger history of dispossession and enclosure.

82.   White, "Bodies that Matter," 28.

83.   Väliaho, "Biopolitics of Gesture," 105.

84.   Tourette, Väliaho points out, is one of the men seated in the room (106). On the back wall, in the painting's background, is the charcoal drawing by Paul Richer called *Periode de contortions*, depicting a woman convulsed into the *arc en*

circle, the hysteric's classic posture. See H. W. Telson, "Une lecon du docteur Charcot a la Salpetriere," *Journal of the History of Medicine and Allied Sciences* 35, no. 1 (January 1980): 58–59, and J. C. Harris, "A Clinical Lesson at the Salpêtrière," *Archives of General Psychiatry* 62, no. 5 (May 2005): 470–472. Later, Freud would hang a lithograph of the Brouillet painting in his study in Hampstead.

85.   The spectator's gaze is blocked from seeing the other episodes of the fits. White notes, *"The Fits* doesn't spectacularize the episodes. They are mostly blocked from view by barriers, bodies, and cell phone screens, or recounted secondhand. In one endearing episode, Toni's new friend Beezy (Alexis Neblett), a scene-stealing sprite in Afro puffs, recounts a fit she's witnessed, miming the victim's choking, twitching, and zombie gaze with gusto. At one remove from the afflicted body, she takes possession of the unknown" (White, "Bodies that Matter," 27). On "African diasporic use of blinding light," see Krista Thompson, Shine (Durham, NC: Duke University Press, 2015), 20.

86.   In addition to everything else at stake, we can see in Toni's slow-motion stepping, outside the step circle and maybe en route to it, a triumph over efforts like that of Tourette to dominate the step and to choreograph, which is to say, *normalize* the body's movements in ways that marginalize as pathological the tics and spasms that, Bradley argues, may well be seen as elements of a gestural vernacular of Black sociality and the history of Black dance. To all this, I would add for consideration Toni's queerness.

87.   We may say that the camera mothers her. Toni's mother is mentioned but never seen on camera; she works late. And in this scene, the camera seems to take her place or that of her brother, who mothers her at the community center and in the neighborhood. On the camera and / as mother-daughter, see Lori Marso on Chantal Akerman's *No Home Movie*: "Find Our Mothers: Chantal Akerman's Camerawork as Motherwork" in *Theory and Event* (forthcoming, 2021).

88.   The music matters, too. It helps lift Toni, actualizing in a way what Tina Campt calls "phonic substance"—which she says is "not simply a sound played over, behind or in relation to an image; one that emanates from the image itself" (81). The effect of the music is to drive the image. They are inseparable. See Tina Campt, "Black Visuality and the Practice of Refusal," *Women and Performance* 29, no. 1 (2019): 79–87.

89.   We can include here the history of witch-hunting, which sometimes also charged men but was focused mostly on women, as detailed by Silvia Frederici, *Caliban and the Witch: Women, the Body and Primitive Accumulation* (Brooklyn, NY: Autonomedia, 2004). For recent engagements with Frederici's work, see "*Caliban and the Witch*: A Verso Roundtable," October 25, 2019, https://www.versobooks.com/blogs/4464-caliban-and-the-witch-a-verso-roundtable, and on Scotland's history of witch-hunting, which swept up some men as well, see Whitney Curry Wimbish, "Thar Be Witches, and Us," *New York Times*, October 25, 2019.

90.   Importantly, says Bradley, this "film indicates a profound interest in improvisation and *even gestural failure as the condition of possibility* for newly consti-

tuted forms of virtuosic movement. The unique physical recalibrations afforded by step open up spaces for the practiced interrogation of the body's composure and control in ways that come to differently organize the gestic" and do not just record its loss (Bradley, "Black Cinematic Gesture," 23, emphasis added).

91.   That walk follows a sequence in which Toni is outside, first in an empty swimming pool and then, shot from below, against the background of trees and sky; birds chirping is the only sound. It seems to be a scene of Thoreauvian contemplation. The song begins, "Must we choose to be slaves to gravity?" and then a straight cut later we are viewing Toni's feet in close-up walking down the community center's white-gray hallway in very slow motion. The hovering instances Campt's account of "black visuality" as a "practice of refusal" in which images "*hover* between still and moving images [and] require the labor of feeling with or through them." Holmer's use of slow motion in *The Fits* resonates with: "the innovative artistic practices deployed by Black artists whose work suspends the presumed distinction between still and moving images . . ." (Campt, "Black Visuality," 81, emphasis added).

92.   White, "Bodies that Matter," 30.

93.   Her first four steps are complete, then—with the sung words "we were born of the sun"—steps five and six are half steps: only heel or only toes step down, not the full footprint sought by Tourette. Here, Toni eludes his grasp. And with step seven until step thirteen, Toni is released. "Shouldn't we be light?" goes the song: "Shouldn't we be treasure?" See "Kiah Victoria—Aurora." YouTube Video, 3:30, April 8, 2017, https://www.youtube.com/watch?v=zJtovqvHKUA.

94.   When Toni's feet dangle in the air, they suggest an alternative to the ordinary walking that is surely a "slave to gravity." Or, better, as Kathy Ferguson notes, "Walking both resists and capitulates to gravity: 'Walking means precisely resigning yourself to being an ambulant, forward-leaning body. . . . Our leaden bodies fall back to earth at every step, as if to take root there again'" ("Anarchist Women and the Politics of Walking," *Political Research Quarterly* 70, no. 4 [2017]: 187). But, for Ferguson, it is also a kind of suspensive rather than the intensive inoperativity; she cites Gros's term, *suspensive freedom.*

95.   On such interruptions, see Carl Schmitt's *Hamlet or Hecuba: The Intrusion of the Time into the Play* (Candor, NY: Telos Press, 2009) and my discussion of it in *Antigone, Interrupted* (Cambridge: Cambridge University Press, 2013).

96.   Agamben, "Notes on Gesture," 136.

97.   Frantz Fanon, *Wretched of the Earth* (New York: Grove Press, 2004), 16–17.

98.   Her eyes closed and seemingly in the grip of impulses she cannot control, Toni's body jerks and heaves, her braids whip around, always in slow motion, as she becomes a silhouette in the bright light of a window and then reappears (in fantasy) on a bridge where she and her brother have trained. She unzips her gray boxer's hoodie to reveal a sparkly dance costume beneath it and raises her outstretched arms, palms up, seeming to summon the bodies that now appear. The dance troupe rushes up the steps to join her for a number that she executes almost

perfectly with them, but not quite. Their assembly reappears to dance in the gym, in the boxing ring, and in the empty pool. In small and large numbers, in all these locations, the girls dance, and Toni smiles. But her smile seems false, actor-y, the forced happiness of a child performing to please. Then we are back to her more mesmerized and mesmerizing self, still in the fits, still in slow motion, in the gym, eyes closed, braids whipping, girls oohing, and Toni silhouetted again, until she falls all the way down to the ground and the girls gasp their way to her. And then, as the credits roll, the "Gravity" song, Kiah Victoria's song "Aurora," gives way to a chant, the *Eta Bakkae* of the neighborhood: "Pride takes the prey! lemme hear you say! Lionesses, Lionesses!" Pride here puns on queerness, too. And the chant shapes the young women's assembly as a dance team.

99.   Manohla Dargis will cast her as "a girl who follows her own beat." And she is, but the issue between Toni and her peers—but which group is her peer group?—is not one of individuality but rather one of queerness. Notably, Dargis's review begins with a still of Toni in the iconic hysteric's *arc en circle* posture with no mention of the imagistic citation noted here. See Manohla Dargis, "Review: In 'The Fits,' a Graceful Tale of a Girl Who Follows Her Own Beat," *New York Times*, June 2, 2016. Will Toni become a dancer who boxes or a boxer who dances? We will recall *The Fits* when we turn to Muhammad Ali, who boxed like a dancer before losing control of his body to Parkinson's: the fits.

100.   In their variety, the fits are legible as a contribution to the history of Black eccentric dance described by Jasmine Johnson ("Choreography," paper presented at the Cogut Institute Political Concepts Conference, Brown University, Providence, RI, December 6, 2019). Johnson describes Black eccentric dance as specifically linked to funeral and mourning. In this context, we may see Toni's return to life in *The Fits*, after her feet momentarily dangle, seemingly lifeless, as belonging to Johnson's archive, which includes the music video *Never Catch Me* in which the adolescents whose funeral is shown get up and dance out of the funeral parlor, commandeer the hearse and drive away. The video is a profoundly moving meditation on anti-Black violence and the Black joy and expression that survive it. Importantly, we could ask whether *The Fits* belongs to the archive of Black eccentric dance, which Johnson describes as a refusal of choreography. If *The Fits* offers such a refusal, it is by way of its contrast of the choreography of the Lionesses' martial dance with the innervations caused by the fits. In keeping with the camera work of *The Fits* tracked here, Johnson notes how one of eccentric dance's most famous practitioners, Snake Hips Tucker, evaded his audiences, slipping in and out of their sights and confusing their expectations.

101.   Where Bradley rightly notes Agamben's inattention to the racial politics of bodily alienation, citing Hartman, Spillers, Cox, and others, Libby Saxton takes Agamben to task for neglecting the ways in which the various apparatuses of capture were enlisted to discipline the working bodies of laborers. As Saxton points out, citing the work of Mary Ann Doane and Deborah Levitt, "Agamben aligns Tourette's method with the famous photographic studies of Jean-Martin Charcot,

Muybridge and Marey, thereby linking the bourgeoisie's loss of gesture with these physiological studies of human movement. We might add to Agamben's series Alphonse Bertillon's comparative photographic charts of the physical features of criminals and Frederick Winslow Taylor's famous industrial efficiency studies (Levitt 197)." Their photographic analyses identified "any individual expressivity contained in the gestures of factory workers" seeking to excise it "in favour of perfectly homogeneous and efficient movements synchronised with the hands of the clock. [I turn in the Appendix to Taylorism and industrial homogenization in my discussion of Chaplin's Tramp in *Modern Times*.] Of the figures Agamben cites, Marey is perhaps the most persuasively emblematic [of the] physiological investigations of human movement, utopian dreams of a pristine and waste-free social hygiene and the impulse to find new imaging technologies converge (Levitt 197)." See Libby Saxton, "*Passion*, Agamben and the Gestures of Work," in *Cinema and Agamben: Ethics, Biopolitics and the Moving Image*, ed. Henrik Gustafsson and Asbjørn Grønstad [New York: Bloomsbury, 2014], 55–70, citing Levitt, "Notes on Media and Biopolitics."

102.   Saxton rightly notes that there is every reason to connect the assembly line itself to cinema's history, itself a form of factory production.

103.   About the possible smile on Toni's face at the end, Patricia White asks, "Is it satisfaction that she's crossed a threshold, or smugness that she's pulled off a ruse?" The film will not decide, but when it closes with the word *pride*, might it be sharing a pun? "After the cut to black, the Lionesses' chant is heard on the soundtrack, riffing on the term 'pride.' Refusing to settle down and privilege a single reading, the film instead takes flight in Toni's gaze, her gait, her gravity" (White, "Bodies that Matter," 31).

104.   In some sense, perhaps I echo Benjamin's claim in his "Work of Art" essay that the actor can triumph over the camera that many assume will triumph over him. But in this case, I attribute the triumph to the film's assemblage not to a singular hero (the director, camerapersons, choreographers, community members, and actors of *The Fits* together), and the triumph does not vanquish the cold camera but redirects its energies.

105.   Agamben, "Notes on Gesture," 153.

106.   Thanks to Tristan Bradshaw for pressing me to clarify the importance to my argument of recovering inoperativity, not use, per se.

2. INCLINATION AND THE WORK OF DIS/ORIENTATION

1.   I have elsewhere argued that care may help prop up and not just unsettle autonomy, working as its supplement, undecidably supportive and subversive. See Bonnie Honig, "Negotiating Positions" in *Political Theory and the Displacement of Politics* (Ithaca, NY: Cornell University Press, 1993), 162–199.

2.   Cavarero describes, in the context of a reading of Levinas, the maternal inclination as on the cusp, positioned for care and / or wounding, in response to the

call of the exposed other. But as a *maternal* inclination, it is nonetheless experiential. I return to the point later in this chapter (Adriana Cavarero, *Inclinations: A Critique of Rectitude*, trans. Amanda Minervini and Adam Sitze [Stanford, CA: Stanford University Press, 2016], 105).

3.   Is there a connection between Bartleby's expression of preference and the term *inclination*, which is an older term for *prefer*? As Neil Saccamano pointed out to me, when David Hume says he finds himself "uninclined," he means he prefers not to.

4.   Cavarero, *Inclinations*. Inclination calls to mind Deleuze and Guattari's displacement of the arboreal (vertical) with the rhizomatic (inclinational).

5.   Henry David Thoreau, "Walking," *The Atlantic* (June 1862), original emphasis.

6.   These women who take to their beds may be precursors to what Lori Marso argues is comedian Ali Wong's "refusal" when she jokes that she does not want to lean in—she wants to "lie down." The joke is in the assumed surrender of the posture, but lying down, as we saw in Chapter 1, can itself be a practice of feminist refusal (in the streets blocking traffic or sleeping outside as part of an occupation). See Lori Marso, "Birthing Feminist Freedom," *HA Journal* 6 (2018): 98–107.

7.   Cavarero, *Inclinations*, 3. Gayle Salomon connects the etymology to *clino*, meaning "to bend": "how might we think through the notion of 'inclination,' which, just like leaning, means "bending out" from the austere vertical' in a contemporary context where 'inclination' names the direction or course of one's sexual desire?" she asks, echoing Ahmed (Gayle Salomon, *The Life and Death of Latisha King: A Critical Phenomenology of Transphobia* [New York: New York University Press, 2018], 50).The reference to *clino* is in a footnote of an Erwin Straus article, noted by Salomon.

8.   Thoreau, *Walking*, emphasis added. Though, when he goes on to "appreciate the beauty and the glory of architecture," Thoreau even invokes on behalf of rectitude the very aesthetic and sacred categories that Agamben affiliates with inoperativity (beauty and glory). George Shulman (private communication) says that in Thoreau's *Walden* the more dominant notes are inclinational: the "climax of the book is about flow, 'downwards' along a hillside." So, too, in *Walking*, there is inclination in the whispers of the two men as they walk. So is it *women's* inclination in particular that discomfits Thoreau?

9.   Perhaps this is not so odd, however, since Thoreau also says "every walk is a sort of crusade," aimed at "reconquer[ing] this Holy Land from the hands of the Infidel."

10.   Euripides, *Bacchae*, trans. Robin Robertson (New York: Harper Collins, 2014), 1095–1113.

11.   Euripides, *Bacchae*, trans. Robertson, 1132–1133.

12.   Cavarero might balk at this since, for her, inclination is a pacifist and altruistic posture, not a violent one. Her aim is not to decapitate or dismember. Neither is mine, of course, but the point here is that what the play figures violently is a

change that may be achieved more pacifically. What is here called regicide may also be a kind of epistemicide. The recent #MeToo slogan "Believe woman" is an example. It switches the default from disbelieving women to believing them when they claim to have been raped or harassed. As we will see at the end of this chapter, when Procne finds out her sister has been mutilated and raped by Procne's husband, Tereus, Procne does not interrogate Philomela. She takes her home. "Believe women" does not mean we must believe all women. It means women get the same defaults as men. We believe them unless given a reason not to. This is by contrast with the misogynist habit of disbelieving women unless and until their claims are forced on us, usually by being multiplied by a chorus of others. On the power of the chorus, see Chapter 3.

13.   See Jean Cocteau's image, *The Language of Love and Hate in "Antigone,"* and Sara Ahmed, *Willful Subjects* (Durham, NC: Duke University Press, 2014).

14.   Elsewhere, the story is referred to as "The Willful Child," and a commentator/translator says, "I have arbitrarily assigned male gender to the child, whose sex cannot be determined by the German text" (Jacob and Wilhelm Grimm, "The Willful Child," trans. D. L. Ashliman [2000], http://www.pitt.edu /~dash/type0779.html#grimm). The painful story resonates with a painful history, recounted by Maria Tamboukou in *Sewing, Fighting and Writing* (a book to which I was drawn as a reader of the *Bacchae* and chronicler of various *"Bacchaes"*): Tamboukou remarks a seamstress's striking depiction "of a destitute mother shaking her daughter's body to keep her awake so that she could go on working for the sake of the family's bread." Tamboukou's subject, Bouvier, found old letters from her mother to her sister complaining about Bouvier's selfishness and the insufficiency of her provision for the family. This, I would argue, is the raised arm being beaten into the grave of motherlessness. Tamboukou's account offers to the otherwise merely misogynist tale by the Grimm brothers a detail that helps account for, though it hardly excuses, the mother's cruelty: poverty. See Maria Tamboukou, *Sewing, Fighting and Writing: Radical Practices in Work, Politics and Culture* (London: Rowman and Littlefield, 2015), 177–179.

15.   The mother seems to be in the service of patriarchal powers. In "The First Fairytales Were Feminist Critiques of Patriarchy," Melissa Ashley traces fairy tales to the seventeenth century's French *conteuses* and charges that what we have now are the result of the nineteenth-century project of the Brothers Grimm, who "dismissed the *conteuses* as inauthentic, as not representative of the voices of the common *volk*." See Melissa Ashley, "The First Fairytales Were Feminist Critiques of Patriarchy. We Need to Revive Their Legacy," *Guardian*, November 10, 2019. This is an example of what we will discuss in Chapter 3: the agonism of fabulation.

16.   Adriana Cavarero, *Relating Narratives: Storytelling and Selfhood*, trans. Paul A. Kottman (New York: Routledge, 2000), 51. Cavarero has her own great reading of the myth in *Relating Narratives*, which has two chapters on Oedipus, the second more centrally on the encounter with the Sphinx. I think her argument in

Inclinations can be extended to generate this third one, compatible with the other two but different.

17.   For the specifics of the Sphinx's puzzle, see Apollodorus, *Library*, trans. James George Frazer (Cambridge, MA: Harvard University Press, 1963), 3.5.8, in which the puzzle appears as follows: "What is that which has one voice and yet becomes four-footed and two-footed and three-footed?" Henri Dorra has suggested that in the Gustave Moreau painting, *Oedipus and the Sphinx* (1864), the poses of the Sphinx and Oedipus, in which the Sphinx is inclined and Oedipus is vertical, are derived from "the Greek etymological meaning of the word sphinx, which is to clutch, embrace, or cling to" ("Oedipus and the Sphinx," Wikipedia, April 8, 2020). Yuan Yuan says "strangle" is the root word in Greek and connects the Sphinx to fears of strangulation by the mother (*The Riddling between Oedipus and the Sphinx: Ontology, Hauntology, and Heterologies of the Grotesque* [Lanham, MD: University Press of America, 2016], 56).

18.   This is not Deleuze and Guattari's radical repurposing of the body: "Why not walk on your head, sing with your sinuses, see through your skin, breathe with your belly?" (Gilles Deleuze and Félix Guattari, *A Thousand Plateaus: Capitalism and Schizophrenia*, trans. Brian Massumi [New York: Continuum], 167). Still, this approach to the Sphinx's riddle bridges to disability studies, which also contests the normativity of rectitude. Andrés Fabián Henao Castro proposes a still-different reading, focused on (non)citizenship status and highlighting the role of Oedipus as a metic king (or, as I have argued, a foreign founder): "Oedipus gets his name, which means 'Swollen-Foot' . . . when he was supposed to be abandoned to die in the arid borderlands." He is so named "in a play where the most important riddle (the riddle of the Sphinx) refers to a four-footed animal (as slaves were pejoratively referred to in Greek antiquity) that became a two-legged creature in the evening (citizen?), and a three-legged-creature at night (metic?)." See Andrés Fabián Henao Castro, "Oedipus at the Border," *Public Books*, November 11, 2019. Elsewhere, Castro connects the four legs of the morning with the two slaves who, respectively, drop Oedipus off to die, without killing him, and later pick him up to save him from abandonment: "Oedipus's four-legged creature would be this corporeal assemblage between the shepherds at the border," Castro suggests. See Andrés Fabián Henao Castro, "Can the Subaltern Smile? *Oedipus* without Oedipus," *Contemporary Political Theory* 14, no. 4 (February 2015): 315–334.

19.   As Gayle Salomon says about Erwin Straus's work on posture, there is a tension in Straus "between the naturalness of uprightness to the human and its nature as an achievement" (Salomon, *The Life and Death of Latisha King*, 46).

20.   This is Sophocles' depiction of Oedipus. On the signifying powers of the cane, see Laurence Ralph, *Renegade Dreams: Living through Injury in Gangland Chicago* (Chicago: University of Chicago Press, 2014). Thinking in terms of the cane and the infirm more generally positions Cavarero's critique of rectitude as a contribution to disability studies, as in this claim: "We are born needing care and die needing care. . . . At brief moments in the middle of life, we hold the illusion

of independence" (Elliot Kukla, "In My Chronic Illness, I Found a Deeper Meaning," *New York Times,* January 10, 2018). See also the interview between Junot Díaz and Samuel Delany, "Radicalism Begins in the Body," *Boston Review,* May 10, 2017.

21.   Cavarero says of Alasdair MacIntyre's book, *Dependent Rational Animals: Why Human Beings Need the Virtues:* it does not "radically contest the paradigm of the liberal individual; he merely reforms and corrects it by interjecting the condition of dependence as a recurrent but temporary possibility for everyone." So, too, we might say, of Oedipus, aware of exceptions to his ideal of autonomy (else he could not have answered the Sphinx's riddle), but they do not challenge or deter him from his determined path.

22.   Cavarero says uprightness is the posture necessary, on Plato's account, for philosophy to exit the cave.

23.   Euripides, *Bacchae,* trans. Richard Seaford (Liverpool, UK: Liverpool University Press, 1996), 1264–1270

24.   Sara Ahmed, *Queer Phenomenology: Orientations, Objects, Others* (Durham, NC: Duke University Press, 2006), 129. (Muhammad Ali will make a similar argument, noting that those deemed foreign by the sovereign power have more in common with him than those deemed conationals. See my discussion of Ali in the Appendix.) The foreignness of Dionysus's followers is underlined when the Asian bacchants' chorus leader praises Bromius, upon hearing of Pentheus's death, and the second messenger says, "What? You rejoice, woman, in the death of my king?" to which the chorus leader replies, "I am no Greek and he was not my king" (Euripides, *Bacchae,* trans. Seaford, 1031–1033).

25.   In a way, I am reading that incline as subversive, not submissive, in an echo of Cavarero's reading of the Madonna and mine of Antigone in *Antigone, Interrupted.* Does care for the dead more perfectly underwrite the altruism that Cavarero puts at inclination's core?

26.   Orientation is a nonstraight posture that polices conformity not only with patriarchy's masculinized moralism but also its mandated heterosexuality. On the normalization and naturalization of heterosexuality, Ahmed notes how "straightness gets attached to other values including decent, conventional, direct, and honest" (*Queer Phenomenology,* 70).

27.   Ahmed, *Queer Phenomenology,* 24.

28.   James Martel, *Unburied Bodies: Subversive Corpses and the Authority of the Dead* (Amherst, MA: Amherst College Press, 2018), 6.

29.   Ahmed, *Queer Phenomenology,* 24.

30.   Euripides, *Bacchae,* trans. Robertson, 1314–1315.

31.   Euripides, *Bacchae,* trans. Robertson, 1299, 1220.

32.   It is uncertain whether Agave just gathers her son together or sews his head back on. The possibility that she reattaches his head, sewing rather than looming, as it were, is one way to fill the text's lacuna. As Robin Robertson puts it, "there is a lacuna in the original text. Agave may have joined her son's head to the rest of his body" (Euripides, *Bacchae,* trans. Robertson, 72).

33.   Martel, *Unburied Bodies*, 56–57. Martel discusses famous dismember-
ments, such as Machiavelli's discussion of the display of Orco by Borgia. For Martel,
this shows how state justice is underwritten by violence (7–8). We can extend the
point to the *Bacchae*, where it is the king who is dismembered, not his servants, and
argue that what is shown is the violence needed to undo sexual enclosure. As I've
noted, this is not to endorse such violence but merely to say there can be no ending
of patriarchy without (metaphorical) dismemberment. Relevant here is the loose use
today of the term *castration* for any and all redistributions of power across gender
lines. Dismemberment is what the end of patriarchy will feel like.

34.   See the Introduction for discussion of the unresolved murder of Semele.

35.   For the details of the lion reading, see Bonnie Honig, "'Out like a Lion':
Melancholia with Euripides and Winnicott," in *Politics, Theory, Film: Critical En-
counters with Lars von Trier*, ed. Bonnie Honig and Lori J. Marso (New York: Oxford
University Press, 2016), 356–388.

36.   Judith Butler sees in the *Bacchae* some acknowledgment of the possibility
that filicide is a maternal desire. She does not raise the issue of regicide. See Judith
Butler, "Breaks in the Bond: Reflections on Kinship Trouble," Housman Lecture,
UCL, London, 2017.

37.   See Hanna M. Roisman for the claim that Pentheus does not deserve his
punishment, assuming contra tragedy as such that the character must be directly
responsible for a wrong, rather than be a carrier of a wrong, for punishment to be
merited. Pentheus is both a carrier and an agent of wrongdoing insofar as he and
Cadmus are content to go on as if Semele's death requires no investigation. Roisman
does not note the crime against Semele in her reading of the play. Hanna M. Roisman, "Euripides' Bacchae—A Revenge Play," in *Looking at Bacchae*, ed. David
Stuttard (London: Bloomsbury, 2016), 121–132.

38.   Sorority is not perfectly egalitarian, and in any case, one could argue that
maternity is a better model for politics *because* of its inequality. In democratic politics, after all, we are always contesting inequalities in the current partition of the
sensible. But that is not Cavarero's argument, perhaps because, for her, the aim is
more ethical than political: maternity exemplifies the relationality that is needed
for an ethics of altruism that is better placed than Levinas's to overcome egoism.

39.   Would it still remain the case that, as Cavarero says, "the oblique line
that traverses the painting is a matrilineal line"? (Cavarero, *Inclinations*, 99). Another reading of the painting, in response to Cavarero, also points out the sorority
of the two women; see Alison Stone's "The Ontology of the Maternal: A Response
to Adriana Cavarero," *Studies in the Maternal* 2, no. 1 (2010): 2: "In his 1910 essay
on Leonardo da Vinci, Freud pointed out that there are two mothers in the painting
(1985, p. 205–7). Reciprocally, there are two *children* in the scene—not only Jesus
but also Mary. Mary is in her mother's lap (indeed, she completely fills it). Although
now an adult and mother herself, Mary comes to her adulthood and mothering from
having been a vulnerable infant cared for by her mother Anne—a vulnerable child
that, psychically, Mary will always in part remain. Mary has grown to occupy a space

delimited by the body of her own mother. Thus the painting shows us that Mary as mother—any mother—is always also the daughter of her own mother." Butler's Housman lecture claims that Dionysus has two mothers: the god is born of Semele and a feminized Zeus who birthed him from his thigh-womb on behalf of the lost mother.

40.   "Confirming a subversive gesture originally performed in the *Virgin of the Rocks* (1483), Leonardo places the child beside the mother, and not in her arms, as in the traditional representations" (Cavarero, *Inclinations*, 99).

41.   This untraditional distance from the mother(s) is what sets the scene for Mary to incline *toward* her child. Also, traditionally, this mother and child do *not* "look at one another," and yet here they do. Diego Millan suggested to me that we could see the leaning of the mother in the painting as a leaning out and not as a leaning in—a sign of distancing rather than closeness. That is, we cannot tell decisively if she is reaching for the child to scoop him up, or if she has just set him down and is leaning back and away from him, toward her own mother (sister).

42.   Cavarero, *Inclinations*, 87.

43.   Cavarero, *Inclinations*, 97.

44.   Cavarero, *Inclinations*, 105. Recall here the potentiality that Agamben, and Deleuze and Guattari thematize, as we saw in Chapter 1: poised on the precipice of an action that can go either way—(im)potentiality or inoperativity.

45.   Cavarero, *Inclinations*, 105.

46.   Cavarero, *Inclinations*, 105.

47.   Projecting maternal murderousness onto the Greek Medea, Cavarero insulates Leonardo's Christian maternity from implication in Freud's (Greek, ambivalent) maternity, characterized at once by "'the promise of unbounded tenderness' and 'sinister menace'" (Miriam Leonard, "Freud and the Biography of Antiquity," in *Creative Lives in Classical Antiquity: Poets, Artists and Biography*, ed. by Richard Fletcher and Johanna Hanink [New York: Cambridge University Press, 2016], 305–326).

48.   The quotations here are from Miriam Leonard, who first called my attention to the relevance of this material. See Leonard, "Freud and the Biography of Antiquity." Notably, Medea, too, took her son(s) in place of her husband when she killed *them* to avenge the wrong for which she wanted to kill *him*.

49.   Cavarero, *Inclinations*, 105.

50.   Leonardo's painting was also called *Saint Anne with Two Others*.

51.   Cavarero may also invite theatricalization of the painting when she says that the unique signification of the Levinasian face that "summons me and commands me not to kill" emerges "from a theater without backdrop" (*Inclinations*, 165).

52.   Notably, Miriam Leonard says, Freud thinks that the picture of Bacchus/St. John is just a compulsive repetition of the St. Anne picture with its enigmatic androgynous smile ("Freud and the Biography of Antiquity," 320).

53.   Said Pozzo (Angela Ottino della Chiesa, *L'opera completa di Leonardo, pittore* [Milan: Rizzoli, 1967], 109, from a document in the Vatican Library, and

see Marilyn Aronberg Lavin, "Giovannino Battista: A Study in Renaissance Religious Symbolism," *Art Bulletin* 37, no. 2 [June 1955]: 85–101).

54.   Also added was a "vine wreath" (S. J. Freedberg, "A Recovered Work of Andrea del Sarto with Some Notes on a Leonardesque Connection," *Burlington Magazine* 124 [May 1982], 285).

55.   Ted Hughes's version ("Tereus," in *Tales from Ovid: 24 Passages from the Metamorphoses* [New York: Farrar, Straus and Giroux, 1999], 236–237) is riveting:

> Still calling to her father
> And to the gods
> And still trying to curse him
> As he caught her tongue with bronze pincers,
> Dragged it out to its full length and cut it
> Off at the root
> The stump recoiled, silenced,
> Into the back of her throat.
> But the tongue squirmed in the dust, babbling on—
> Shaping words that were now soundless.
> It writhed like a snake's tail freshly cut off,
> Striving to reach her feet in its death-struggle.

56.   There is some debate about whether the weaving would have been of words, a written message, or images. See Ingo Gildenhard and Andrew Zissos, "Barbarian Variations: Tereus, Procne and Philomela in Ovid (*Met.* 6.412–674) and Beyond," *Dictynna* 4 (2007): 1–25. See also Dan Curley, "Ovid, *Met.* 6.640: A Dialogue between Mother and Son," *Classical Quarterly* 47, no. 1 (1997): 320–322, whom they cite as well.

57.   Gildenhard and Zissos say that the cannibalization allows the women to "literally 'penetrat[e]' Tereus. . . . Feminizing and grotesquely 'impregnating' her hateful spouse" ("Barbarian Variations," 12). This is a "figurative rape" that, just like Tereus's rape of Philomela, "throws all familial relation into confusion" (12). (The distinction between literal and figurative is also here thrown into confusion.) Notably in Ovid's version of the *Bacchae*, as retold by Hughes, Tiresias's prophecy also depicts a filicidal banquet of flesh, though here the mother and aunts, not the father, consume the son: Tiresias tells Pentheus he has dreamed "Of a banquet / Bacchus will hold for you, Pentheus, / At which you will be not only the guest of honour / But the food and drink. . . . / Your pedigree carcase / Ripped by unthinking fingers." Pentheus is angered by this, but it is "A lifetime too late / To alter himself or his fate" (Hughes, "Bacchus and Pentheus," *Tales from Ovid*, 184–185).

58.   Ovid likely drew on the tragedies. "Ovid transformed tragedy—the *Tereus* of Sophocles [414]—into epic," says Dan Curley, who suggests that Ovid may have drawn also on Euripides's *Medea* (431) and his *Bacchae* (405) (Curley,

"Ovid, *Met*. 6.640," 320). But the lines of influence are complicated. Jennie Marsh argues that Sophocles's *Tereus*, now lost, was itself likely influenced by the *Medea*, since Sophocles's version of the story introduced a new, recognizably Euripidean detail: the deliberate infanticide of Itys by his mother. That detail is in Ovid, too. So do we trace it to the *Medea* (as Curley argues) or to the *Tereus* (which got it from the *Medea*, as Marsh argues)? And what about the *Bacchae*, which Curley says influenced Ovid? Euripides's version of the story might have been influenced by the playwright's own *Medea* and by Sophocles's *Tereus*, too. Curley provides great evidence for some of the lines of influence in "Ovid, *Met*. 6.640." On Sophocles's *Tereus*, see David Fitzpatrick's essay by that name in *Classical Quarterly* 51, no. 1 (July 2001): 90–101, and N. C. Hourmouziades, "Sophocles' *Tereus*," in *Studies in Honor of T. B. L. Webster* (Bristol, UK: Bristol Classical Press, 1986,) 134–142. Nicole Loraux notes, drawing on Hourmouziades, that in "the tragedy that was probably called *Tereus*, . . . despite all his efforts to give an important role to Tereus," Sophocles's "plot revolves around the feminine solidarity between Procne, Philomela, and a chorus of women" (Nicole Loraux, *Mothers in Mourning*, trans. Corinne Pache [Ithaca, NY: Cornell University Press], 57n1).

59.   Why two times: "Mother, Mother"? The dual address may represent the (Kleinian) mother's capacity to love *and* wound: recognizing the wounding mother, the child tries to summon the other, loving, mother. Curley argues that Itys's "Mater, Mater" in Ovid borrows from the story of the *Bacchae*, which was part of the prelude or postlude in Sophocles's *Tereus*. In both, the son recognizes the mother(s) and the mother does not return the favor.

60.   Curley implies in "Ovid, *Met*. 6.640" that Procne's costume as a bacchant is a displacement of the missing disguise of Pentheus as a bacchant, which, in Ovid's retelling of the story of the *Bacchae*, does not occur.

61.   Unlike the sisters in the *Bacchae* who dispute their sister Semele's claim, Procne believes her sister. The line about how to rank sister and son resonates with Antigone's in Sophocles's play, about how there are things she would do for a (natal) brother that she would not for a (conjugal) husband or child. Procne may perhaps even reprise the logic to which Sophocles's Antigone appeals in prioritizing the natal over the conjugal family: with parents dead or too old, the sibling is irreplaceable. But child or husband? I can always have another. See my *Antigone, Interrupted*, chapters 4 and 5, for a detailed reading of the line. I am suggesting now that both Antigone and Procne (and maybe Agave, too) give voice to the tensions of various conflicting kin relations, between the conjugal and natal family, between marital and sororal ties in the double binds of patriarchy.

62.   Gildenhard and Zissos, "Barbarian Variations," 16, emphasis added. Not so in the *Odyssey*'s version of the story, however. Loraux says, "In the *Odyssey*, the murderous mother is not (not yet?) called Procne, but simply Aedon (Nightingale). Mother of an only son, she is jealous of her sister-in-law. . . . Nightingale cannot refrain from killing her rival's eldest son. . . . During the night, Nightingale *mistak-*

enly kills her own son Itylos" (Loraux, *Mothers in Mourning*, 58, emphasis added). Here, the filicide is a mistake committed in "a moment of madness" (Loraux, *Mothers in Mourning*, 60, quoting Homer, *Odyssey*, 19.511–534).

63.   If women's care work is to nurse, as some theorists of care suggest (see Joan Tronto, *Caring Democracy: Markets, Equality, and Justice* [New York: New York University Press, 2013], and Elizabeth K. Markovits, *Future Freedoms: Intergenerational Justice, Democratic Theory, and Ancient Greek Tragedy and Comedy* [New York: Routledge, 2018]), Procne shows here she knows how to do it, nursing her grudge against Tereus for his violence against Philomela and thus furthering her resolve to repay it in kind.

64.   Curley says both become maenads without noting this difference. Other commentators note the difference without underlining the commonality: "Although Procne is dressed up as a maenad in this scene, Ovid makes clear that her Bacchic ecstasy is feigned, a veneer, which, on the level of plot, merely conceals her real intentions and, on the level of poetics, indicates the presence of a different narrative force: the Furies" (Gildenhard and Zissos, "Barbarian Variations," 6).

65.   Bernice Johnson Reagon, "Coalition Politics: Turning the Century," in *Home Girls: A Black Feminist Anthology*, ed. Barbara Smith (New York: Kitchen Table: Women of Color Press, 1983), 343–356.

66.   On the importance of rehearsal to emergency politics but also to the politics of emergence, see Elaine Scarry's *Thinking in an Emergency* (New York: Norton, 2011) and my "Three Models of Emergency Politics," *boundary 2* 41, no. 2 (2014): 45–70. My early reading of Johnson's "Coalition Politics" is in "Difference, Dilemmas, and the Politics of Home," *Social Research* 61, no. 3 (Fall 1994): 563–597, and was revised and republished in *Democracy and Difference: Contesting the Boundaries of the Political*, ed. Seyla Benhabib (Princeton, NJ: Princeton University Press, 1996), 257–277.

67.   Reagon, "Coalition Politics," 355.

3. FABULATION AND THE RIGHT TO THE CITY

1.   As well as "African religion and philosophy," Morrison adds. See Morrison, *Unspeakable Things Unspoken: The Afro-American Presence in American Literature* (The Tanner Lectures on Human Values, University of Michigan, Ann Arbor, 1988.) Thanks to Vaughn Rasberry for reminding me of Morrison in this context. I document below Hartman's debt to Greek tragic forms. My treatment of Hartman's text as a *Bacchae*, like my earlier reading of *The Fits*, is in keeping with some branches of Classical Antiquity Studies in which "reception" is not restricted to texts or images that relate referentially to the ancient world's 'originals.' I hope this reading of *Wayward Lives* and the earlier reading *The Fits* contribute to the great work already ongoing at the intersection of classics, political theory and Black studies by Patrice Rankine, Emily Greenwood, and others including most recently the work of Ferris Lupino on "American Stasis" which studies the reception of classical sources in the

work of Ellison, Baldwin, and Du Bois ("American Stasis," PhD diss., Brown University, 2020).

2.   For my more detailed reading of Morrison's *Home*, see *Shell Shocked: Feminist Criticism After Trump* (Fordham, New York, 2021).

3.   The risk of turning to individuality to remediate the archive's erasures is that the result is a kind of unworlding. I see Hartman as responding to this risk in two ways. First, she makes each life into a world, a Whitmanesque undertaking. Second, she then sets her wayward lives in relation to choruses that offer both worldly and unworldly belonging.

4.   "Sometimes defiant acts may be useless, harmful, and destructive" (138) says Nazan Üstündağ in an excellent essay, "Antigone as Kurdish Politician: Gendered Dwellings in the Limit between Freedom and Peace" (*History of the Present* 9, no. 2 [Fall 2019]: 113–141). She has in mind a death-drive reading of Antigone, which she prefers to what she characterizes as my "sociological" one. I could quibble with that. But she is correct to think I am not willing to allow even failure to fail.

5.   Saidiya Hartman, *Wayward Lives, Beautiful Experiments: Intimate Histories of Social Upheaval* (New York: Norton, 2019), xv.

6.   Hartman, *Wayward Lives*, xiv.

7.   Hartman, *Wayward Lives*, xv. Hartman's wayward women recall the wild roses of June Jordan's "Letter to the Local Police": a "regular profusion . . . growing to no discernible purpose, and according to no perceptible control," made cause for complaint by a neighbor who asks police to curb their growth (*Directed by Desire: The Collected Poems of June* Jordan [Port Townsend, WA: Copper Canyon Press, 2005], 267). Jordan and Hartman retell the story of the wild from the vantage point of loving affirmation.

8.   On Black workers, in a 1993 article, Kelley says, "The most pervasive form of black protest [of work] was simply to leave" (95). Such actions, he called infrapolitical. Kelley charted practices of inoperativity and inclination as infrapolitical practices. He singled out waywardness in particular: "the ability to move represented a crucial step toward empowerment and self-determination; employers and landlords understood this, which explains why so much energy was expended limiting labor mobility and redefining migration as 'shiftlessness,' 'indolence,' or a childlike penchant to wander" (95). Political commentators looking for an organized strike might miss the significance of such protests. See Robin D. G. Kelley, "We Are Not What We Seem," *Journal of American History* 80, no. 1 (June 1993): 75–112.

9.   Hartman, *Wayward Lives*, xiv.

10.   On kinship's possibilities and perversions under slavery, see Felicia Denaud, "Renegade Gestation: Writing Against the Procedures of Intellectual History" in *Black Intellectual History: A JHI Blog Forum*, Oct 23, 2020.

11.   See Shatema Threadcraft, *Intimate Justice: The Black Female Body and the Body Politic* (New York: Oxford University Press, 2016).

12.   The director of *The Fits*, Anna Rose Holmer, is white. In the film, the public health representative who says she is "still working on [her] degree" is likely

white and perhaps so too is the newscaster on television who reports on the fits, but the tiny television screen is blurred and, although Toni seems to be watching, we can only hear the newscast. *The Fits* was originally conceived as a film about dance and contagion, not focused on race. It took its final shape from its (re)location in a Black neighborhood and dance community in Ohio.

13.   Key here is Hartman's decision to include but to render opaque a photograph of a young child, a girl photographed with no clothes on by Thomas Eakins. This recalls the camera work of *The Fits* which both showed and did not show its protagonist, Toni, and the other girls. Kevin Quashie poses questions about the decision to include this image in Hartman's book in his contribution to *Online Roundtable: Saidiya Hartman's* Wayward Lives, Beautiful Experiments (https://www.aaihs.org/online-roundtable-saidiya-hartmans-wayward-lives-beautiful-experiments/).

14.   Hartman describes her text as a "fugitive text of the wayward" (*Wayward Lives*, xv).

15.   I imagine a staging of the play in which the earlier scene where Pentheus preens in front of Dionysus is silently screened, ghostlike, behind Agave as she crows to Cadmus and is then absorbed by his mesmerism, just as Pentheus was, earlier, lured by the god's. This would highlight the parallels between and equal importance of the two agons and it would add to the sense of the first scene's prefigurative powers: it foresees not just Pentheus' doom but also Agave's eventual failure.

16.   Euripides, *Bacchae*, trans. Robin Robertson (New York: Harper Collins, 2014), 1243.

17.   A recent essay highlights the lost liberatory, freedom-oriented qualities of feminism's much criticized second wave, citing Germaine Greer's rather bacchic sentiments at the time: "'We need only set up the preconditions for a free sexuality: whatever forms it took would be assuredly an improvement on what we have now, "natural" in the truest sense. . . . Love and sexuality would be reintegrated, flowing unimpeded.' Writing about this intoxicating moment later, in 1999, Greer recalled that she and many of her cohort had been embarrassed by the contemptuous phrase 'women's lib,' short for 'women's liberation.' Yet she realized that it had signified something essential: 'When the name "Libbers" was dropped for "Feminists" we were all relieved. What none of us noticed was that the ideal of liberation was fading out with the word. We were settling for equality. . . . Women's liberation did not see the female's potential in terms of the male's actual; the visionary feminists of the late sixties and early seventies knew that women could never find freedom by agreeing to live the lives of unfree men. . . . Liberationists sought the world over for clues to what women's lives could be like if they were free to define their own values, order their own priorities and decide their own fates.'" See Liza Featherstone, "Moving beyond Misogyny: Why Do They Hate Us?" *New Republic*, November 4, 2019.

18.   Euripides, *Bacchae*, trans. Robertson, 1206–1207, 1174.

19.   For critiques of recognition's conservative powers, see Patchen Markell, *Bound by Recognition* (Princeton, NJ: Princeton University Press, 2003), and

Glen Coulthard, *Red Skin, White Masks: Rejecting the Colonial Politics of Recognition* (Minneapolis: University of Minnesota Press, 2014).

20.   I discuss the Lacanian idea in Žižek and Zupancic of reformatting the ethical situation in chapter 6 of *Antigone, Interrupted* (New York: Cambridge University Press, 2013).

21.   Euripides, *Bacchae*, trans. Robertson, 1271–1284.

22.   Yulia Ustinova calls it "therapy by words" (*Divine Mania: Alteration of Consciousness in Ancient Greece* [New York: Routledge, 2017]). Butler and Nussbaum differ, but on this one point, the two seem to converge: "At the end of *The Bacchae*, it seems we are in the world of the fully awake, having undergone a quick and painful detoxification and moral awakening" (Judith Butler, "Breaks in the Bond: Reflections on Kinship Trouble," Housman Lecture, UCL, London, 2017). See Martha Nussbaum, Introduction to Euripides, *The Bacchae of Euripides: A New Version*, trans. C. K. Williams (New York: Noonday Press, 1990), vii–xliii. Goff (*Citizen Bacchae*) says Agave is "groping towards normality" (351).

23.   On periperformatives, see Eve Sedgwick, *Touching Feeling: Affect, Pedagogy, Performativity* (Durham, NC: Duke University Press, 2003), and my introduction to *Antigone, Interrupted*.

24.   Euripides, *Bacchae*, trans. Robertson, 1271–1284.

25.   Wohl's reading and mine converge here: "Cadmus recalls Agave to her senses by reconstituting an Oedipal structure and placing her within it. She must remember first her marriage to Echion (1273; marriage exchange is the inverse of Oedipal incest) and then her house, child, and husband" (Victoria Wohl, "Beyond Sexual Difference: Becoming-Woman in Euripides' *Bacchae*," in *The Soul of Tragedy*, ed. Victoria Pedrick and Steven M. Oberhelman [Chicago: University of Chicago Press, 2006], 152n13). I would add that first of all, she must remember her father. Hence her opening, in reply to him, "Yes, Father."

26.   The shepherd admired by Foucault for his truth-telling in Foucault's mention of the *Bacchae* is valued by Foucault for refusing sovereign propaganda. But this thinker who said, "We need to cut off the king's head; in political theory that has yet to be done," misses the moment in the *Bacchae* where that is precisely what happens (Michel Foucault, *Power/Knowledge*, ed. Colin Gordon [New York: Pantheon, 1980], 121).

27.   Raquel Gutiérrez Aguilar, "Against the Day," *South Atlantic Quarterly* 113, no. 2 (July 2018): 676.

28.   I considered this objection earlier but from a different angle, noting that in tragedy as such, people are held responsible for things they do unknowingly.

29.   Euripides, *Medea and Other Plays*, trans. Philip Vellacott (New York: Penguin, 1973), 1078–1081.

30.   Euripides, *Medea and Other Plays*, trans. Vellacott, 1107–1108.

31.   In Chapter 2, I referred to James Martel's work on this topic. I note here the interesting exploration by Marisa J. Fuentes in *Dispossessed Lives: Enslaved*

Women, Violence and the Archive (Philadelphia: University of Pennsylvania Press, 2016), especially chapter 4, concerning the legal decrees regarding the burial of executed slaves in the eighteenth century. Arguably, the new burial laws, which Fuentes charts and which seek to disappear the dead body into the sea, testify also to the corpse's power, as well as its powerlessness. Thanks to Tim Huzar for directing me to Fuentes's work.

32.   The who and the what are Arendt's terms. Who we are is the performative product of action in concert and the basis of stories to be told of our actions. What we are is our sociological identity, the traits from which, Arendt says, though I have disagreed, nothing new can come. For Arendt's view, see *The Human Condition* (Chicago: University of Chicago Press, 1998). My critique is in *Political Theory and the Displacement of Politics* (Ithaca, NY: Cornell University Press, 1993), and "Toward an Agonistic Feminism," in *Feminist Interpretations of Hannah Arendt* (University Park: Pennsylvania State University Press, 1995).

33.   This idea that the women's actions attenuate their proper roles and that the play, through Cadmus, illustrates the power and costs of their restoration fits with Sheila Murnaghan's claim that Euripides and tragedy as a genre explore the difficult transition from daughter to wife amid tragedies of single motherhood (especially in the *Ion* and the *Bacchae*, which she compares). See Sheila Murnaghan, "The Daughters of Cadmus: Chorus and Characters in Euripides' *Bacchae* and *Ion*," *Bulletin of the Institute of Classical Studies, Supplement, Greek Drama III: Essays in Honour of Kevin Lee* 87 (2006): 99–112.

34.   Cadmus is the keeper of the archive (Thoreau credits him with the invention of letters in "Walking") and Agave is its disturbance.

35.   See, for example, Olga Taxidou, "Dionysus and Divine Violence: A Reading of 'The Bacchae,'" *Journal of Literature and Trauma Studies* 1, no. 1 (2012): 1–13. And Sheila Murnaghan: "In keeping with the play's meta-theatrical character, each group of women reflects more openly than most tragic choruses do, the conditions of being in a chorus" ("The Daughters of Cadmus," 100).

36.   Euripides, *Bacchae*, trans. Robertson, 295–298.

37.   Other commentators see the play as a warning to the city about the excesses of Dionysian revelry.

38.   Hartman, *Wayward Lives*, 65. This is her description of Mattie Nelson, but it applies also to Hartman's writing practice: a craft that works with limited resources "to make a feast of meager opportunities" (55). An errancy of its own.

39.   Euripides, *Bacchae*, trans. Robertson, 1236–1237.

40.   Hartman, *Wayward Lives*, 128.

41.   Hartman, *Wayward Lives*, 92.

42.   Relatedly, see Noga Rotem, *(Post) Paranoid Politics from Hobbes to Arendt*, (PhD. Dissertation, Brown University, Fall 2020) on the salon of Rahel Varnhagen as a refusal to be pathologized.

43.   Thanks to Lori Marso for calling my attention to this important near miss, a nod to the a-political anonymity of the city and its political possibilities at

the same time. On Goldman, see Kathy Ferguson, *Emma Goldman: Political Thinking in the Streets* (Plymouth, UK: Rowman and Littlefield) 2011. On anarchist walking, see Ferguson, "Anarchist Women and the Politics of Walking" and responses by Marso and Annie Menzel in *Political Research Quarterly* 70 (4): 708–719, 720–727, and 728–734.

44.   See W. E. B. Du Bois, *Black Reconstruction in America: Toward a History of the Part Which Black Folk Played in the Attempt to Reconstruct Democracy in America, 1860–1880* (New York: Harcourt, Brace, 1935). Du Bois rejected the Dunning school's historiography, which cast the enslaved as docile and subservient pawns in a Civil War that was a white man's conflict proclaimed to be about anything but slavery. Du Bois noted that when enslaved people left the plantations in droves, this was not mere flight or even fugitivity but a "swarming" out in a general strike and into the Union armies to fight. Active agents of their own emancipation, Black men were engaged in a massive refusal and were themselves the ones who redirected the meaning of the war from the preservation of the Union to slave emancipation. On the historiography then and since, see Guy Emerson Mount: "The North and the South had apparently fought gallantly over just about anything and everything but slavery—emerging in the end as a divinely unified and thoroughly perfected nation. Du Bois fought back" ("When Slaves Go on Strike: W. E. B. Du Bois's *Black Reconstruction* 80 Years Later," December 28, 2015, https://www.aaihs .org/when-slaves-go-on-strike/). The noun and verb swarm/ed recur in Du Bois's text (e.g., 65, 68, 84) as in Hartman's, part of her effort to enter the wayward into Du Bois' ledger of refusal.

45.   Saidiya Hartman, "The Belly of the World: A Note on Black Women's Labors," *Souls*, Vol. 18, No. 1, January–March 2016, 166–173: "So where exactly does the sex drudge, recalcitrant domestic, broken mother, or sullen wet-nurse fit into the scheme of the general strike? If the general strike is a placeholder for political aspirations that Du Bois struggles to name, how does the character of the slave female's refusal augment the text of black radicalism? Is it at all possible to imagine her as the paradigmatic slave or as the representative black worker?" Thanks to Nica Siegel for questions that led me back to this essay by Hartman. Hartman builds on Alys Eve Weinbaum, who notes the agency of women on the plantation and as part of the general strike, and cites Angela Davis's "Reflections on the Black Woman's Role in the Community of Slaves" as the first in a series. Weinbaum says, "One of the central 'truths' *Black Reconstruction* proffers is that of the slave as 'the black worker' and of slaves, en masse, as agents of human emancipation. But what of the other 'truths'? . . . It is here that black feminism enters [with] a unique, future-oriented response. . . . When read in and through its exchange with *Black Reconstruction*, black feminism emerges as nothing less than a new 'propaganda of history'—a counternarrative insistent on accounting for enslaved women and, too, for the continued relevance of the story of enslaved women's protest against their reproductive and sexual exploitation in the moment of black feminist elaboration" (Alys Eve Weinbaum, "Gendering the General Strike: W. E. B. Du Bois's *Black Reconstruction*

and Black Feminism's 'Propaganda of History,'" *South Atlantic Quarterly* 112, no. 3 [2013]: 447).

46.   Euripides, *Bacchae*, trans. T. A. Buckley (London: Henry G. Bohn, 1850), 680–682.

47.   Hartman, *Wayward Lives*, 282. Book 3 opens with an image of action in concert: women holding hands in neatly arranged rows like soldiers or a church chorus, at a 1917 anti-lynching march. On the other side of the same page, another image of another concerted action: an organized parade made up almost entirely of men standing in groups (215–216). The sign at the center of the second image says, "THE NEW NEGRO HAS NO FEAR." An image labeled "Girls fleeing police during riot" is one prior image of collective action (Hartman, *Wayward Lives*, 170).

48.   Hartman, *Wayward Lives*, 279, 282. "This riot, like the ones that preceded it and the ones that would follow, was not unusual. What was unusual was that the riot had been reported at all" (280). The "chorus spoke with one voice" and rioted "collectively" (279). The words Hartman uses to describe the women who rioted are *en masse, ensemble, crowded, huddled, complete revolution,* a *collective body,* and a *discordant assembly* (283). Also featured are *anarchy, tumult, gathering together,* and *refusal to be governed* (285). With their "collective utterance," the women are said to express a "utopian impulse," which in the face of all evidence to the contrary, assumed that someone outside the walls of the prison might care.

49.   Hartman, *Wayward Lives*, 279. The *Times* said the incarcerated women "pounded the walls with their fists, finding a shared and steady rhythm that they hoped might topple the cottage and make the walls crumble, smash the cots, destroy the reformatory" (279).

50.   For example, Bedford Hills sentenced parolees to work in the homes of White people in upstate New York, treating servitude as rehabilitation. "Parole meant being barred from the city, separated from family and friends, and forced into the grueling work that made the Mr. and Mrs. of the private home into wardens of the state, bureaucrat and overseers of domestic space. General housework was the sentence that awaited you after the first sentence had been completed. To the eyes of a conscripted domestic, the white household was an extension of the prison" (Hartman, *Wayward Lives*, 267).

51.   Hartman, *Wayward Lives*, 263.

52.   Hartman, *Wayward Lives*, 276.

53.   Hartman, *Wayward Lives*, 299. The words used by Hartman to describe this chorus are *dreamers, artists, idlers, faggots, communists, lady lovers,* and more. They engage in acts of "flight," "escape," and "migration," and when they move, they either "rush" (into the city), "stroll" (down Lenox Avenue), or dance (299). Later, they are a "multitude," and their members "anonymous members of the ensemble," "the crowd," or "one among the chorus" (301).

54.   Gender conformism and social conservatism are traits of the ancient chorus, though not all classicists agree on this. For classicist Page duBois, the

chorus is one of the three features of tragedy on behalf of which the calls for "toppling the hero." See Page duBois, "Toppling the Hero: Polyphony in the Tragic City," *New Literary History* 35, no. 1 (Winter 2004): 63–81. But the chorus in the ancient world may also recenter the hero, if Sheila Murnaghan is right that the institution manages women's transition from girl to wife to mother (i.e., from father to husband to son) in accordance with social expectations. (This would put that chorus in the same place, psychologically and socially speaking, as the dance troupe in *The Fits*.) Between the socially assigned roles of daughter and wife are moments of individuation and desire that exceed the social roles' powers to domesticate women. These moments of individuation or desire interrupt the otherwise reliable "traffic in women." The chorus and even tragedy itself thematize this problem of individuation, Murnaghan argues, "Many female choruses were concerned specifically with the initiation of young women into the stage of life in which they would become eligible for marriage" ("The Daughters of Cadmus," 103).

55.   Hartman, *Wayward Lives*, 302.

56.   The chapter follows the chorus line members from theater to cabaret to dance floor. It is sometimes unclear in Hartman's text which of these she is describing when she attributes to the dancers a "shared body" and "a common rhythm," moving "in concert" and "communicating . . . as if all were coordinated." It may not matter since, as Hartman says, the chorus line, the theater, the cabaret, and the dance floor offered their "own constraint and [their] own freedom" (*Wayward Lives*, 303). So, too, does the orgy or, as I called it earlier, the salon of sexual inquiry, another scene of collectivity, to which Mabel is brought by her white girlfriend, Ruth (321–323). Here, the chorus and the acts imagined by Pentheus finally converge over two thousand years after the fact, as "the public sex and collective lovemaking . . . effaced the lines of social division, unmade men and women . . . [and made] eros into communal luxury" (324–325).

57.   Hartman, *Wayward Lives*, 299.

58.   Hartman, *Wayward Lives*, 302.

59.   Hartman, *Wayward Lives*, 347.

60.   As its members, Hartman lists "Muses, drudges, washerwomen, whores, house workers, factory girls, waitresses, and aspiring but never-to-be stars" (*Wayward Lives*, 345).

61.   "The Greek etymology of the word *chorus* refers to *dance within an enclosure*," Hartman says. Dance and enclosure signal the twin conditions of tragedy: freedom and constraint. And when Hartman says of the last of her three choruses, that it "bears it all for us," she recurs to the work of tragedy as an art form: to make the pain of living bearable. "All sorrows can be borne if put into a story," Arendt said, quoting Isak Dinesen (perhaps already thinking of the city whose enclosure will bear it). This is Hartman's move, too, and Du Bois's when they discuss the sorrow songs.

62.   The Theban chorus is made up of three, we find out from the messenger who refers to three bands of women on Cithaeron: Agave and her sisters, Ino and Autonoe, each leads one of the bands. The Asian chorus arrives in Thebes with Dio-

nysus from afar; there are also the men who seek to join the worship wittingly (Cadmus and Tiresias) and unwittingly (Pentheus himself).

63.   Hartman, *Wayward Lives*, 348.

64.   On wilderness as ritual, see Delores S. Williams, *Sisters in the Wilderness: the Challenge of Womanist God-Talk*, noting "A connection between the wilderness and religious experience has been made by African Americans for hundreds of years" (98). Williams quotes William Allen who "described the kind of ritual movement slaves associated with the wilderness in the nineteenth century" as comparable to "the ancient bacchants" (99). I am grateful to Dan-el Padilla Peralta for this reference.

65.   Although as I noted earlier in the Introduction, there is some ambiguity about how handholding signifies in the classical context.

66.   Hartman, *Wayward Lives*, 349.

67.   Arendt, *The Human Condition*, 198.

68.   It is important to note, though, that even as she assigns fabulation to the city, Arendt offers her own fabulation, which is her vying for the right to the city. Also, notably, Arendt says the Greek polis is not "its physical location"—it rather "arises out of acting and speaking together," and this alone constitutes its "true space" (*The Human Condition*, 183, 198), but she also talks about the need for a walled place for the stories of the in-between to be told and retold. And something like this combination of portability and discreteness seems to appeal to Judith Butler as well. Meeting the body's needs in a public setting, joining together to provide food, water, toilets, and so on, the assembled "enact the very principles of democracy for which [the assembly] struggles," Butler explains (*Notes toward a Performative Theory of Assembly* [Cambridge, MA: Harvard University Press, 2015], 217–218). The pressing needs of the body, which, Butler notes critically, Arendt wanted to make irrelevant to politics, here occasion a politics of common cause. Together, prompted by these needs, the assembled build an infrastructure. The toilets do not just meet needs; they are part of a public, shared infrastructure that is needed for independent reasons: as infrastructure, it unites and separates those it gathers.

69.   Euripides, *Bacchae*, trans. Robertson, 1169–1212.

70.   Arendt, *The Human Condition*, 199.

71.   Arendt, *The Human Condition*, 198.

72.   David Harvey, "The Right to the City," *New Left Review* 53 (Fall 2008). See also Pauline Lipman, *The New Political Economy of Urban Education: Neoliberalism, Race, and the Right to the City* (New York: Taylor & Francis, 2011). David Harvey's *Rebel Cities: From the Right to the City to the Urban Revolution* (New York: Verso, 2013) develops a critique of the right to the city as still a right, meaning it is sovereign and individualizing. But Margaret Kohn replies, building on Henri Lefebvre's work, to argue in favor of the right to the city as a hetero-right, "dialectical-political" rather than "abstract-philosophical" (*The Death and Life of the Urban Commonwealth* [New York: Oxford University Press, 2016], 11). Kohn "tries to sustain a productive tension between an account of the common-wealth [or city] as an

object of struggle and a course of solidarity" (3). Her call to trade in the tragedy of the commons for the "comedy of the commons where we build something and enjoy it together" (12) resonates with the practices of urban claiming and play explored in Davina Cooper's *Feeling like a State: Desire, Denial, and the Recasting of Authority* (Durham, NC: Duke University Press, 2019).

73.   Or better, we could say that rather than reject the city as a lost cause, an affirmative politics of refusal might embrace it for that reason. On the politics of the lost cause, see Lida Maxwell, *Public Trials: Burke, Zola, Arendt, and the Politics of Lost Causes* (New York: Oxford University Press, 2014), and Jack Halberstam, *The Queer Art of Failure* (Durham, NC: Duke University Press, 2011). In my view, the project of highlighting the affirmations of refusal developed here finds affinities with Tina Campt's development of Black visuality as a practice of refusal in which she casts refusal as "a rejection of the status quo as livable and the creation of possibility in the face of negation . . . using negation as a generative and creative source of disorderly power to embrace the possibility of living otherwise" (Tina Campt, "Black Visuality and the Practice of Refusal," *Women and Performance* 29, no. 1 [2019]: 83).

74.   The *Bacchae*'s "narrative of female aggression offer[s] to the women's violence only one, self-incriminating male scapegoat," Pentheus, not "the entire masculine polity," says Barbara Goff (*Citizen Bacchae*, 137). But Goff does note the bacchants are a "city of women" (214), which could suggest they have designs on the city.

75.   Hannah Arendt, *On Revolution* (New York: Penguin, 1990), 133, emphasis added.

76.   Arendt, *On Revolution*, 133–134. For Nietzsche, we know, the Dionysian was partnered with the Apollinian. He is echoed when Arendt identifies happiness with the American revolution and connects a kind of drunkenness with that of the French. She worries that the Americans need a little more Dionysus and the French a little less. She does not note it but such public drunkenness would signify differently on the policed American streets of the wayward in 1920 than in the vicinity of the Paris commune.

77.   But how to (re)tell the story? The question of genre is raised by Ta-Nehisi Coates in *Between the World and Me* (New York: Spiegel & Grau, 2015), commenting on a museum that tells the US Civil War story "as though the fall of the confederacy were the onset of a tragedy, not jubilee." W. E. B. Du Bois's *Black Reconstruction in America* sequenced the two genres and argued that what began as jubilee became tragedy, "the unending tragedy of Reconstruction." From the general strike of the Civil War era to the backlash of Jim Crow, Du Bois said, the United States authored "a tragedy that beggared the Greek." Du Bois details the massive violence that was leveraged against people of color whom he ennobles in iconic tragic terms: faced with unbearable suffering, they "have made withal a brave and fine fight" (*Black Reconstruction*, 708). Similarly, Hartman dusts off the so-called deviant Black women of last century's turn and finds in their non-normative practices the "brave and fine fight" of a noble social movement whose revolutionary, riotous noise is blanketed by claims of docility, idleness, deviance,

and pathology. Her fabulation collects from the past the salons, backyards, and alleyways that are familiar grounds to political organizers now. When she absorbs Du Bois' vocabulary into her own account of the wayward women, she presses for the full inclusion of the women he slighted.

78.   On new rights as parts of a transformative politics, see Bonnie Honig, *Emergency Politics: Paradox, Law, Democracy* (Princeton University Press, 2009).

79.   I owe the argument developed in these last few pages, which I added late to Chapter 3, to Annette Gordon-Reed's Fall 2020 review of Hartman's book in the *New York Review of Books* ("Rebellious History," *NYRB*, October 22, 2020); to Neil Roberts who read some early pages on it; to Vaughn Rasberry, whose unspoken hesitations provoked a rethinking on my part, late in the day; to the Yale Classics colloquium, which discussed the review with me the day after it came out; and specifically to the discussant comments and questions posed in that forum by Nica Siegel, Nebojsa Todorovic, and Katherine Ponds, as well as Emily Greenwood and Lindsay Stern.

80.   Presumably this is why Keeanga Yamahtta Taylor calls it genre defying ("Saidiya Hartman's 'Beautiful Experiments,'" *Los Angeles Review of Books*, May 5, 2019). I think its genre is tragedy. What it defies is familiar disciplinary specialization. As Gordon-Reed points out, "*Wayward Lives* won a 2019 National Book Critics Circle Award in the category of 'Criticism,' perhaps indicating some difficulty in classifying it."

81.   See *Thomas Jefferson and Sally Hemings: An American Controversy* (Charlottesville: University of Virginia Press, 1997) and *The Hemingses of Monticello: An American Family* (New York: W.W. Norton, 2008).

82.   To "topple the hero," Page duBois says, is the aim of her own readings of Greek tragedy, and Hartman cites her. Hartman hero-topples too (and I do not just mean her critique of Du Bois' Philadelphia study). Here is an example: the title of Hartman's book names as wayward not certain women, but *lives*. I have not attended to this, but we could see this as a move to de-personalize the bits of biography she finds in the archive. It puts a commons in place of heroes. Turning the archive's pathologized "cases" into trajectories and its biographical bits into swarms, as she says with Du Bois, Hartman's next move, alongside this one, is to biographize. She personifies those trajectories and swarms in a counter-archival storytelling that brings certain women and their joyous freedom to life.

CONCLUSION

1.   When Agamben turns his attention later in the *The Use of Bodies* (trans. Adam Kotsko [Stanford, CA: Stanford University Press, 2015]) primarily to use (not inoperativity), the result is a monastic rumination that ends in the embrace of contemplation.

2.   Things have changed since then in the world of political theory, where rioting, like marching and other practices of protest and dissent, is now seen as le-

gitimately expressive and possessed of normative import. On this convergence in the 1960s and 1970s, see Jonathan Havercroft: "Three of the giants of 20th century political theory, Hannah Arendt, John Rawls, and Michael Walzer all wrote on rioting and political protest in the wake of the 1960s riots in the U.S. All three argued that riots were illegitimate because they were violent, whereas non-violent civil disobedience was a legitimate mode of political protest. . . . I've come to see these three texts as a crucial moment of foreclosure that made rioting simply beyond the pale of legitimate political action. This is doubly frustrating with Walzer given his central role in reviving the just war tradition in light of the Vietnam War." Havercroft also notes that "the best analyses of riots and rioting had been done by historians" and highlights "E. P. Thompson's work in particular." See Jonathan Havercroft, "Riots and Political Theory: A Reading List," June 11, 2020, https://www.jonathanhavercroft.com/blog/2020/6/11/riots-and-political-theory-a-reading-list.

3.   Hannah Arendt, *Crises of the Republic* (New York: Harcourt Brace, 1972), 65.

4.   On this and criticizing Walzer on this precise point with regard to Ali, see Lionel K. McPherson, "Individual Self-Defense in War," in *The Cambridge Handbook of the Just War*, ed. Larry May (New York: Cambridge University Press, 2017), 135–151.

5.   See especially recent work by Juliet Hooker ("Black Lives Matter and the Paradoxes of U.S. Black Politics: From Democratic Sacrifice to Democratic Repair" in *Political Theory* 44, no. 4 (August 2016), 448–-469; Alexander Livingston, "Martin Luther King Knew That There's Nothing Peaceful About Nonviolence If You're Doing It Right," in *Jacobin*, June 10, 2020; and Erin Pineda, *Seeing Like an Activist: Civil Disobedience and the Civil Rights Movement* (New York: Oxford University Press, 2021).

6.   On the importance of "threads" as a figure for the work of theory and especially criticism, see Bonnie Honig, *Shellshocked: Feminist Criticism after Trump* (New York: Fordham University Press, 2021).

7.   Jane C. Hu, "What's Really Going On at Seattle's So-Called Autonomous Zone?" *Slate*, June 16, 2020.

8.   I draw on the subtitle of Jane C. Hu's article: "Failed Experiment by Radical Anarchists, a New Sort of Utopia, or Just a Place?" *Slate*, June 16, 2020.

9.   "One major misconception about CHAZ is that protesters 'seized' the space from the police. It's really more like the police left the area, and the protesters who were already invested in a round-the-clock occupation of the Seattle Police Department's East Precinct continued staying there. On June 1, protesters began demonstrating at SPD's Capitol Hill precinct building nightly, and most nights, police used flash-bangs and chemical irritants like pepper spray and tear gas to disperse the crowd around the barriers it erected in the blocks surrounding the precinct—including June 7, just two days after Mayor Jenny Durkan announced a 30-day moratorium on tear gas. On June 8, the SPD removed its barricades and suddenly vacated the building. SPD and the city government braced for violence, saying it

had received 'credible information about a potential intent to set fire to the East Precinct.' At the time, it was not clear to the general public why the SPD left the East Precinct or whether it would be back. It's since become clear that Durkan had ordered the decision, one police Chief Carmen Best said she was angry about. At a press conference Thursday, Durkan said she made the decision in hopes it would de-escalate the conflict between police and protesters" (Hu, "What's Really Going On").

10.   Bernice Johnson Reagon, "Coalition Politics: Turning the Century," in *Home Girls: A Black Feminist Anthology*, ed. Barbara Smith (New York: Kitchen Table, 1983), 355.

APPENDIX

1.   Corey Robin, "Lavatory and Liberty: The Secret History of the Bathroom Break," *Boston Globe*, September 29, 2002. "But," Robin continues, "where Ford sought to speed up the meal's entrance into the body, his successors—from store managers in the Midwest to fashion moguls in New York—have concentrated on slowing down its exit" so as not to lose time to the bathroom break. In Naomi Klein's *The Shock Doctrine: The Rise of Disaster Capitalism* (New York: Picador, 2007), we learn that Ford exported hunger, in this case, to Argentina: "Before the coup," she says, "Ford had been forced to make significant concession to its workers: one hour off for lunch instead of twenty minutes," for example. Afterward, things changed. "While Ford provided the junta with cars, the junta provided Ford with a service of its own—ridding the assembly lines of troublesome trade unionists" (42). For more on the bathroom break and its mirror, the drug test, see Alex Gourevitch and Corey Robin: "The first obligation of the employee is to abide by the rule or obey the command of their employer. That can mean that they must urinate—or are forbidden to urinate. It can mean that they should be sexually appealing—or must not be sexually appealing. They may be told how to speak, what to say, whom to say it to, where to be, where to go, how to dress, when to eat, and what to read—all in the name of the job" ("Freedom Now," *Polity* 52, no. 3 [July 2020]: 384–398).

2.   On the sit-down strike, see Marc Stears, *Demanding Democracy: American Radicals in Search of a New Democracy* (Princeton, NJ: Princeton University Press, 2010).

3.   Gabriel Winant, "Life under the Algorithm: How a Relentless Speedup Is Reshaping the Working Class," *New Republic*, December 4, 2019. According to Winant, this "spread rapidly across the world's workplaces. The bargain between [Noll] and Taylor represented the explicit formulation of what would become the defining compromise of twentieth-century American capitalism: increase your output, get paid more: wages go up with productivity" until they don't.

4.   What Benjamin calls Chaplin's "innervation" is the corporeal partner to Deleuze's stutter. "The writer who becomes a stutterer in language . . . makes the language as such stutter: an affective and intensive language and no longer an af-

fectation of the one who speaks," says Gilles Deleuze in "He Stuttered," in *Essays Critical and Clinical*, trans. Daniel W. Smith and Michael A. Greco (Minneapolis: University of Minnesota Press, 1997), 107–114.

5.   In *The Human Condition*, Arendt puts food and the machinery of production into two different categories, as we saw above regarding the *Bacchae*: labor (fermentation/food preparation for consumption) and work (loom/making of lasting objects for use). The acceleration of food consumption, depicted by Chaplin and promoted by Ford, violates Arendt's distinctions, which is a way to mark the wrong. In a different way, all three of Arendt's categories of activity—labor, work, and action—are suspended and violated by Butler, deliberately, to criticize Arendt for her failure in *The Human Condition* to understand how bodily needs that we all have (for food, shelter) might generate the powerful community-building that results from concerted action to meet them. When protestors occupying a public place or square organize to meet the bodily needs of comrades and allies with tents, food, and toilets, the assembly invokes (culinarily and otherwise) a future whose ordinary operations can be like this extraordinary present in which provisions are collectively provided and enjoyed, needs are used not to rank people against one another (say, on a scale of resilience) but to join them together in shared vulnerability, and the proximity of shared membership inspires collectivity. This is what it means to join the "assembly" and take part in it. For a more critical take on Butler's focus on bodily vulnerability, on behalf of something more such as solidarity, and closer to an Arendt-style reading of the scene, see Ali Aslam, who asks, "What are the limits of conceiving of democracy in terms of mutual vulnerability?" (*Ordinary Democracy: Sovereignty and Citizenship beyond the Neoliberal Impasse* [New York: Oxford University Press, 2017], 22). Aslam criticizes Butler for focusing on the ethical and neglecting, therefore, democracy's dependence on both "extra juridical [presumably, ethical] and juridical forms of power." If fear of the other was transcended at the assembly in Cairo, it was not as a result of tending to universal bodily needs but rather as a result of activists' work "to address the fear—fear of the police and fear of sectarian violence—that the regime had used to extend its rule [through] exemplary spectacles of interfaith cooperation . . . involving human chains of Christians protecting Muslim worshippers on Fridays and Muslims standing guard during Sunday Mass. Together these spectacles conveyed and generated evidence of cooperation and trust among all Egyptians" (23).

6.   Winant, "Life under the Algorithm."

7.   See June Purvis, "Cat and Mouse: Force Feeding the Suffragettes," *BBC History Extra*, November 26, 2018, https://www.historyextra.com/period/edwardian /cat-mouse-force-feeding-suffragettes-hunger-strike/. On contemporary force-feeding of hunger strikers, see Banu Bargu, *Starve and Immolate: The Politics of Human Weapons* (New York: Columbia University Press, 2016), Anna Terwiel, "Hungering for Change" (PhD dissertation., Northwestern University, 2014), and Charles P. Pierce, "Force-Feeding Is Torture, and the United States Government Is Doing It in Your Name," *Esquire*, February 4, 2019. On control of the workday and its rechoreography of

the working body, see these videos (for which I thank Shannon Mattern) on "voice picking": "How Voice Picking Works—Voice Beyond," YouTube Video, 1:46, April 6, 2019, https://www.youtube.com/watch?v=gzoz8khyyUs; Honeywell Intelligrated, "Voice Picking System," YouTube Video, 0:49, November 28, 2017, https://www.youtube.com/watch?v=U4EJOiCwSR8.

8.   This would fulfill Ford's dream, but after a promising start, the machine accelerates too fast. The next glitch of the machine is caused by an upper level manager's mistake, when he puts on one of the plates some nuts from bolts he has removed. The machine starts up again and gives the Tramp the metal to swallow instead of food. When he spits some of them back out again, he mirrors another scene in which he is swallowed by the machine on the line and is then spit back out again. This is significant, since if the feeding machine were to work, the Tramp and all humans would become machine(-like): eating on command. There is some sad irony in the fact that Ford's son Edsel died of stomach cancer (David Lanier Lewis, *The Public Image of Henry Ford: An American Folk Hero and His Company* [Detroit, MI: Wayne State University Press], 365).

9.   Jason Zinoman, "A Bird's-Eye View of Both Romance and Horror," *New York Times*, February 17, 2012.

10.   BWW News Desk, "Erin Courtney's *A Map of Virtue* to Make West Coast Debut in November," *Broadway World*, September 21, 2017, https://www.broadwayworld.com/los-angeles/article/Erin-Courtneys-A-MAP-OF-VIRTUE-to-Make-West-Coast-Debut-in-November-20170921.

11.   Margaret Gray, "Review: 'A Map of Virtue' Leads in New Directions, but Do We Really Want to Join the Ride?" *Los Angeles Times*, November 16, 2017.

12.   Courtney, *A Map of Virtue*.

13.   But, he says, the twist "is ultimately less important than the way it exposes the relationships in the play." Zinoman, "A Bird's-Eye View."

14.   Later, in the Vassar production I saw, all three of the hostages are seen alive but wet and bedraggled (*A Map of Virtue*, Erin Courtney, directed by Turner Hitt, produced by the Philaletheis Society, Vassar College, Poughkeepsie, NY, April 12–14, 2018). This test has a history. Gordon L. Rottman records the use of it in *US Marine Rifleman 1939–45: Pacific Theater* (Oxford: Osprey, 2006) and (writing with Derrick Wright) in *Hell in the Pacific: The Battle for Iwo Jima* (London: Bloomsbury, 2008). It is later featured routinely in anime as a school punishment "local" to Japan until 1970. Earlier, right after the war, the punishment was used by the Japanese in Korea, as recorded in the Kang Kwi-Mi story, "A Tale of Music" (in *Literature from the "Axis of Evil": Writing from Iran, Iraq, North Korea and Other Enemy Nations*, ed. Alane Mason [New York. Words Without Borders, 2006], 103–129).

15.   Richard Henry Pratt, *Battlefield and Classroom: Four Decades with the American Indian, 1867–1904* (New Haven, CT: Yale University Press, 1964). See also the story of Bill Wright, sent as a child to the Stewart Indian School in Nevada at the age of six, as told by NPR ("American Indian Boarding Schools Haunt Many,"

NPR Morning Edition, May 12, 2008, https://www.npr.org/templates/story/story
.php?storyId=16516865). See also Toby Rollo, "Consent and Colonial Pedagogies:
Decolonizing Education from Residential to Public Schooling," in *Troubling Truth
and Reconciliation in Canadian Education Critical Perspectives*, ed. Arlo Kempf
and Sandra Styles (Edmonton: University of Alberta, in press) on the continuities
between the residential system and public school systems that pursue "assimilation"
of Native children, and Steve Burgess, "They Hid Him from Residential School, He
Grew to Be Chief," *Tyee*, October 30, 2019.

16.   Courtney, *A Map of Virtue*.

17.   Courtney, *A Map of Virtue*.

18.   Lucy Tapahonso, "For More Than 100 Years, the U.S. Forced Navajo
Students into Western Schools. The Damage Is Still Felt Today," *Smithsonian Magazine*, July 2016. I read now about the incredibly cruel Mohawk Institute Residential School in Toronto and the small resistances of the young children there who
squirreled away candies and other "treasures," such as a silver gum wrapper. See
Louise Brown, "Giving a Voice to Residential School Ghosts," *Toronto Star*, July 2,
2016. Another such "treasure," found recently in a box concealed in a wall, is a
picture of a bird on the back of a matchbook. Only several hours after seeing the
photograph do I realize it reminds me of a Joseph Cornell box (photographed by
Lucas Oleniuk/Toronto Star, 2016).

19.   Courtney, *A Map of Virtue*.

20.   In this sense, she reminds me of John Coetzee's Elizabeth Costello,
haunted by the Holocaust, who sees skin and the flesh of human and animal dead
everywhere. She is tuned in to something to which others are deaf(ened). Her inclination is at the center of Coetzee's *The Lives of Animals* (Princeton, NJ: Princeton
University Press, 1999).

21.   NATE: Since when do you have to earn a tattoo?

> SARAH: I just feel like I stole them, that's all.
> NATE: Oh, you paid for them; I was there.
> SARAH: I just want to start over.
> NATE: Oh-kay.
> SARAH: It doesn't mean anything. It doesn't mean a thing. (Courtney,
>   *A Map of Virtue*.)

22.   The desire to start over can be damaging—those who seek a new world or
new beginning too often do violence to the old—but it can also be a reckoning. For
my critique of Hannah Arendt on "new beginnings," see "What Is Agonism?," in
"The 'Agonistic Turn': *Political Theory and the Displacement of Politics* in New Contexts," *Contemporary Political Theory*, 18, no. 4 (December 2019): 640–672.

23.   The frescoes hang in the Palazzo Pubblico. It is assumed they were hung
there to influence governmental decision making.

24.   *What Is Democracy?* directed by Astra Taylor (The National Film Board
of Canada, 2018).

25.   In *States without Nations: Citizenship for Mortals* (New York: Columbia University Press, 2010), Jacqueline Stevens points out that after a while, the newly drawn spaces generated new interests of their own.

26.   Josiah Ober, "'I Besieged That Man': Democracy's Revolutionary Start," in *Origins of Democracy in Ancient Greece*, ed. Kurt A. Raaflaub, Josiah Ober, and Robert W. Wallace (Berkeley: University of California Press, 2007), 87. The debate among classicists was canvassed in the 1990s by Charles W. Hedrick: "Some have seen [Cleisthenes] as a selfless aristocrat who wanted to help the common people (Victor Ehrenberg); others as a cynical schemer who tried to gerrymander the state to increase the influence of his own family and failed (David Lewis). Most recently, Josiah Ober has argued . . . that the foundation should be understood as the awakening of a collective political consciousness, the occasion of which was an uprising, a moment of violence" ("Review of *Cleisthenes the Athenian: An Essay on the Representation of Space and Time in Greek Political Thought from the End of the Sixth Century to the Death of Plato* by Pierre Lévêque, Pierre Vidal-Naquet, David Ames Curtis; and *Taming Democracy: Models of Political Rhetoric in Classical Athens* by Harvey Yunis," *Political Theory* 26, no. 3 [June 1998]: 413–418).

27.   Ober, "'I Besieged That Man,'" 88.

28.   Wikipedia attributes the "father of Athenian democracy" reference to Thomas R. Martin, Barbara H. Rosenwein, and Bonnie G. Smith, *The Making of the West, Peoples and Cultures: A Concise History, Volume I: To 1740* (Boston and New York: Bedford / St. Martin's, 2007), 44.

29.   For conversation about Ali, I am grateful to Tricia Rose, Andre Willis, Rudy Sayres, Ariella Azoulay, George Shulman and the CSREA at Brown University.

30.   Caroline Alexander offers a less outrageous, more conventional but also enlightening classicizing comparison in her book on the *Iliad*, *The War that Killed Achilles: The True Story of Homer's Iliad and the Trojan War* (New York: Penguin, 2009). Says reviewer Dwight Garner, she compares Achilles's speech refusing Agamemnon to "Muhammad Ali's refusal ('I ain't got no quarrel with the Viet Cong') to fight in the Vietnam War. . . . Achilles, among whose first acts, early in 'The Iliad,' is to challenge the authority of his commander, Agamemnon [says]: 'I for my part did not come here for the sake of the Trojan spearman to fight against them, since to me they have done nothing,' Achilles declares. 'But for your sake, o great shamelessness, we followed, to do you favor.'" See Dwight Garner, "Beneath a Sheen of Glory, the Ugly Horror of War," *New York Times*, October 13, 2009.

31.   Joyce Carol Oates, "Muhammad Ali: 'The Greatest,'" in *Uncensored: Views & (Re)views* (New York: Harper Collins, 2005), 209–210.

32.   Oates, "Muhammad Ali," 217.

33.   Oates, "Muhammad Ali," 217.

34.   Roger Ebert, "Watching *Rocky II* with Muhammad Ali," RogerEbert .com, July 31, 1979, https://www.rogerebert.com/interviews/watching-rocky-ii -with-muhammad-ali. In an essay on the transition in American politics since the 1850s from "character" to "personality" or "celebrity," L. D. Burnett contrasts the

"yeoman" and the "showman" and lights on the show *This is Your Life* as a pivotal point in the trajectory away from character to celebrity. Muhammad Ali, whose episode of *This is Your Life* I discuss here, is an interesting addition to Burnett's archive, since he understood well how to play the celebrity game but showed great character, in the 1850s sense, while doing so. That is to say, historicizing *This Is Your Life* as a show of its era and part of a trend to life-narrative and away from character may lead us to miss how it was enlisted on behalf of refusal (L. D. Burnett, "Is Character Making a Comeback?," *Arc Digital*, October 23, 2020, https://arcdigital .media/is-character-making-a-comeback-402245c46185.

35.   Dance and poetry, for which Ali had a particular penchant, are two of the three art forms embraced by Nietzsche as cures for the ills of philosophy (for Nietzsche, as for Plato, poetry was tragedy). The third is music, the one of the three that best teaches the arts of inclination and is possessed of the Dionysian power to, as Deleuze and Guattari say, "unleash becomings" (Gilles Deleuze and Félix Guattari, *A Thousand Plateaus: Capitalism and Schizophrenia*, trans. Brian Massumi [New York: Continuum], 272). Ali recorded an album with Sam Cooke. They can be seen singing together live on the Dust-to-Digital Facebook page, "Sam Cooke and Muhammad Ali—'The Gang's All Here' (1964)," January 22, 2019, https://www .facebook.com/dusttodigital/videos/355140115216650/?v=355140115216650; for the recorded version, see "'The Gang's All Here' sung by Muhammad Ali," YouTube Video, 3:04, January 31, 2007, https://www.youtube.com/watch?v=E03mTh5_We4.

36.   Partly recording his time with Ali, George Lois of *Esquire* released a memoir titled, *$ellebrity: My Angling and Tangling with Famous People* (New York: Phaidon, 2003), with Ali on the cover. See Tim Grierson, "How Muhammad Ali's Iconic 'Esquire' Cover Helped Cement a Legend," *Rolling Stone*, June 5, 2016. On voice, see also Dave Zirin, "Don't Remember Muhammad Ali as a Sanctified Sports Hero. He Was a Powerful, Dangerous Political Force," *Los Angeles Times*, June 3, 2016: "We haven't heard Ali speak for himself in more than a generation, and it says something damning about this country that he was only truly embraced after he lost his power of speech, stripped of that beautiful voice."

37.   When he was called to step forward at the scene of army induction, he did not move. Three times his name was called, three times he did not move, "despite being warned by an officer that he was committing a felony offense that was punishable by five years in prison and a fine of $10,000" (Krishnadev Calamur, "Muhammad Ali and Vietnam," *Atlantic*, June 4, 2016). Here is one of Ali's most famous accounts of his decision to refuse the draft: "My conscience won't let me go shoot my brother, or some darker people, or some poor hungry people in the mud for big powerful America," he said at the time. "And shoot them for what? . . . They never lynched me, they didn't put no dogs on me, they didn't rob me of my nationality, rape and kill my mother and father. . . . Shoot them for what? How can I shoot them poor people? Just take me to jail." See "Muhammad Ali on the Vietnam War-Draft," YouTube Video, 2:37, February 20, 2011, https://www.youtube.com/watch ?v=HeFMyrWlZ68. As Krishnadev Calamur pointed out forty years later, the "remarks

and actions were even more controversial than the former Cassius Clay's conversion to Islam in 1964. The Vietnam War was popular at the time in the U.S., and the sight of [a] man, especially a black man, who not only refused to serve—but did so eloquently—incensed the sporting, media, and political establishments." The venerated Jackie Robinson came out against the young boxer: "'He's hurting, I think, the morale of a lot of young Negro soldiers over in Vietnam,' Robinson said. 'And the tragedy to me is, Cassius has made millions of dollars off of the American public, and now he's not willing to show his appreciation to a country that's giving him, in my view, a fantastic opportunity'" (Krishnadev Calamur, "Muhammad Ali and Vietnam," *Atlantic*, June 4, 2016).

38.   Ashfaq Khalfan, "Muhammad Ali: The World's 'Greatest' Conscientious Objector," *Amnesty International*, June 14, 2016, https://www.amnesty.org/en/latest /news/2016/06/muhammad-ali-the-worlds-greatest-conscientious-objector/. Importantly, "it was not judges who kept Ali from prize fighting in the United States while his draft evasion case was litigated. It was boxing commissioners and politicians— sometimes on their own, sometimes under pressure from veterans' groups, the press, and various self-appointed protectors of our 'national honor.' The ban was started by Edwin Dooley, President of the New York State Athletic Commission. During the afternoon of April 28, 1967, a few hours after Ali had formally refused induction but before he had been charged with a crime, Dooley announced that Ali's license to box in New York had been 'indefinitely suspended' because 'his refusal to enter the service is regarded by the commission to be detrimental to the best interests of boxing.' Boxing commissions around the country quickly copied New York" (Hampton Delinger, "When Muhammad Ali Took on America," *Slate News & Politics*, June 6, 2016).

39.   Calamur, "Muhammad Ali and Vietnam."

40.   Zirin, "Don't Remember."

41.   T. J. Quinn, "A Will Stronger than His Skull: The Biggest Fight Ali Won Was the Battle to Be Himself," *Undefeated*, June 4, 2016, https://theundefeated .com/features/a-will-stronger-than-his-skill/.

42.   David Remnick, "The Outsized Life of Muhammad Ali," *New Yorker*, June 4, 2016. Liebling comes in for particularly excoriating criticism from Joyce Carol Oates, who calls his writing "jokey, condescending and occasionally racist" (*On Boxing* [New York: Harper Perennial, 1987], 53).

43.   Remnick, "The Outsized Life of Muhammad Ali."

44.   See "Muhammad Ali on the *Eamonn Andrews Show* (1966)," YouTube Video, 2:12, March 15, 2015, https://www.youtube.com/watch?v=-xf5HSES14w. "He apparently worked on the premise that there was something obscene about being hit," was Norman Mailer's observation (quoted in Oates, *On Boxing*, 25). Sugar Ray Robinson who reportedly in his youth had tap danced for pennies, was famously quick-footed in the ring, but he was not a heavyweight.

45.   Someone else recently noted the similarity and made a brilliant mash-up of the two called "Charlie Chaplin vs Muhammad Ali" (YouTube Video, 0:54,

December 28, 2016, https://www.youtube.com/watch?v=CwPujL6NQDA). Notably, Oates connects Chaplin and Ali, noting that the two of them, along with Paul Robeson, stand out as public figures because they were persecuted by the United States for their political beliefs ("Muhammad Ali," 213, 221).

46.   The words are Jonathan Eig's. See Jonathan Eig, "'What's My Name?': The Title Fight in which Muhammad Ali Asserted His Identity," *Undefeated*, June 4, 2016, https://theundefeated.com/features/whats-my-name/.

47.   Oates, "Muhammad Ali," 222.

48.   Oates, "Muhammad Ali," 212.

49.   Absorbing the blows of opponents calls to mind the civil disobedience training noted by Martin Luther King Jr. in his "Letter from Birmingham Jail" (August 1963, 2): "We started having workshops on nonviolence and repeatedly asked ourselves . . . : 'Are you able to accept blows without retaliating?'"

50.   See Associated Press, "Muhammad Ali's Old Training Camp Sold to John Madden's Son," ESPN, July 21, 2016, https://www.espn.com/boxing/story/_/id/17119284/muhammad-ali-old-training-camp-sold-john-madden-son-mike.

51.   In addition to being a coach, Joe Martin was also a policeman. He had recruited Ali, then Clay, into boxing, when Ali's new bike was stolen and Ali swore he would catch the thief and beat him up. You'll have to learn how to fight, first, said Martin inviting him to the gym, and so Ali's career began. The bike and its theft are an incredible thread throughout the Ali / Christmas episode of *This Is Your Life*. The loss of the bike, a gift from his father, is a story told by his father on the show. Ali half-jokingly interrupts him a few times to tell him to hurry it up. The theft led Ali to a father figure, Joe Martin. The bike was a gift for Christmas and this particular episode of *This Is Your Life* is the Christmas show. When the story of the bike theft is told and host Eamonn Andrew says, "and now . . . ," Ali brightens up and says, "Do you have my bike?" Ali is not just joking. The theft has stayed with him (much as it does for the ten-year-old in the Dardenne brothers film, *A Kid with a Bike* [2011], in which the bike and the father are also, as for Ali, all bound up with each other. See Peter Bradshaw, *"The Kid with a Bike*—Review," *Guardian*, March 22, 2012). But Eamonn Andrew says no, it is not the bike. He brings out Ali's two coaches from his childhood. Later Andrews asks Martin, did you ever find the bike? Martin says no, "we have never found it yet, but we will eventually." The hollow promise of the law reverberates in the gaze of Ali in that moment. But the episode is also a bit reparative it seems, since toward the end of it, Ali says, "I feel like a little bitty boy just getting a new toy for Christmas." Surrounded by friends, family, and acquaintances from a life in boxing, Ali was not talking anymore about what was stolen, that long lost bike; or perhaps he was.

52.   See Editors of GQ, "Colin Kaepernick Will Not Be Silenced," *GQ*, November 13, 2017.

53.   Jonathan Eig, "The Cleveland Summit and Muhammad Ali: The True Story," *Undefeated*, June 1, 2017, https://theundefeated.com/features/the-cleveland-summit-muhammad-ali/.

54.   Here, see also Adriana Cavarero on "Adam Pierced by the Arrow of Mer-
cury," in *Inclinations: A Critique of Rectitude*, trans. Amanda Minervini and Adam
Sitze [Stanford, CA: Stanford University Press, 2016], 153). As scholars of classical
reception know, sometimes the reception reshapes the original. Modeling Kaepernick on Ali elevates the quarterback's worthy struggle, but it also models Ali on
Kaepernick, and this in a way, again, Christianizes Ali. Others did the same, casting
him as a martyr: Martin Luther King Jr. said Ali was to be admired for his sacrifice:
he "is giving up fame. He is giving up millions of dollars to do what his conscience
tells him is right" (Delinger, "When Muhammad Ali Took on America"). These
great sacrifices, and Ali's eventual success, call attention to the American demand
that Black people suffer before they can contribute, or that their suffering *is* their
unique contribution to the country. For great critical interventions on this, see Juliet
Hooker, "Black Lives Matter and the Paradoxes of U.S. Black Politics: From Democratic Sacrifice to Democratic Repair," *Political Theory* 44, no. 4 (April 2016) and
Ferris Lupino, "American Stasis" (PhD diss., Brown University, 2020).

55.   There is some irony in the saint's affiliation with soldiers; only a few years
later, in 1976, Derek Jarman would make a film about Saint Sebastian.

56.   "When the cover hit newsstands, on April 4, 1968, the loaded metaphor
wasn't lost on the American public. That same day, Martin Luther King Jr. was as-
sassinated, endowing the image of Ali with even deeper significance." See Alexxa
Gotthardt, "The Photograph that Made a Martyr out of Muhammad Ali," Artsy,
November 7, 2018, https://www.artsy.net/article/artsy-editorial-photograph-made
-martyr-muhammad-ali.

57.   A critic of sovereignty because, as Corey Robin points out, Ali "wasn't
merely claiming conscientious objector status, though he was. He wasn't simply
claiming the authority of a higher being, though he was. He was asserting the right
of the citizen to be the final judge of what threatens or endangers him. In asserting
that right, Ali was posing the deepest, most fundamental challenge to the power and
authority of the state. That he also claimed to be more threatened by his own fellow
citizens and government than by an officially declared enemy of the state only added
to the subversiveness of his challenge." See Corey Robin, "Muhammad Ali, Thomas
Hobbes, and the Politics of Fear," June 4, 2016, http://coreyrobin.com/2016/06/04
/muhammad-ali-thomas-hobbes-and-the-politics-of-fear/.

58.   Ali's claim that "I have gained a peace of mind. I have gained a peace of
heart" is the statement of a conscientious objector, as Arendt defines it: someone
who cares most about being able to live with himself. But he said it in answer to questions about whether he had regrets (Calamur, "Muhammad Ali and Vietnam").
Peace of mind was not his motivation; it was his compensation. Care for the world—
on behalf of what might be—was surely his motivation. I think here of Foucault's
mention of "the heterotopia, not of illusion, but of compensation" ("Of Other
Spaces," *Diacritics* 16, no. 1 [Spring 1986]: 22–27).

59.   Ali fought Ernie Terrell in 1967 in a fight that became known as the
What's My Name Fight. In prefight publicity meetings, Terrell had referred to Ali

as Cassius Clay. But Terrell was not criticizing Ali for his conversion to Islam, as many others did, both in boxing and outside of the sport. Terrell claimed he had known Ali a long time and was just using the name he had always known him by, but Ali called him an "Uncle Tom" and declared he aimed to teach him a lesson. "'I want to torture him,' Ali said. 'A clean knockout is too good for him'" (Eig, "'What's My Name'"). During the fight, Ali taunted Terrell repeatedly: What's my name? Say my name!" but not, Jonathan Eig argues, as so many assumed at the time, because Ali wanted to prolong his torture of Terrell. It was, as Ali told announcer Howard Cosell right afterward, simply because he was unable to end it. Could you have knocked him out earlier? asked Cosell in front of the crowd. "No, I don't believe I could've," Ali said. "After the eighth round I laid on him, but I found myself tiring." The still-dominant version of the story, however, is that Ali was particularly brutal that night and that this was in the name of Islam. As Jonathan Eig puts it, "The white men covering the bout, who by now looked for any and every reason to criticize Ali . . . called him a torturer and a thug. They said he lacked dignity, that he was no Joe Louis, no Gentleman Jim Corbett. They called it 'a disgusting exhibition of calculated cruelty'" and intimated its excessiveness was attributable in some way to Ali's conversion. Jimmy Cannon actually called Ali's treatment of Terrell "'a kind of a lynching'" (Eig, "'What's My Name'").

60.   Ali won on the TKO, Wepner said. "I pressed the whole fight, and I landed 30-something punches. I don't think he landed 10. All he did was dance around and show off, but they had him winning the fight" (Fox Sports, "Chuck Wepner Calls the Day He Lost to Muhammad Ali the Greatest of His Life," June 4, 2016, https://www.foxsports.com/boxing/story/muhammad-ali-chuck-wepner -the-bayonne-bleeder-knockdown-060316). Wepner litigated for compensation from Stallone. Filing suit in 2003 and settling in 2006: "Wepner's 1975 fight with Muhammad Ali has been widely acknowledged by Stallone as the inspiration for the original 1976 film. 'Sly' even said on the 2001 DVD release: 'What I saw was pretty extraordinary, I saw a man they call "the Bayonne Bleeder" who didn't have a chance at all against the greatest fighting machine supposedly that ever lived. But, for one moment (when he knocked Ali down in the ninth), this stumblebum was magnificent'" ("Seconds Out, Wepner Gets Payout for Being 'Real Rocky,'" Eurosport, July 8, 2006, https://www.eurosport.com/boxing/us-news/2005/wepner-gets -payout-for._sto940601/story.shtml.)

61.   Ebert, "Watching *Rocky II* with Muhammad Ali."

62.   Joseph Santoliquito, "Statue of Boxing Legend Joe Frazier Unveiled in South Philly," *Philly Voice*, September 12, 2015, https://www.phillyvoice.com/statue -boxing-legend-joe-frazier-unveiled-philly/.

63.   Mark Kram Jr., "Long Overdue Statue of Joe Frazier a Sign of Love from Philadelphia," *Sports Illustrated*, September 11, 2015, https://www.si.com/boxing /2015/09/11/joe-frazier-statue-philadelphia.

Acknowledgments

I gave the Flexner Lectures in fall 2017 at Bryn Mawr, a college that is part of the history of what Yopie Prins calls ladies' Greek. In the nineteenth century, one could not gain admission to Bryn Mawr without knowledge of classical languages. I have always assumed the requirement was a filter for elites, a sign of social or class power. But rereading Patricia Yaeger's work as I completed the revised lectures for this book, I wondered if the requirement was, rather, a marker of the radical power of bilingualism that Yaeger finds in Charlotte Brontë's *Villette*.

Yaeger says that Brontë's bilingual Lucy learns "to play in the space between words, to decenter and demythologize both her primary language and her secondary." Is this "play" in play when in the ritual Lantern Night to this day, Bryn Mawr sophomores welcome incoming freshmen with a song in Greek? Under cover of class capital and elite tradition, do they pass on a feminist heritage of transgressive bilingualism? Praising Athena as a goddess of learning and initiation, they may not just classicize; they may also participate in what Yaeger calls a tradition of "repair" that overcomes "the limitation language imposes on their lives."

I was aware, when I gave these lectures theorizing feminist refusal in connection with Euripides's *Bacchae*, that Bryn Mawr hosted a production of the *Bacchae* as part of the college's fiftieth anniversary celebrations in 1935. Such classicization likely reassured those who might have worried back then about how educated women, ensconced in a college heterotopia, might get ideas. That is certainly the aim here: *to get ideas.*

I was not aware, but was excited to learn later on, as I finished this book, that in advocating feminist refusal I am in the company also of the Flexner family, which founded and supported institutions of education early in the twentieth century. Mary Flexner, for whom these lectures are named, was aunt to Eleanor Flexner, author of the pioneering history of women's activism, *A Century of Struggle* (1959). Uncannily, just as I completed the final copyedits on this project, on October 16, 2020, Eleanor Flexner was memorialized, over twenty years after her death, in the *New York Times*' belated obituary feature, "Overlooked No More." Its author, Ellen Carol DuBois, notes that when Eleanor Flexner "brought an early draft" of *A Century of Struggle* "to Harper & Brothers, she was told to remove the material on Black women because it would be of no interest to general readers." She refused. The book was later published whole by Harvard University Press. Flexner's next book, on Mary Wollstonecraft, focused in particular on her relationship with her sisters. As I note in my conclusion: sister is an anagram for resist.

I am grateful to President Kimberley Wright Cassidy of Bryn Mawr College for the invitation to deliver the 2017 Flexner Lectures, and to her and the faculty, students, and administrators for the hospitality extended to me during my time there. Thanks to those who organized the visit, hosted me in their classrooms, and participated in *Riot Antigone*, a fantastic K-pop-style production of *Antigone* directed by Soenjae Kim and performed during my time there. Thanks as well to all those who attended the lectures and shared with me their questions, thoughts, and doubts along with suggestions for further reading. I want to single out Ruth Lindeborg for her role in all of it.

Besides Bryn Mawr College, early versions of these lectures were given at the universities of Alabama (Gender and Race Studies) and Toronto (Center for Ethics), Bocconi University in Milan (interdisciplinary seminar on "Identities, Boundaries, and Representations"), and the University of Verona (Hannah Arendt Center for Political Studies), University Adolfo Ibáñez in Santiago, Chile, the University of Illinois at Chicago's Humanities Center, Wellesley College's Humanities Center, Stanford University's *materia* research group, UC Santa Barbara's Series on the New Faces of Citizenship, Cornell University's Society for the Humanities, the Mellon School of Theater and Performance Research Annual Summer School at Harvard, the Center for the Study of Race and Ethnicity in America (CSREA) at Brown and the Political Theory Colloquium at Brown, Victoria University in Wellington, New Zealand, the

Classics and Contemporary Theory workshop at University of Sydney, Australia National University gender and sexuality studies group (where a meeting with an emergent scholars group at ANU gave me my book title), Pomona, Kenyon, Denison, and Gettysburg Colleges as the Inaugural Carl F. Cranor Phi Beta Kappa scholar for Phi Beta Kappa, as (co-) keynotes, at the joint conference of the Society for European Philosophy and the Forum of European Philosophy (SEP-FEP) at the University of Essex, UK, and at Brighton University's conference on Adriana Cavarero's book *Inclinations*; and at the Yale Classics Colloquium, the Stanford University Political Theory Colloquium, and Cambridge University's Political Theory Workshop. I am grateful to all who organized and attended, including Helen Morales, Victoria Wohl, Carol Dougherty, Catherine Gilhuly, Laura Grattan, Diego Rossello, Utz McKnight, Clare Woodford, Tim Huzar, Ximena Briceño, Héctor Hoyos, Judith Butler, Adriana Cavarero, Alison McQueen, Beth de Palma Digeser, Paige Digeser, Catherine Conybeare, Bethany Schneider, Mark Canuel, Emily Beausoleil, Tristan Bradshaw, Fiona Jenkins, Des Manderson, Ainsley LeSure, the Political Theory group at Brown. I owe particular thanks for comments on early drafts to Lori Marso (who also read the penultimate draft on short notice), George Shulman, James Martel, Miriam Leonard, Jill Frank, Lida Maxwell, John Seery, and Jacques Khalip.

The work here was developed alongside students in my Brown University undergraduate and graduate seminars (2013–2017) in Modern Culture and Media (MCM) and Political Science—*Democracy among the Ruins, Politics of Precarity and Resilience* (with Amanda Anderson), *Pedestrian Theory: Agamben and Inoperativity* (with Jacques Khalip), *Conscientious Objection and Civil Disobedience, Greek Tragedy in Politics, Literature, and Film,* and *Political Theories of Refusal.* I benefited from working with colleagues in the 2016–2017 Pembroke Seminar on *Theaters of War: Inoperativity and the Politics of Refusal,* and thank the Pembroke Center for hosting that seminar. Early on, Rebecca Schneider pulled me into a staged reading of the *Bacchae,* where I met Connie Crawford, whose Agave was an inspiration. Ferris Lupino provided valuable research assistance. I profited from conversations with Noga Rotem,

Diego Millan, and Valentina Moro. Colleagues at Brown to whom I am grateful for conversation, commentary, and their own work on related topics include Amanda Anderson, Ariella Azoulay, Tamara Chin, Mark Cladis, Leela Gandhi, Juliet Hooker, Jacques Khalip, Sharon Krause, Tal Lewis, Adi Ophir, Kevin Quashie, Melvin Rogers, Tricia Rose, Rebecca Schneider, and Andre Willis.

Deirdre Foley provided valuable staff support on this project and Karen Bouchard, Arts and Humanities Librarian at Brown, provided the expertise needed to upgrade images and seek permission to use them. Bouchard also connected me with Matthew Martin who provided the vulture version of the Leonardo painting discussed in Chapter 2. Claire Grandy prepared the manuscript for publication. I am deeply grateful for all these contributions to this project.

Conversations about this book with friends and family were also key: thanks to Naomi Honig, Michael Whinston, Noah Whinston, Kim Gray, Sucosh Norton, Roni Donnenfeld, Melanie Simon, and John Connell for insight, sources, and inspiration. College friends of Noah suggested a perfectly apt title that might have made this book a best seller: *Sorority Politics and Greek Life*. I already regret not using it.

Chapters One and Two build on ideas first discussed in "How to Do Things with Inclination? Antigones, with Cavarero" in *Toward a Feminist Ethics of Nonviolence*, edited by Tim Huzar and Clare Woodford (Fordham University Press 2020); and my reading of the *Bacchae* here draws on a first, brief, preliminary attempt in "'Out Like a Lion: *Melancholia* with Euripides and Winnicott," in *Politics, Theory, and Film: Critical Encounters with Lars von Trier*, edited by Bonnie Honig and Lori Marso (Oxford University Press, 2015).

Finally, I am grateful to Brown University for sabbatical and other kinds of institutional support that enabled me to bring this project to completion, to Harvard University Press's Lindsay Waters for help shaping the ideas at the start, to readers for the press whose comments guided the final revisions, to Mary Ribesky for editorial guidance, to Scott Smiley for indexing, and to Emily Marie Silk for adopting *A Feminist Theory of Refusal*.

Index